WHAT SO PROUDLY WE HAIL

ALSO BY MAYMIE R. KRYTHE

All About American Holidays
All About Christmas
All About the Months

What So Proudly
We Hail

All About Our American Flag,
Monuments and Symbols

═══ ☆ ═══

Maymie R. Krythe

HARPER & ROW, PUBLISHERS

NEW YORK, EVANSTON, AND LONDON

1817

To Albert John Kirschbaum, Ph.D.

Contents

Contents

During these modern times that "try men's souls," we Americans still have our distinctive national symbols, which have inspired the growth and development of our country.

Thomas Crawford, the sculptor who created the famous statue of Freedom that surmounts the great dome of the Capitol in Washington, once declared:

A country puts its dreams and its ideals into symbols—a flag, a plot of ground, a monument. The people grow to love these symbols, fight for them, die for them. A symbol and what it stands for must stay together. They are indivisible!

1

Our National Flag

SEVERAL unidentified writers have expressed their ideas about national flags in these paragraphs:

> Every nation uses a special flag to represent its unity and independence. A nation's flag stands for the gains, hope, and ideals of its people. In its own land a flag carries the honor and love of its citizens; abroad, it is respected as the emblem of a self-governed people.

> A flag is more than just a brightly colored piece of cloth. It is a symbol or sign, that stands for an idea, a cause, or a purpose.

> Each country in the world has a flag of its own. Such a flag has a special meaning for the people who live in that country. A country's flag can stir people to joy and sadness, to courage and sacrifice, according to when and how it is used.

For 190 years our "Star-Spangled Banner" has waved "o'er the land of the free" and is "the proud and sacred symbol of the freedom, equality, justice and humanity for which our country stands."

The American flag, called at times "Old Glory," the "Stars and Stripes," the "Star-Spangled Banner," and the "Red, White, and Blue," is one of the oldest national ensigns in the world. It was adopted on June 14, 1777. (Since 1916, June 14 has been celebrated as Flag Day; it was first proclaimed by President Woodrow Wilson.) Only the basic flags of Great Britain, Austria, Denmark, Holland, Sweden, and Switzerland are older. Today the sun never sets on our

American flag, for it flies all around the globe over our embassies, legations, and consulates.

When the colonists started their rebellion against England, they had no common flag. These continentals followed the British custom and did not fly a banner over their troops on the march. Each colony or regiment and many companies had their own individual ensigns. These were of various colors and designs.

The insignia included such diverse things as beavers, pine trees, coiled rattlesnakes, anchors, a crescent, a rifleman, and a chain of links. It is said that General Washington used the New England Pine Tree flag on his ships in Massachusetts Bay. These different banners carried such slogans as "An Appeal to Heaven," "Hope," "Liberty or Death," "Don't Tread on Me," "We Are One," and "Conquer or Die."

Since something "continental" was needed, a committee from the Continental Congress, headed by Benjamin Franklin, probably discussed the matter with General Washington when they conferred with him at Cambridge in 1775 about the organization of the new army.

On January 1, 1776, the soldiers who had been serving as militia or as volunteers were inducted as members of the troops of the Continental Congress. A flag called the Great (or Grand) Union or Congress Colors was hoisted to the top of a 76-foot mast on Prospect Hill, Somerville, near Boston. A great cheer arose when it was put in place. This act is said to have brought much hope to the troops and helped to unite them.

George Washington, on January 4, 1776, wrote to Colonel Reed, his military secretary:

> On the day that gave being to the new army, we hoisted the union flag in compliment to the united colonies.

Even after this ensign was adopted as official, all sorts of flags and colors continued to be used. The Grand Union, "a dignified banner with a clear meaning," was raised on the flagship *Alfred* as the naval ensign of the thirteen states after Commodore Esek Hopkins took command of the ships Congress had authorized.

The Grand Union had thirteen stripes for the new states. The blue canton (the rectangle in the corner), with the crosses of St. George and St. Andrew, indicated the relationship with the mother country. There were several months of skirmishing and bloodshed—with some hope of patching up the quarrel—before the ties were completely severed; then the canton was replaced by a blue field containing thirteen white stars.

On November 16, 1776, the *Andrea Dorea*, an American ship of war flying the Grand Union, saluted the Dutch fort on the island of St. Eustatius in the West Indies. Captain Robinson presented a copy of the Declaration of Independence to the Governor of the island. After he had read it, the governor ordered a return of the nine-gun salute; this was the first international recognition of a United States flag.

When the Declaration of Independence, which marked the separation of the United States from Great Britain, was approved, the new republic needed a distinctly American flag to replace the half-American, half-British Grand Union, for the American ships were going out to hamper enemy communications and to prey on British commerce. If a ship sailed under its own colonial flag, it was likely to be considered a private vessel, and its crew could be hanged as pirates.

Therefore, on June 14, 1777, Congress resolved:

> That the flag of the thirteen United States be thirteen stripes, alternately red and white, that the Union be thirteen stars, white in a blue field, representing a new constellation.

However, the Congress did not specify the arrangement of the stars, so the early flags often showed different arrangements of them in the blue field. It is not certain where this flag was first flown, but its first official announcement is said to have been on September 3, 1777.

Although the story has not been authenticated, George Washington has long been credited with this explanation of the symbolism of the flag:

> We take the stars from heaven, the red from our mother country, separating it by white stripes, thus showing that we have separated

from her, and the white stripes shall go down to posterity, representing liberty.

Congress passed a resolution that each time a new state was added the flag would have a new star and a new stripe. Therefore, after Vermont was admitted in 1791 and Kentucky in 1792, our national flag had fifteen stars and fifteen stripes. This unique ensign served for twenty-three years—from 1795 to 1818—as our national symbol.

THE BANNER WITH FIFTEEN STARS AND FIFTEEN STRIPES

During the years 1795 to 1818 much American history was made under Old Glory. After the War of 1812 a wave of nationalism swept over the land, and our flag began to take on the characteristics of a mighty symbol of sovereignty.

Philip Freneau, the foremost poet of the era, mentioned the flag in several poems; in one, he wrote:

> Go on, great man, to scourge the foe,
> And bid the haughty Britons know
> They to our thirteen stars shall bend . . .

It was the fifteen-star flag that those two intrepid explorers Lewis and Clark carried in 1805 across our continent to the Pacific coast, over lands that later would be divided into the states of Missouri, Iowa, Kansas, Nebraska, North Dakota, South Dakota, Montana, Idaho, Oregon, and Washington.

This distinctive banner, too, led us to victory in three wars: the first for the suppression of French privateers, from 1798 to 1800; against the pirates of Tripoli, 1801–1802; and against England, 1812–1815.

For many years it had been customary for nations to pay tribute to the pirates of Tripoli in order to sail their vessels safely through the Mediterranean. In 1801, when Captain William Bainbridge paid the usual tribute, the ruler of the pirates declared that he would wage war on the United States if he did not receive a larger sum within six months.

The monarch carried out his threat, but to his surprise a small American fleet, flying the fifteen-star flag, bombarded his city. He was forced to surrender and had to release his American prisoners and pay damages; thereafter the Mediterranean was safe for foreign shipping.

It is said that the first American flag to be flown over a fortress in the old world was raised above a stronghold at Derne, Tripoli, by Lieutenant P. N. O'Bannon of the Marine Corps and Midshipman Mann of the Navy.

The fifteen-star and fifteen-stripe ensign also played an important role in the War of 1812. Under it General Andrew Jackson won much fame by defeating the British at the Battle of New Orleans.

On September 10, 1813, "Old Glory snatched victory from the jaws of defeat" on Lake Erie. Earlier, in June of that year, Captain James Lawrence, when dying, had cried out, "Don't give up the ship!" And using those words as his slogan, Commodore Oliver Perry was victorious over the British on Lake Erie, near Put-in Bay. At once he sent the President his famous message: "We have met the enemy and they are ours—two ships, two brigs, one schooner and one sloop."

THE NEW FLAG

After this special flag had served for twenty-three years, new territories were clamoring for admission. Many soon realized that if a new stripe and a new star were added each time, the national banner would become very unwieldy. One representative to Congress declared:

If the Union keeps on increasing at the present rate, you will soon find that the tallest pine in the forests of Maine will not be high enough to serve as a flagstaff.

Several members of Congress kept urging a change in the law. Finally, on April 4, 1818, the body approved this resolution:

That from and after the Fourth of July next, the Flag of the United States be thirteen horizontal stripes, alternate red and white: that the Union be twenty stars, white in a blue field.

That on the admission of every new state in the Union, one star be added to the Union of the Flag; and that such addition shall take effect on the Fourth of July next succeeding such admission.

(By 1912, with the addition of Arizona and New Mexico, we had forty-eight stars in Old Glory. The forty-ninth state was Alaska, admitted in 1959, and the fiftieth Hawaii, in 1960.)

Now the stars in Old Glory hold us

> Together by the bond of our national government—while the thirteen stripes preserve the traditions and ideals of the thirteen colonies, or original states, which so nobly laid the foundations of this great independent nation.

In early pictures of revolutionary battles some artists painted various types of American flags. It is said that when Washington crossed the Delaware River on Christmas, 1776, the ensign over his boats was a white one, with a liberty cap and the words "Liberty or Death." However, the German artist Emmanuel Leutze (1818–1868), who created the widely known picture of this historic event long after it occurred, depicted the Stars and Stripes, a flag which was not adopted until the next year—1777.

During the Mexican War, Old Glory played a vital role. In September, 1847, General Winfield Scott's men stormed Vera Cruz and planted the Stars and Stripes on a high crest. That same month his troops took Chapultepec, where "flag after flag was flung from the upper walls." When the Americans captured Mexico City, our banner flew over the palace.

At the approach of the Civil War, northern papers were full of allusions to the Stars and Stripes. For instance, the Philadelphia *Press* declared:

> Henceforth, each man, high and low, must take his position as a traitor, as a foe or a friend of his country, as a supporter of the flag of the Stars and Stripes, or of the rebel banner.

After Fort Sumter was bombarded and taken by the southerners, there was a great patriotic awakening in the North. One reporter wrote in *The New York Times:*

> From one end of the land to the other, in the crowded streets of cities, and in the solitude of the country, where the splendor of the

Stars and Stripes, the glittering emblem of our country's glory, meets the eye, come forth shouts of devotion and pledges of aid.

During the course of the Civil War, President Abraham Lincoln did not suggest altering the flag; the stars of the seceding states remained on it.

Until 1866 American flags were made of bunting manufactured in foreign lands. Some companies had tried to make the material here but had not been successful. Bunting is a thin, woolen stuff used mainly in flags. In 1865 Congress put a duty of more than 400 per cent on imported bunting, which caused flag makers really to try. Within a year one company, in Lowell, Massachusetts, presented the United States Senate with a flag made from American bunting and it was hoisted over the Capitol. Thus for the first time in our national history an ensign fashioned from material made here floated over Congress.

In 1912, during the administration of President William H. Taft, some important requirements in regard to Old Glory were set forth. The proper legal dimensions were: height, 1 unit; length, 1.9; width of each stripe, 1/13 unit; height of canton or union, 7/13 unit. The 48 stars were to be arranged in 6 even rows of 8 each.

THE PLEDGE OF ALLEGIANCE

The initial pledge was first published in *The Youth's Companion* for September 8, 1892. It was used in connection with the national public schools' celebration of Columbus Day in October, 1892. More than 12 million schoolchildren took part in this nationwide affirmation, which read as follows:

I pledge allegiance to my Flag and the Republic for which it stands—one nation indivisible—with liberty and justice for all.

For some years there was conflicting evidence as to the correct author—Francis Bellamy, of Rome, New York; or James Upham, of Alden, Massachusetts. Both were members of the editorial staff of *The Youth's Companion* when the pledge first appeared. In 1939 the United States Flag Association appointed a committee of two historians and a political scientist to settle the disputed question. On

May 18, 1939, they submitted their findings and declared Francis Bellamy the author.

In 1923 the words "my flag" were deleted and the phrase "the Flag of the United States" substituted. In 1954 the words "under God" were added, giving the pledge its final form:

> I pledge allegiance to the Flag of the United States of America and to the Republic for which it stands, one nation under God indivisible, with liberty and justice for all.

FLYING THE FLAG AT NIGHT

The American flag always flies over the Capitol in Washington, D.C. This building is not governed by the military regulations that require the emblem to be furled at sunset. It is raised on the wing of the two chambers when they are in session. If a session continues after dark, a light flashes from the lantern at the top of the dome. The custom of flying Old Glory continuously over the Capitol started during World War I. This building was selected as the one site where our patriotic symbol could be seen without interruption.

There are several other places where the Stars and Stripes may fly both night and day, except in inclement weather. By presidential proclamation, it waves continuously over the Iwo Jima monument in the national capital. Other locations include the birthplace of Francis Scott Key, composer of *The Star-Spangled Banner*, at Keyville, Maryland, and his grave, in the same state, at Mount Olivet Cemetery, Frederick; the War Memorial at Worcester, Massachusetts; and Fort McHenry, near Baltimore, where the national anthem was written.

STORIES ABOUT OLD GLORY

Sergeant Jasper

When the colonists rebelled against the mother country, each colony and certain groups such as military companies had their own ensigns.

South Carolina's flag was "the pride of the colony." Displayed at Charleston, it is said to have been designed by Colonel William

Moultrie. It was blue, with a white crescent, and carried the words "Liberty or Death." Moultrie's troops also wore blue uniforms, and there were crescents and the motto on the front of their caps. While this blue flag was not one representing all the new states, it was the first "banner of American freedom" displayed in the South.

Although the conflict began in New England in 1775, during the following year acts of war occurred on the South Atlantic coast. Just a week before the Declaration of Independence was approved in Philadelphia, a British fleet of nine vessels tried to enter Charleston harbor, South Carolina.

The blue-crescent flag was flying over the log ramparts of Fort Sullivan. On June 26, 1776, the shore batteries fired at the English vessels and stood them off by their fierce cannonade.

Early in the attack the flagstaff on Fort Sullivan was hit by a British cannonball, and the banner fell outside the parapet. At once daring Sergeant William Jasper jumped out from an old gun embrasure, ran the length of the fort, and amid a rain of bullets called out, "Don't let us fight without a banner!" Then he leaped down, caught the flag, and scrambled up the parapet, while his comrades cheered his brave action.

A gunner passed him a staff, to which Jasper fastened the ensign; he quickly thrust it into the breastworks and jumped back to safety.

This fight at Charleston continued that night for ten hours. When the British withdrew the next morning, the blue flag was still waving proudly. The enemy had to leave behind their best vessel as a wreck. After their failure, Charleston and the South were safe for two years from British invasion.

The name of Fort Sullivan was changed to Fort Moultrie, in honor of the brave officer who had defended it so successfully. Sergeant Jasper later was honored by having a square in Savannah, Georgia and a county named for him. And the famous blue flag, with the addition of a palmetto, is still the state emblem of South Carolina.

When the state governor offered Jasper a commission, the honest man admitted that, as he could not read or write, he was "not fit to keep company with officers." Instead, the official gave him "a roving commission." Afterward the sergeant often went out with a few comrades and came back with prisoners.

Some time later William Jasper was killed in attempting to repeat his feat. After three color bearers had been shot down in battle, he caught the flag, waved it, and had just put it back in place, when a British bullet downed the brave southerner. He helped keep the South's most famous colonial flag flying and sacrificed his life for it, thus becoming one of the South's famous Revolutionary heroes.

John Paul Jones and the Stars and Stripes

In 1775 the Continental Congress authorized the building and fitting out of five warships in the Delaware River, to be used to prey on British shipping. There was some talk about conspicuous colors to be used on these vessels.

In February, 1776, John Paul Jones, a young, ambitious, Scottish Navy lieutenant "impatient to distinguish himself in action," hoisted on the *Alfred*, the flagship of the five vessels commanded by Commodore Esek Hopkins, a yellow silk flag with a coiled rattlesnake on it. This ensign bore the warning "Don't Tread on Me!"

Jones did not like this flag and openly expressed his dislike for it. The *Alfred* flew two other banners; one was a Union Jack with a snake, while the third was the Grand Union, much more to Jones's liking, for it had thirteen stripes for the original colonies, or states, as they were now calling themselves. The fleet, headed by the *Alfred*, sailed to the Bahamas in 1776 to try to capture military supplies left there by the British.

On June 14, 1777, the very day Congress had approved our first national flag, John Paul Jones was named commander of the new sloop-of-war, the *Ranger*. He wrote in his diary:

> The flag and I were twins, born in the same hour. We cannot be parted in life or death. So long as we can float, we shall float together. If we must sink, we shall go down as one.

Jones went to Portsmouth, New Hampshire, where the *Ranger* was being built. He was delighted to command a ship flying the new ensign, the first Star-Spangled Banner to wave over an American vessel. Later he wrote: "It was my fortune as senior of the lieutenants to hoist the flag of America, the first time it was displayed."

The story goes that one summer day in 1777 a group of patriotic young ladies held a sewing bee in Portsmouth. Then they went to the *Ranger* and presented its skipper with a handsome flag in the new, approved congressional design. It is said that this banner had been fashioned from the materials of some of their very best silk gowns.

John Paul Jones sailed the *Ranger* to France and sent word to Benjamin Franklin in Paris that the British General Burgoyne had surrendered at Saratoga. This piece of good news helped persuade the French to enter the conflict on the American side.

On February 13, 1778, the *Ranger* sailed to Quiberon Bay, in France. It anchored near the French fleet. Jones was determined that America should be recognized as an independent country. So he saluted thirteen times and the French vessels replied. Of course he and his men were delighted with this recognition. The surgeon on the *Ranger* wrote in his diary: "This is the very first salute ever paid an American flag."

Later a contemporary of the commander of the *Ranger* said of him: "He hath made the Flagg of America respectable among the Flaggs of all nations."

Not long afterward, on April 24, 1778, the *Ranger*, flying the new ensign, met the British ship *Drake*. The latter was forced to strike its colors—the first time a British man-of-war was conquered by an American vessel.

The *Ranger* was sent back to America, and Jones transferred his flag to "a condemned French ship, a wornout old trader." He named it the *Bon Homme Richard*, honoring his good friend Benjamin Franklin, the author of *Poor Richard's Almanac*. It had only forty-two guns, while its opponent, the *Serapis*, was a new British man-of-war with fifty guns.

On September 23, 1779, off the east coast of England was fought one of the most famous battles in all American naval annals. It was a desperate sea encounter and was waged for four hours by moonlight.

At first it appeared that the *Serapis* would be an easy winner. Many of Jones's men were killed when one of the guns on the *Bon Homme Richard* exploded, blowing up part of its main deck. Then Commander Pearson on the *Serapis* asked, "Have you struck your colors yet?" And the American commander defiantly replied, "No, I have just begun to fight!"

When the main mast on the *Serapis* began to wobble, its captain surrendered. So John Paul Jones lost the *Bon Homme Richard* but boarded the *Serapis* as victor.

For a day and a half the "splintered remnant" of the *Bon Homme Richard* rolled on the surface of the ocean, while Jones and his men watched from the deck of the *Serapis*. Finally, on the morning of September 25, 1779, with her dead on board her, and still proudly carrying the flag made by the Portsmouth ladies, the *Bon Homme Richard* sank, bow first. Of her last moments her commander said: "Her tattered Stars and Stripes floated for a brief moment on a sweeping wave, and then trailed beneath the blue that mingled with a field of stars."

Afterward John Paul Jones told why he had not taken the flag off before she sank:

> I couldn't bear to strip it from the poor old ship in her last agony, nor could I deny to my dead on her decks, who had died to keep it flying, the glory of taking it with them.

A quarter gunner, John Kilby, wrote this tribute to the *Bon Homme Richard:* "She went down, head foremost, with all sails set . . . and that beautiful ensign she so gallantly wore in action and when we conquered. A most glorious sight!"

A New York Woman and Her Flag

An interesting story has come down to us in connection with an American flag; it happened in New York City, just at the close of the American Revolution. November 25, 1783, was the date for the evacuation of the British troops from that city. That morning, a Mrs. Day, "a large, muscular woman, a zealously loyal American," in defiance of British orders that they would be in control until 12 o'clock noon, ran up the American flag on a pole in front of her home.

Soon some British soldiers came marching down the street, headed by William Cunningham, provost marshal, and "a stern oppressor of loyal Americans." He was angry when he saw the banner up before its time. Mrs. Day was calmly sweeping away in front of the house.

At once he ordered her in no uncertain terms to haul down the flag, but the stubborn lady refused to lower it one inch. "Then came the last pitched battle of the American Revolution." Cunningham seized the halyards and started to pull down the Stars and Stripes.

That was too much for Mrs. Day. Without a moment of hesitation she fell upon him like a thunderbolt. The irate woman banged him on the head time and time again with her broom. His wig became twisted and the white powder from it flew in all directions.

The officer raised one arm to try to fend off the "stout whacks" of the determined American, but all his efforts were in vain. It must have been an ignominious moment for the haughty Britisher, especially in front of his men.

Finally the servant of his Britannic Majesty, baffled by the unceasing shower of blows on his head, had to give up his attempt to make Mrs. Day obey orders. He and his men made their retreat in disorder. For "the Flag, the woman and her broom had won a sweeping victory."

Old Glory Reaches England

The period from October, 1781, to November, 1783, was a hard one for the new nation; for the peace treaty with England was not signed until the latter date. Then the sea became open to American merchantmen. At once they started out, looking for trade.

An English magazine in February, 1783, wrote of seeing an American flag on a ship in the Thames. It was the *Bedford*, with a cargo of whale oil, which had reported at the London Custom House. The writer commented:

> She is American built, manned wholly by American seamen, wears the rebel colors. . . . This is the first vessel which has displayed the rebellious stripes of America in any British port.

British officials were stupefied to see an American ship carrying Old Glory, before the treaty had been signed by the two nations.

Stars and Stripes' First Time Around the World

There was another first for our flag five years later, in 1788, when the vessel *Columbia*, sailing from Boston and skippered by Captain Robert Gray, carried the ensign around the globe for the first time.

The *Columbia* sailed around Cape Horn, then wintered in our Northwest, where "Old Glory fluttered in the wind." In the spring the captain took the *Columbia* to Canton, China, then via the Cape of Good Hope back to New England. He reached home safely with the flag intact, after making its first round-the-world voyage.

The First United States School Flag

It is believed that the first schoolhouse in our land over which the Stars and Stripes waved, from the top of a pine staff, was a log one on Catamount Hill, Colrain, in the center of Massachusetts.

The loyal women of Colrain got together and made the flag which was first flown on the schoolhouse in May, 1812. Then, almost a century later, on June 3, 1903, the Catamount Hill Association erected a monument on the site of the small school, to honor this significant event of 1812.

The Original Star-Spangled Banner

Francis Scott Key, a young lawyer of Baltimore, Maryland, on September 13, 1814, went aboard a vessel of the British fleet in Chesapeake Bay to get a friend released. The friend was Dr. William Beanes, who had been captured after the burning of Washington.

The lawyer succeeded in his mission, but the two men were not permitted to go ashore that day, as the British fleet intended to bomb Fort McHenry. They were put on board the tender *Minden*, out of range of gunfire, but they were within sight of the fort.

All through that night Francis Scott Key watched anxiously as the heavy bombardment continued against the American fort. And when morning finally dawned, Key was overjoyed to see that the flag with its fifteen stars and stripes was still there, waving triumphantly over Fort McHenry. This inspired Key to write what later became our national anthem. He took an old letter from his pocket and on the envelope jotted down some of his feelings. Of course, he never dreamed that his words would later become world famous. Soon the poem was published and set to the music of an old English tune called *Anacreon in Heaven*. Congress made it our national anthem on March 3, 1931.

The original Stars and Stripes flag is 42 feet long, and it was flown from a staff 87 feet high. The stripes are 2 feet wide, the stars are in five rows of three each. It is said that it took several men to handle this 200-pound banner. It remains the largest United States flag to have flown through an American battle. This was made by Mrs. Mary Pickergill and her daughter, Mrs. Caroline T. Purdy. Although it was "tattered and torn," it was mended by skillful needlewomen. Today it is carefully preserved in the Smithsonian Institution in Washington, D.C.

He Named Her "Old Glory"

Captain William Driver, who was born in Salem, Massachusetts, where he became a shipmaster, is generally credited with naming our ensign "Old Glory."

In 1824, on Driver's twenty-first birthday, his mother and several other women called at his ship and gave him a beautifully made flag with twenty-six stars, made of 110 yards of bunting. At once he hoisted it on the masthead of his ship, the *Charles Daggett*. It floated proudly in the breeze, and the captain looked up at it in admiration and called out, "There it is; I name thee, Old Glory!" Another version of the story is that he exclaimed, "My ship, my country, and my flag, Old Glory!" The term was so appropriate that others soon began to call it by this name.

The flag presented by the women sailed on many trips with the Yankee sea captain, who considered it his chief possession and greatest treasure. On one occasion he was asked to rescue the mutineers from the British ship *Bounty* skippered by the notorious Captain Bligh.

Some time before the Civil War broke out, Captain Driver settled in Nashville, Tennessee. When the war came, he stood firmly by the North. At first he hung out his widely traveled flag, but some of his southern neighbors tried to get possession of it to destroy it. Captain Driver then decided to sew the precious banner inside the coverlet on his bed. During the day it would be completely hidden, and at night he would have it with him.

In February, 1862, the federal soldiers entered Nashville. At once Captain Driver asked permission to fly his ensign over the state capitol. Some of the soldiers came to his home and ripped open the coverlet that contained his great flag. Captain Driver himself carried it to the Capitol; there he had the joy of seeing Old Glory again waving in the breeze. However, as it was badly worn, he replaced it with a new one. He was thrilled that he had lived long enough to see the Union flag again flying over the Tennessee capitol. With tears in his eyes, Captain Driver declared:

> There, those Texas Rangers have been hunting for these six months without finding it, and they knew I had it. I have always said that if I could see it float over the Capitol, I should have lived long enough. Now Old Glory is up there now, gentlemen, and I am ready to die.

At his death, in 1886, Old Glory was sent to Essex Institute in Massachusetts for safekeeping.

Our Flag Reaches Japan

For more than 200 years the islands that make up the land of Japan were closed to the world by their monarchs. However, in 1853 Admiral Matthew C. Perry of the United States Navy went there to perform the ceremony of "showing the flag" (by force, if necessary). He demanded that our flag be saluted and that vessels carrying it should be allowed to trade in Japanese ports.

It is said that since the Japanese had no navy then of their own, they were really compelled to accede to the admiral's demand. On July 14, 1853, he was received by the Lord of Toda. A treaty was discussed to open Japan to American ships. This was ratified on March 8, 1854.

The machine age was now underway, and the visit of Perry to Japan brought the Kingdom its first glimpses of modern civilization.

The Stars and Stripes at Fort Sumter

Today Fort Sumter, at Charleston, South Carolina, is a national monument, for it was here that the Civil War began. The Confederates under General P. G. T. Beauregard in April, 1861, bombarded and captured it and held it until February, 1865.

When Fort Sumter was forced to surrender, Major Robert Anderson and his men saluted Old Glory with fifty guns. Next the banner was lowered, and the officer and his troops marched out of the fort "with colors flying and drums beating."

Four years afterward, when the conflict was almost over, on April 14, 1865, General (formerly Major) Anderson was ordered by President Lincoln to raise the American flag over Fort Sumter—the banner he had been forced to lower.

This was an outstanding occasion for the Union. Hundreds of people came from long distances and were taken out to the fort in a special steamer. Among the crowd were many army officers, along with 200 from the navy.

When it was time to run up the colors, Sergeant Hart opened a carpetbag and took from it the identical ensign the Yankees had been forced to lower four years before. As Old Glory was hoisted and unfurled to the breeze, a mighty cheer arose at seeing the beloved symbol back in its proper place. Hats were tossed into the air, the band played *The Star-Spangled Banner*, and there was a salute by the guns of Fort Sumter. Nearby forts responded; and the day was long remembered. The famous Henry Ward Beecher was the orator of the day and gave a speech that thrilled his listeners:

> There flies the same flag that was insulted. . . . Lifted to the air, today it proclaims, after four years of war, "Not a state is blotted out!" . . . And glory be to God, who . . . hath ordained victory, and shall ordain peace.

When General Anderson died, he was carried to his grave with this flag on his casket. At his wife's death, by her request, this very special banner was given to the War Department.

Flags at Libby Prison

Many federal troops were held at Libby Prison in the South during the war. For July 4, 1862, twenty-five men of the Ninth Massachusetts Infantry, including Timothy J. Regan of Company E, decided they would have a flag for this important anniversary.

Later, the Boston *Globe* reported how they managed to do this. Regan donated his blue flannel trousers; and through the guards the men were able to buy some red worsted and unbleached white cotton. They used a white shirt as material for the stars. After working hard, they completed the flag by the morning of Independence Day. Then Regan climbed up into the rafters and unfurled it, "to the delight of the little band of patriots."

There is an unusual and interesting sequel to this story. Old Glory was cut into twenty-two pieces so it would not be captured by the Confederates. Each man who had helped make it got a piece, and when he was finally released from prison, he concealed it in his clothing.

After the conflict was over, Regan wanted to unite the flag again. However, it was thirty-five years before he got the pieces and completed the flag, which was 11 feet, 9 inches, by 6 feet, 7 inches. Then it was kept at a Grand Army of the Republic post in Roxbury, Massachusetts.

A similar event happened at the same Libby Prison the following year, 1863. The prisoners heard through a slave that General Robert E. Lee had been defeated at Gettysburg. At once the men joined in singing *The Battle Hymn of the Republic*. Then "the sick, starving fellows" decided to make a flag and display it. The noted Chaplain C. C. McCabe, of the 121st Ohio Infantry, was one of the prisoners; later he told of this incident:

> A man was found who wore a red shirt; another had a blue one; white shirts were plenty. From the combination of these, at last emerged the emblem of liberty with all its thirty-four stars. I never saw men gaze so long and earnestly at a flag before.

The Flag of the Rough Riders

In the Spanish-American War, in 1898, the Rough Riders, composed of men from the Southwest, cowboys, and eastern college men, assembled in Arizona. The Women's Relief Corps of Phoenix volunteered to make a standard for them when they discovered the troop didn't have one. So they worked all night to complete a handsome silk banner.

The governor of Arizona presented the flag to the Rough Riders. As this company went through the South on their way to Tampa, Florida, they were warmly greeted. Theodore Roosevelt, a member of the organization, was said to have been "the spirit of Old Glory incarnate."

He reported that everyone came out to greet them and to cheer their progress. Former Confederates declared they had never dreamed in the bitter days after the war that they would welcome the Stars and Stripes so warmly. But now they were sending their sons out "to fight and die for it."

The Rough Riders were the first volunteer regiment organized in the Spanish-American War. They were also the first military unit to raise the United States flag over a foreign land since the time of the Mexican War.

Some of them hoisted Old Glory at the crest of Loriltires. Three men had climbed the hill to place a flag at its summit. They were trying to clamber up the slippery tin roof of a deserted blockhouse but were not making much progress. Luckily, an American sailor came up and was able to plant the Rough Riders' flag at the top—the same ensign made by the women in faraway Arizona.

Down in the bay below, on American transports, the soldiers saw the Stars and Stripes fluttering over Cuba. Then came bedlam: there were cheers, yells, band music, and sounds of gunfire.

This Rough Rider flag was carried in many battles on Cuban soil. During one conflict Color Sergeant Wright was hit in the neck by bullets, and four holes were made in the silken banner.

Admiral Peary's North Pole Flag

On the afternoon of September 6, 1909, a dramatic message was flashed by telegraph and cable around the world:

> The pole at last! The prize of three centuries, my dream and goal for 20 years, mine at last! I cannot bring myself to realize it! Stars and Stripes nailed to the North Pole.
>
> —Peary

At last the long fight and search was over; the North Pole had been won. For hundreds of years men had been trying to reach it. Explorers from numerous lands had sacrificed their lives in attempts. Thus far it had defied all who had tried. However, in 1909 Rear Admiral Robert Peary was the first man to do so.

At age twenty-five he was a civil engineer with the United States Navy. In 1886, at thirty, he made his first expedition to the North. From that time on, "the lure of the north" was in his blood.

For eighteen years this determined man worked toward his goal. Each time he returned from an unsuccessful trip, he had learned much from the failure. He brought back knowledge of scientific value; for example, Peary proved that Greenland was an island.

In 1905 the admiral set out again to try to reach the pole, this time in the *Roosevelt,* built especially for the exploration. His party left the ship on the north coast of Grant Land and pushed northwest on sleds. Finally hardships forced them to turn back, 200 miles from the pole.

In 1894 Mrs. Peary had made him a silk flag. At each of his farthest-north points, on his unsuccessful journeys, he had left a small piece of this standard, with a record, in a bottle.

Admiral Peary, on his eighth expedition, in 1908, again set out in the *Roosevelt*. His men divided into several parties, but because of shortage of supplies, one group after another had to turn back.

Peary's party consisted of his Negro aide, Matthew A. Henson, and four Eskimos. At noon on April 6, 1909, he called a halt; they were just 3 miles from the pole. In order to be sure that he had reached it, the admiral went back and forth across it several times, passing over the point where the north, east, south and west blend into one. Although the party reached the North Pole on April 6, 1909, his message did not get to the people of the world until September 6 of that year.

The group remained 36 hours at the pole. Before leaving, Peary, Henson, and the Eskimos built a great cairn of ice cakes. At its summit fluttered the United States flag which Mrs. Peary had made years before.

When the party left, Admiral Peary deposited a glass bottle in the cairn with a strip of Old Glory and this letter:

90 N. Latitude, North Pole
April 6, 1909

I have today hoisted the national emblem of the United States of America at this place, which my observations indicate to be the North Polar axis of the earth, and have formerly taken possession of the entire region, and adjacent, for, and in the name of the President of the United States of America.

I leave this record and the United States flag in possession.

—Robert E. Peary, U.S.N.

The Flag on Mother's Day

Perhaps some do not know it is fitting and proper to display the flag on Mother's Day, the second Sunday in May of each year. This custom was started by the following joint resolution of Congress, on May 8, 1914:

Whereas, the service rendered the United States by the American mother is the greatest source of the country's strength and inspiration; and

Whereas, We honor ourselves and the mothers of America when we do anything to give emphasis to the home as the fountainhead of the State; and

Whereas, The American mother is doing so much for the home, the moral uplift and religion, hence so much for good government and humanity: therefore, be it Resolved by the Senate and House of Representatives of the United States of America in Congress assembled, that the President of the United States is hereby authorized and requested to issue a proclamation calling upon government officials to display the United States Flag on all government buildings, and the people of the United States to display the Flag at their homes, or other suitable places, on the second Sunday in May, as a public expression of our love and reverence for the mothers of our country.

Sec.2. That the second Sunday in May shall hereafter be designated and known as Mother's Day, and it shall be the duty of the President to request its observance as provided for in this Resolution.

Two Memorable Flags of World War II

A memorable American flag is the one that was flying over the national Capitol on December 7, 1941, when Pearl Harbor was attacked by the Japanese. That same flag was raised the next day, when Congress declared war against Japan; and also three days afterward, when a like declaration was made against Germany and Italy.

President Franklin D. Roosevelt termed this banner the "Flag of Liberation" and took it with him to the conference at Casablanca, and also displayed it on other historic occasions. On September 1, 1945, this same ensign flew at the mast of the USS *Missouri*, during the formal surrender of the Japanese.

Another historic Old Glory was waving over Pearl Harbor on December 7, 1941. It rippled over the United Nations Charter meeting in San Francisco in the spring of 1945 and over the Big Three Conference at Potsdam, Germany, held later that year. This same ensign flew over the White House on August 14, 1945, when the Japanese accepted the terms of surrender.

The Flag of Iwo Jima

If you should ask people to recall a photograph in which the Stars and Stripes is prominent, no doubt many would answer, "Raising the flag at Iwo Jima." This picture that thrilled the world was taken by thirty-three-year-old Joe Rosenthal. When he was climbing an extinct volcano, Mount Suribachi, on the small island of Iwo Jima in the Pacific, he hastily snapped the picture of some soldiers on their way to plant an American flag on the summit.

After he had taken it, Joe thought, "That ought to make a good picture—if I caught it." Cameraman Joe Rosenthal didn't realize it, but he had made a photograph that will live forever. Millions of Americans soon knew that Joe *had* caught it. For, "Perfect in composition, sculptural in effect, the photo of the flag raising at Iwo Jima was the 'Spirit of 76' in modern combat dress."

Joe Rosenthal was an Associated Press cameraman from San Francisco. When Pearl Harbor was attacked, he tried to enlist. But he was turned down by the army, navy, marines, and seabees. He was only 5 feet, 5 inches tall, had one-twentieth normal vision, and was classified as 4-F. He wore thick-lensed glasses and always carried two extra pairs with him.

It was not until 1944 that he arrived in the Pacific area as a photographer. He not only covered the Hollandia campaign but also made landings with the marines at Guam and Peleliu and with the army at Angauer.

He reached Iwo Jima with his unit, under heavy fire. That morning, while transferring to a landing craft, he fell into the water and was almost crushed between the two craft. Luckily he had just handed over his cameras, but in the accident Joe lost his helmet.

As their boat was making its way to the shore, the coxswain pointed out a small party of men going up the slope to plant a flag on Mount Suribachi. If successful, this incident would boost the men's morale.

When Joe Rosenthal reached land, he grabbed a fire-blackened helmet that a dead marine had worn and put it on. As he started up the rise, he often had to heed the call "Down!" as a marine threw a hand grenade into a dugout just ahead of the climbing photographer.

At the top Joe saw a small flag waving. Five marines and a navy corpsman (the group he had seen from the boat) were going to put up a larger flag and keep the smaller one as a souvenir.

He quickly studied the setup, moved back 35 feet, and "clicked his shutter at exactly the right split second." As soon as he got back to the ship, Joe wrote captions and sent the films to Guam. His noted photo was made on February 23, 1945. The marines reached the summit of Mount Suribachi on the fifth day of the attempt. However, it was three weeks before the small island was won, following "a desperate and bloody struggle."

Within 24 hours after Joe had snapped the picture, it was thrilling millions of Americans; for ". . . in the photo Americans beheld the vision of victory—the surrender of Germany in May, the capitulation of Japan and the end of the war on August 14."

In San Francisco, Joe Rosenthal's draft board issued this announcement: "A registrant doing the work this man is doing is deserving of better than a 4-F classification." The board made him a 2-A F (an essential deferment).

Not knowing about this praise, Joe got a pay raise and an order to return to the United States, where he was received as a celebrity. He was sent to New York for a series of banquets, speeches, and interviews. He received the Pulitzer prize and other awards. And Joe Rosenthal became "the world's most photographed photographer." When he was asked for a comment on his picture, he modestly replied, "I like it. I think it reflects credit on the marines."

When the famous scene appeared on a green 3-cent stamp, it broke all records for first-day issues. It is claimed that this photo has been reproduced more times than any other in our history. The flag raising on Iwo Jima has been the inspiration for poems, pageants, medallions, and paintings in oil and water colors, and for statues in stone, bronze, wood, and once even in ice for a banquet in San Francisco. On the top of Mount Suribachi there is a bronze bas-relief of the unforgettable incident.

A plaque given Joe Rosenthal by the Catholic Institute of the Press hangs in the Associated Press lobby in New York and carries this tribute:

> Faith in God was his armor,
> His weapons, valor and skill.

"He served in the best tradition of the American press photographer."

One of the most inspiring sights in our national capital is the distinctive scene of six weary men on their way to raise the flag, which has been perpetuated in a heroic bronze work. This outstanding re-creation was presented by the Marine Corps as a gift to the people of America. It honors not only those six fighters on Iwo Jima but also all the brave marines who made history while serving in this branch of our armed services.

Felix de Weldon was the artist who created this 75-foot-high piece of sculpture. It stands on 7½ acres of land bordering Arlington National Cemetery—about 350 yards to the north—and is under the care of the U.S. Interior Department.

This unique monument was dedicated on November 19, 1954. Three of the six men who had taken part in the historic episode were there; the other three had been killed on Iwo Jima. President Eisenhower took part in the ceremonies and declared: "But they will live forever in the hearts of the American people, heroically depicted by the side of the Potomac."

About three months later, February 2, 1955, the marines gave a final salute and an honored grave to an American Indian who was one of the flag raisers at Iwo Jima. Corporal Ira Hayes died at his home on the Gila River reservation in Arizona on January 24. His body was brought east, and comrades buried him on a tree-shaded hillside at Arlington. His grave is not far from the great statue "which immortalizes in bronze the deed performed by six soldiers on a barren volcanic island in the Pacific in 1945."

A light snow started as they neared the grave. Leading the group and paying final honor was the commandant, General Lemuel C. Shepherd. Standing close by was Pfc. René A. Gagnon, who had helped Ira Hayes raise the flag.

The "Little" Flags

More than a million veterans of the United States wars are buried in national cemeteries. Only on Memorial Day, May 30, is it permissible to place a "little flag" on a soldier's grave. "It's a custom that simply grew through the years, a way for the country to show its respect for those who fought its wars and served it in peace-time."

Therefore, on Memorial Day, a miniature flag flies over the grave of John F. Kennedy, the simple headstone of General J. J. Pershing, the common grave of 2,111 unknowns of the Civil War, and many other comrades. Often Boy Scouts assist in placing the small flags and gathering them the next day. Each year the government re-places many of them.

TRIBUTES TO OLD GLORY

In the story "The Man Without a Country," by Edwin Everett Hale, Philip Nolan said:

> No matter what happens to you, no matter who flatters you or who abuses you, never look at another flag, never let a night go by, but you pray God to bless that flag. . . . There cannot be a man who loves the old flag as I do, or prays for it as I do, or hopes for it as I do.

> We join ourselves to no party that does not carry the flag and keep step to the music of the Union.
>
> —Rufus Choate

> A thoughtful mind, when it sees the flag, sees not the flag, but the nation itself. And whatever may be its symbols, its insignia, he reads chiefly in the flag, the government, the principles, the truths, the history that belong to the nation that sets it forth. The American Flag has been a symbol of Liberty and men rejoiced in it.
>
> —Henry Ward Beecher

> God pity the American citizen who does not love the flag; who does not see in it the story of our great free institutions, and the hope of the home as well as the nation.
>
> —President Benjamin Harrison

> You can't appreciate home until you've left it, money till it's spent, your wife till she's joined a woman's club, nor Old Glory until you see it hanging on a broomstick on the shanty of a consul in a foreign town.
>
> —O. Henry

There is the national flag. He must be cold, indeed, who can look upon its folds, rippling in the breeze, without pride of country. If in a foreign land, the flag is companionship and country itself with all its endearments.

—Charles Sumner

The Stars and Stripes is the sign of national sovereignty and unity. It is the symbol of the Constitution as the Cross is of Christianity.

—Charles W. Stewart

The flag stands for all that we hold dear—freedom, democracy, government of the people, by the people, and for the people . . . then it is our duty to defend the flag which stands for them all.

—Henry Cabot Lodge

It is my conviction that one of the gravest misjudgments by the professed evaluators of American public opinion is their under-estimation of the profound, intellectual, and emotional, the fervent and the sentimental attachment, the average, everyday American has for his flag.

—Wayne L. Hay

This flag, which we honor, and under which we serve, is the emblem of our unity, our power, our thought, and our purpose as a nation. It has no other character than that we give it from generation to generation . . . and yet though silent, it speaks to us—speaks to us of the past, of the men and women who went before us, and of the records they wrote upon it.

We celebrate the day of its birth; and from its birth until now, it has witnessed a great history, has floated on high, the symbol of great events, of a great plan of life, worked out by a great people. . . .

Traditionally a symbol of liberty, the American Flag has carried the message of freedom to many parts of the world.

—President Woodrow Wilson

No flag ever devised by man has so clearly expressed the ideals of true democracy in its design. . . . It has been literally the guiding star of our pioneers, explorers, humanitarians and soldiers. It has interwoven its threads into the texture of every chapter of our national romance. No man or child can comprehend the majesty of the history of the United States who is ignorant of the story of Old Glory.

—Samuel Abbott

2

The Great Seal
of the United States

WHEN our young republic was in the throes of organizing its government, the Founding Fathers decided to adopt a national seal with which to authenticate their important documents; for "European countries had long used seals; so the new nation signified its equal rank by adopting its own seal."

On July 4, 1776, the Continental Congress meeting in Philadelphia set up a committee consisting of Benjamin Franklin, John Adams, and Thomas Jefferson "to bring in a device for a seal for the United States of America."

After Congress rejected the report by this committee, a second group brought in a drawing. This did not meet with congressional approval either. The third committee appointed for the purpose asked William Barton of Philadelphia, a specialist in heraldry, to assist them in the project. One authority states that Charles Thomson, secretary of Congress, selected ideas from all three reports, and with the aid of William Barton designed our Great Seal.

After long delays a design was finally accepted by Congress on June 20, 1782. It was described in detail in a law of 1782, but no picture or drawing was made of it. After its official adoption, it was cut into brass. Since then seven dies have been cut. The one made in 1903 is still in use.

One source states that on September 12, 1872, our Great Seal was used for the first time on the following document:

A grant of full power and authority for George Washington to arrange with the British for the exchange, subsistence, and better treatment of prisoners of war.

If you are interested in knowing what both sides of this seal look like, you can study the reverse side of a one-dollar bill. There both sides of this important American symbol are shown. It is one of the few places where one can see the reverse. It has never been cut or used as a seal.

The design of the present one-dollar bill was created in 1935; however, the symbols used on it stem from the first days of our existence as an independent nation. The Great Seal is not found on any other denomination.

You may want to know what the various mottoes and symbols on both sides signify. Several years ago, Congressman Clyde Doyle of California wanted an answer to this question. He wrote the Library of Congress for an explanation. Mr. Doyle inserted the Library's 2,000 word reply in the *Congressional Record* for other interested Americans to read.

The face of the Great Seal has a dominating feature—a distinctive national emblem—the American eagle, with wings and talons outstretched. On its breast is a shield, borne without any support, symbolizing American self-reliance "to denote that the United States of America ought to rely on its own virtue."

The pose of the bird is considered to be "rather stiff, because it is displayed in heraldic style." Naturally, the thirteen stripes on the shield represent the original states, while the blue "chief" above the stripes was a symbol for Congress in 1782 and the union of all the states. Since the year 1789, it is said, the "chief" has stood for all the branches of our government.

In its beak the eagle holds a scroll with the Latin phrase "E Pluribus Unum," signifying "One from many"—the uniting of the thirteen states.

The eagle's right talon holds an olive branch, symbol of peace; and its left talon a bundle of thirteen arrows, denoting "military readiness, with defense as a last resort." One writer declares that while the eagle can wage war, it prefers to live in peace.

Above the bird's head is a circular field with thirteen stars— "thirteen pieces argent." The designer, William Barton, described this as "a glory, or a breaking through a cloud . . . forming a constellation argent on an azure field."

On the back of the Great Seal is an uncompleted pyramid—thirteen layers of stone—representing the original states. These signify "strength and duration—the building for the future of the Union." Above the pyramid, in a triangle backed by a "glory, or burst of light," is the "All-seeing Eye" of God or Providence, indicating that "the spiritual is above the material."

Also over the pyramid is the Latin motto "Annuit Coeptis," which can be translated as "He has favored our undertaking." The base of the monument carries the date MDCCLXXVI, or 1776. And below are the words "Novus ordo seclorum," or "a new order of the ages."

The Great Seal is in the custody of the Division of Protocol of the State Department.

Since the seal gives official status to the nation's most important documents, law forbids its use on any document not signed by the Secretary of State.

According to an official booklet about this important American emblem:

> It is affixed to such Civil Commissions as those of the Cabinet Officers, Ambassadors, and Ministers, and to exequaturs issued to foreign consular officers; and by individual warrants signed by the President it is affixed to such documents as instruments of ratification of treaties, full powers to negotiate a treaty, or to exchange ratifications, and Presidential proclamations, and to envelopes that contain letters of credence or other ceremonial communications to heads of foreign governments.

Mrs. Clydia M. Richardson became Keeper of the Seal in 1943. For several years it was kept in a small back room, where it was almost hidden from sight. For a long time she kept trying to get it properly displayed, and in an interview declared: "After all, it belongs to the people, and it is one of our great heritages."

At last she won the fight; and now the Great Seal is shown in a fitting place on the second floor of the State Building. Mrs. Richardson sent out notices about the new location so that people could come to see it.

She often tells visitors that when the design was being planned, Benjamin Franklin believed that a turkey, rather than an eagle, should be the proper emblem. "But it was felt that the turkey gobbler was a bluffer and a show-off, while the eagle soared above and was aggressive—more symbolic of what we wanted to be as a nation."

The Keeper and two assistants are the only persons who have access to the Great Seal. It is stated that Mrs. Richardson has never made a mistake in stamping more than sixty thousand documents. These have included numerous treaties and ratifications.

The importance and significance of this widely known American symbol is set forth in a pamphlet issued by the State Department:

> The Seal of the United States—the symbol of our nation's sovereignty—enters prominently into our country's foreign and domestic affairs. Impressed on certain documents by the direction of its custodian, the Secretary of State, the Seal authenticates the President's signature on various acts of our government. The design of the Seal was the product of various minds and hands belonging to some of the most illustrious of our Founding Fathers, and it represents the ideas and idealism of the stirring days of our War of Independence.
>
> The design of the Seal constitutes our nation's coat of arms, and as such, it has various official uses as decorations—from buttons on military uniforms to the plaques above the entrances of U.S. Embassies and Consulates.
>
> Most of the details of the design are symbolic: the qualities of purity, valor, vigilance, perseverance, and justice; the dedication to peace; the capacity for self-defense—all find expression in the device on the Seal.

Today the face of the seal is used not only on important papers but also on medals, to ornament the caps of army and air-force officers, on official stationary, on various national publications, on the buttons of soldiers' uniforms, and as an architectural decoration. It is displayed before every American embassy, legation, and consulate in the world.

3

The Presidential Seal and Flag

THE presidential seal, symbolizing the authority of our chief executive, dates to 1880 and was first used by President Rutherford B. Hayes.

The eagle on this seal is similar to that on the Great Seal of the United States. The bird has the shield, or escutcheon, in front of it and holds the olive branch and the thirteen arrows in its talons. And above the eagle's head is the inscription "E Pluribus Unum." This emblem is identical with the presidential coat of arms, except that these words surround it: "The Seal of the President of the United States."

This seal appears on the President's flag; a circle of fifty stars encloses the heraldry of our coat of arms. In the eagle's beak is a white scroll with the words "E Pluribus Unum."

The first presidential flag appeared in the year 1916, when it was approved by President Woodrow Wilson. He had requested Assistant Secretary of the Navy Franklin D. Roosevelt and Commodore Bruce McCandless, aide to the Secretary of the Navy, to plan a suitable emblem. On May 29, 1916, President Wilson signed the order that made this design official.

The ensign carried the presidential coat of arms on a blue field, with four stars, one in each corner. It was used until the design was superseded by a new one, by executive order of President Harry Truman, on October 25, 1945.

This chief executive had suggested a star for each state, so the eagle appeared within a circle of stars, representing the states collectively. As additional ones entered the union, more stars were added to the circle.

On the President's flag the eagle and seal are shown in natural colors, rather than in white, as on the former banner. The red, white, and blue on the eagle's breast are symbolic of our national colors. In the original seal and on the first flag, the eagle faced toward the left; but in the newer design the national bird is shown looking to the right, facing the olive branch of peace instead of the arrows of war.

The presidential flag is featured in the White House; for example, in the room that President Truman used as a study, the white colonial mantel was flanked by the chief executive's personal ensign.

Above the doorway to the Oval Room in the White House the President's seal is displayed. It is also woven into the hand-tufted rug which is in the center of the Green Room.

When the chief executive is aboard a U.S. warship, his flag is flown on the masthead during his visit. And if the vessel flying his flag passes others, the latter parade the full guard, eleven ruffles are given on a drum, four flourishes sounded by a bugle, and *The Star-Spangled Banner* played by the band as officers and men salute.

All saluting ships, on meeting a vessel carrying the President's flag, fire a national salute, as do the naval batteries. At a military post the chief executive is received with regimental colors; officers and men salute; drums and bugles sound; the national anthem is played, or bugles sound "To the Colors"; and a salvo of twenty-one guns is fired. When the President departs, he is given another such salute.

THE VICE-PRESIDENT'S FLAG

The current Vice-President's flag was adopted in 1948; it replaced the first one, which had been designed in 1936. The earlier one was simply the presidential flag in reverse. The present ensign has a white background, and the eagle is enclosed by a circle of thirteen stars.

Recently, when Vice-President Hubert Humphrey was explaining the difference between the presidential and vice-presidential flags, he joked and declared that the presidential eagle "is a grand martial bird, wings upspread, fist full of arrows." But:

> The eagle of my vice-presidential seal is holding up only one little old arrow. And the wings are spread as if coming in for a landing, hopefully a soft one.

4

"In God We Trust"

ALTHOUGH "In God We Trust" was adopted as our national motto as late as 1956, there had been frequent previous references in American history to the idea that our country was under the guidance of a divine Providence. Many statesmen and other notable Americans did not hesitate to mention the name of God and to assert their belief that He was leading the destiny of our national government.

After the famous Boston Tea Party, on December 16, 1773, the English Parliament ordered that port closed until the American colonists paid for the tea that had been destroyed. Four regiments were shipped to Boston; meetings by the citizens and elective representation in the town were suppressed.

The Americans disputed the right of the mother country to these actions. Joseph Quincy (1744–1775) made in 1775 "Some Observations on the Boston Port Bill," which included these words:

> Blandishments will not fascinate, nor will threats of a "halter" intimidate. For under God, we are determined that whatsoever, whensoever, or howsoever, we shall be called upon to make our exit, we shall die free men.

Colonel Valentine Blacker (1778–1823) is credited with having given this famous order to his men: "Put your trust in God, my boys, but keep your powder dry!"

General George Washington was inaugurated as the first President of the United States on April 30, 1789, in the city of New

York—then the nation's capital—on the balcony of Federal Hall, at Wall and Broad streets. After the official ceremony, the new chief executive offered the following prayer, a copy of which was found in Washington's pew in St. Paul's Chapel a few blocks away (this seat is still preserved there):

> Almighty God, we make our earnest prayer that Thou wilt keep the United States in Thy Holy protection; that Thou wilt incline the hearts of the citizens to cultivate a spirit of subordination and obedience to government; to entertain a brotherly affection and love for one another and for their fellow citizens of the United States at large.

According to Thatcher's *Military Journal* of December, 1777, the first prayer in the American Congress was given by the Reverend J. Duche, and contained these passages:

> O Lord, our Heavenly Father . . . who . . . reignest with power supreme and uncontrolled over all the Kingdoms, Empires, and Governments; look down in mercy on these American States, who have fled to Thee from the rod of the oppressor, and thrown themselves on Thy gracious protection; desiring henceforth to be dependent only on Thee, they have appealed for the righteousness of their cause. . . .
>
> Give them wisdom in Council and valor in the field; defeat the malicious designs of our cruel adversaries. . . . Be Thou present, O God of wisdom, and direct the councils of this honorable assembly; enable them to settle things on the best and surest foundation . . . that order, harmony, and peace may be effectively restored . . . religion and piety prevail and flourish among Thy people.
>
> . . . and crown them with everlasting glory in the world to come. All this we ask in the name and through the merits of Jesus Christ, thy Son, our Saviour. Amen.

Thomas Jefferson declared: "The God who gave us life, gave us liberty at the same time."

And he ended his famous Declaration of Independence with these lines:

> And for the support of this Declaration, with a firm reliance on the protection of Divine Providence, we mutually pledge to each other our Lives, our Fortunes, and our sacred Honor.

A poet in later times, Richard Hovey (1864–1900), wrote this about Thomas Jefferson:

> The guns that spoke at Lexington
> Knew not that God was planning then
> The trumpet word of Jefferson
> To bugle forth the rights of man.

Another stalwart statesman and eminent orator, Daniel Webster (1782–1852), in an important speech affirmed: "God grants liberty only to those who love it and are always ready to guard and defend it."

On another notable occasion, when Webster was eulogizing John Adams and Thomas Jefferson at Faneuil Hall in Boston on August 12, 1826, he made this long-remembered statement: "It is my living sentiment, and by the blessing of God, it shall be my dying sentiment—Independence now and Independence forever!"

More than a century ago, our Civil War President stated these beliefs:

> I recognize the sublime truth announced in the Holy Scriptures and proven by all history that those nations only are blest whose God is the Lord.
>
> I believe it is the duty of nations as well as of men to own their dependence upon the overruling power of God and to include the influence of His Holy Spirit to confess their sins and transgressions in humble sorrow, yet with assured hope that genuine repentance will lead to mercy and pardon. . . .
>
> We have been the recipients of the choicest bounties of heaven; we have grown in numbers, wealth and power as no other nation has ever grown. But we have forgotten God. . . .

President Franklin D. Roosevelt, in a speech to Congress on January 6, 1941, outlined the famous Four Freedoms considered essential for mankind; he declared: "The second is freedom of every person to worship God in his own way, everywhere in the world."

The "Code of the U.S. Fighting Man" is a pamphlet that was published in Washington in 1964 by the Armed Forces Information and Education, Department of Defense. In the introduction is this paragraph:

The foundations of this code are faith in God, knowledge of the basic truths and advantages of America's democratic institutions, pride in one's Service, and respect for national, military, and unit history and traditions.

The impressive Code of Conduct for Members of our Armed Forces was first promulgated on August 17, 1955, by President Dwight D. Eisenhower. The code and its basic philosophy were re-affirmed by a directive sent out by the Department of Defense in 1964:

Although the Code was first expressed in its written form in 1955, it is based on time-honored concepts and traditions that date back to the days of the American Revolution.

This code has an introduction, followed by six sections, setting forth what is required of our fighting men. The final part asserts:

I will never forget that I am an American fighting man, responsible for my actions, and dedicated to the principles which made my country free. I will trust in my God and in the United States of America.

In several American patriotic songs there is mention or praise of God in connection with the varied events of our national annals. *Hail Columbia*, written by Joseph Hopkinson in 1798, contains these words, "in heav'n we place a manly trust." Francis Scott Key in *The Star-Spangled Banner* used the words of our national motto in a slightly different way:

Blest with victory and peace, may the heav'n rescued land
Praise the Pow'r that hath made and preserv'd us a nation!
Then conquer we must, for our cause it is just,
And this be our motto: "In God is our trust."

America, with words written by the Reverend Samuel F. Smith, of Boston, was first sung at a children's celebration on July 4, 1832, at the Park Street Church in Boston. Its last stanza is a prayer to Divine Providence.

Our fathers' God! to Thee,
Author of Liberty,
To Thee we sing;
Long may our land be bright
With freedom's holy light;
Protect us by Thy might,
Great God, our King.

The Battle Hymn of the Republic, by Julia Ward Howe, composed in 1861 during the Civil War, is a triumphant expression of the power of a higher Being and His ability to win out for the right. Mrs. Howe concluded her distinctive hymn with:

In the beauty of the lilies, Christ was born across the sea;
With a glory in His bosom that transfigures you and me;
As he died to make men holy, let us die to make men free,
While God is marching on.

A few years later, when the United States was celebrating its centennial in 1876, the Quaker poet John Greenleaf Whittier wrote a *Centennial Hymn*, containing these lines:

Our fathers' God! from out whose hand
The centuries fall like grains of sand.

America, the Beautiful, was composed by Katharine Lee Bates; she was visiting in Colorado from the East and was deeply impressed by the magnificent view from the top of Pike's Peak. In her hymn, Miss Bates describes the beauty of our land; and in each stanza she prays that God will direct our people, ending with:

O beautiful for patriot dream
That sees beyond the years
Thine alabaster cities gleam,
Undimmed by human tears!
America! America! God shed His grace on thee
And crown thy good with brotherhood
From sea to shining sea!

On November 13, 1864, when the morale of the Union forces was at a low ebb because of various defeats on the battlefields, Secretary of the Treasury Salmon P. Chase received a letter from the Reverend M. R. Watkinson of Ridleyville, Pennsylvania, who wrote: "From my heart I have felt our national shame in disowning God as not the least of our present national disaster." Then the minister suggested to the Secretary that there should be "recognition of the Almighty God in some form on our coins."

At once Secretary Chase took up Mr. Watkinson's proposal and ordered designs to be prepared with the inscription "In God We Trust" on them. He also sponsored legislation that authorized the use of this motto.

It first appeared on some American coins after April 22, 1864, when Congress voted to produce two-cent pieces bearing these words. The use of this national motto was then extended to other coins. In 1955 Congress ordered the slogan to be placed on all coins and paper bills. On July 20, 1956, "In God We Trust" was officially accepted as our national motto.

In an article in the Long Beach *Press Telegram*, July 17, 1966, L. A. Collins, Sr., declared that religion in schools *is* a part of education. He discussed the findings of a recent Gallup poll conducted by the *Catholic Digest*, which showed that religion "is still a major factor in public as well as parochial schools":

> Many are disturbed by the U.S. Supreme Court's prohibition of officially sponsored prayers and devotional readings of the Bible in public schools. But few are aware of the many doors the Court leaves open for the recognition of God in the classroom.
>
> Within the Court's limits, educators can make the curriculum reflect the recognition of God as an integral part of American life and the religious influences in man's development.

Mr. Collins called attention to the fact that the Mayflower Compact, which the forty-one Pilgrims drew up on shipboard before landing on Plymouth Rock in 1620, began with the words, "In the name of God, Amen." The voyage, so the Compact stated, had been "undertaken for the glory of God." And this important paper was signed "solemnly and mutually in the presence of God."

That "cornerstone of American freedom," the Declaration of Independence, makes four specific references to the dependence of our nation on God.

Also, from the early days of our country we have our annual Thanksgiving Day, set apart to give thanks to Almighty God. Each year, our President calls upon all citizens on that day to "express gratitude to a bountiful Creator."

We have already seen that the reverse of the Great Seal of the United States shows the eye of God above the pyramid.

Our national belief in a higher Being is revealed also by the fact that government employees, court witnesses, and applicants for passports are obliged to take an oath containing the words, "So help me God," a practice begun by our first President. Forty-nine state constitutions "recognize our dependence upon God himself as the source of human rights and liberties."

A bill passed by both houses of Congress and signed by President Eisenhower on June 14, 1954, brought about a change in the pledge of allegiance to the flag. The words "under God" were added to it. So, not only the words but also the spirit of our national motto have pervaded many important events of our national history.

5

The American Eagle

THE bald eagle is the official emblem of the United States. Without doubt it is the most-pictured bird in America; it appears with outspread wings on the Great Seal, on the President's flag, on countless documents stamped with the Great Seal, on several of our coins, and on billions of one-dollar bills.

This American eagle is shown in different positions on coins and in military insignia. Sometimes the bird is seen in flight, other times at rest. Both front and side views are depicted.

Today this American symbol is a familiar sight in various places in Washington. In the main reading room of the Library of Congress a large eagle surmounts the clock. In the historic marble-columned hall where the Senate and Supreme Court once held their sessions, a spread-winged eagle still looks down.

The mace of the House of Representatives is an important emblem—the symbol of the authority of the House. On its summit is "a high-flying eagle." This mace is a means of giving information to the members of the chamber.

When the House is called to order each day, an assistant sergeant-at-arms places the mace at the right of the Speaker. It remains in this position as long as the House is in session. When it is set on a lower pedestal, this signifies that "the House has resolved itself into a Committee of the Whole on the State of the Union."

These signals in connection with the mace are important because 218 members make up a quorum for House action, while only 100 must be present when the House is gathered as a Committee of the Whole.

The 40-inch mace was created by William Adams of New York and reproduced from the design of the original, which was destroyed by the fire set by the British in 1814. It is "a superb example of the silversmith's art," but it cost the United States only $400.

This mace with its surmounting eagle is regarded with so much respect that it needs only "to be presented to an unruly House member to restore order."

The eagle, long known as the "king of birds," has been for many centuries in various countries the symbol of freedom, strength, courage, and military prowess. It is said that 5,000 years ago the people of Sumer (an ancient region of Lower Babylonia) used the "spread eagle" as their emblem of power. In Roman and Greek ruins figures of this bird have been discovered on coins, medals, and other objects.

In imperial Rome military authorities placed a gold eagle on the head of a spear, and this was carried before each legion. By 104 B.C. the eagle was accepted as the chief Roman emblem. Later it was used by Emperor Charlemagne, and noblemen of the Middle Ages often had eagles as insignia on their shields.

In Prussia the black eagle was favored, while the double-headed bird of the ancient land of Assyria became the symbol of the Byzantine Empire and was later also found in the imperial coats of arms of Austria and Russia. Napoleon I of France adopted the eagle as his standard.

There was a long and rather bitter dispute in the American Congress when the members of the new nation along the Atlantic coast of America were trying to decide on a national emblem. And it wasn't until 1789—after six years of discussion—that the young country finally chose the bald eagle with its outspread wings. One source stated:

The most violent opponent was Benjamin Franklin. The eagle was not, he complained, a truly American bird; for it had long been the symbol of European, Asiatic, and African kings and conquerors.

However, the rest of the members did not favor Franklin's idea of selecting the wild turkey, a native of this continent, for the honor.

The great statesman, in a letter to a friend, wrote on January 26, 1784:

> I wish the bald eagle had not been chosen as the Representative of our Country; he is a Bird of bad moral Character; like those among Men who live by sharping and robbing, he is generally poor, and often very lousy.
>
> The Turkey is a much more respectable Bird and withal a true, original Native of America.

But Congress ignored Franklin's suggestion. However, it did select the one variety—the bald eagle—found only in our country and unknown in Europe. And since then most persons agree that the early Congress made a wise choice. For "he is indeed a true monarch of the skies." A writer for *Britannic* has well stated:

> The bald eagle was adopted as the emblem of the United States probably because of the bird's magnificent majesty in flight—an almost effortless mastery of the air.

The first time an eagle was used on an American coin was in the year 1776, on a Massachusetts penny. Since 1789 several coins bearing eagles have been minted in the United States. These have included half-dollars, quarters, and some gold coins of varying denominations.

For many years a ten-dollar gold piece, named an "eagle," was quite popular. This coin was first made in 1795 and discontinued in 1934. It had an eagle's head stamped on the back. There have also been double-eagles, half-eagles, and quarter-eagles.

And, strange to say, for some time the eagle has been invading American houses. One person suggested that whenever there is a special outburst of patriotism, "the eagles flap right into our homes." Nowadays these birds are very popular for decorations and can be found on rugs, fabrics, lamps, wallpaper, towel racks, door knockers, wall plaques, and pitchers.

Canada and the United States have only two kinds of eagles—the golden and bald types. The latter is more common, is distinctly

American, and makes its home in temperate and warm regions. When bald eagles are one or two years old their feathers are grayish or a smoky brown color, with some white spots. At the age of three or four years the head and tail feathers turn white. The strong beaks, powerful claws, and bare legs are bright yellow. Because the early American settlers were used to the gray sea eagle of the old world, they named these birds "bald-headed" eagles, for the word "bald" formerly meant white. From a distance the birds may have looked bald to them.

The bald eagle is one of the largest of the bird family, stands 3 feet high, and may live to be thirty or forty years old. The male weighs about 8 pounds and has a wingspread of about 7 feet. The females are larger and may weigh 12 pounds, while their wingspread is 12 feet.

This bird is a strong flyer, with remarkable speed and stamina. One expert told of finding an eagle with a dated aluminum band; it had flown from Florida to a place in Georgia, a distance of more than 600 miles, in less than forty-eight hours.

The bald eagle, "a sea eagle," does not wander very far away from the seashore, river, or lake. It feeds on fish, carrion, small reptiles, mammals, and birds. Some say these eagles are excellent fishermen and can spot fish from incredible distances. (The term "eagle-eyed" has become part of our language.)

Often one of these great birds soars high overhead, scanning the water and nearby shore. Then he "glides effortlessly above the water to spot prey, sets wings for long diagonal flight, skims the surface, and dips extended talons into the water to make a catch."

One writer has stated that the eagle is *not* a good fisher and that he prefers to rob the osprey or fish hawk of its catch. The eagle swoops down between the osprey and the water. It forces its victim to fly higher and higher until it tires. When the fish hawk has to drop its prey, the eagle catches it in midair.

If the eagle is flying over land and sees a rabbit or other little animal, it keeps circling over it, then plummets down. If it misses its prey, the big bird tries again before the animal can escape.

These birds migrate—so it is claimed—only if the water freezes over. Each year they return to the same nest, or eyrie, often "a huge home in a tall tree" or on a cliff, from which the couple has a wide view. The story goes that one eagle's nest in Ohio was used for thirty-six years. The pair builds the nest of sticks; sometimes it is as large as 10 feet across and 20 feet deep. Each year the eagles repair and expand the nest by using sticks and grass.

One man wrote that some of the great birds have a "flair for interior decoration." He reported that a nest in Florida had been furnished with "human clothing, a tennis shoe, laundry-bleach bottle, gunnysack, a photographer's flash bulb, and a copy of a weekly magazine." Another nest, "made largely of torn popcorn boxes and peanut bags," was used in a zoo by one eagle family.

Two or sometimes three eggs are laid by the female in a grass-lined spot in the middle of the nest. She incubates the eggs for about thirty-five days, during which time the male guards and feeds her.

When the young ones are hatched, they are covered with white down; in about four weeks they wear "a dark gray felt-like down." Both parents share in feeding their offspring. They tear a fish apart and offer small bits to the eaglets.

As they grow older the eaglets are taught to feed themselves. The young birds remain in the nest for nine or ten weeks. They are protected from falling out by a railing of sticks around their home. When they are about ten weeks old, they begin to exercise by walking about the nest and by raising their wings and jumping into the air. Next, they start to fly away from their home.

Unfortunately, the bald eagle becomes scarcer each year. It is believed that the bird was at its zenith about the time Congress chose it as our national emblem in 1789, when it "roamed the continent with no enemies, except an occasional Indian or white settler." But, as more pioneers arrived and the country began to fill, this eagle became the prey of "collectors, chicken-raisers, or misguided citizens who thought eagles carried off lambs and children." Authorities maintain that the bald eagle cannot lift more than ten pounds; there is not a single authenticated case of a child's being carried off by this bird.

Since the birds have been hunted so much and so long, they have become rare, although still fairly common in Florida and up and down the Atlantic coast. "But elsewhere in America, its majestic presence is a rare sight." The bald eagle—so authorities report—had been fighting a losing battle until 1940, when Congress passed a law to protect the bird from being captured or killed. However, the Audubon Society believes that at least ten per cent of those remaining are killed annually.

In 1961, after a five-year study, an expert reported at the annual meeting of the Audubon Society that there were probably fewer than 5,000 of these birds left in our country. At this convention there was "serious concern for the future of the bald eagle." One speaker said:

> The lordly flight of the bald eagle may soon be confined to the Great Seal of the United States, the dollar bill, and the buttons of military uniforms.

Alexander Sprunt, director of research for the society, declared that it may be lucky that we admitted the state of Alaska to the union, for it is the one location where the bald-eagle population seems to be surviving.

President Kennedy sent the society a telegram, with which, no doubt, all patriotic Americans will agree:

> The Founding Fathers made an appropriate choice when they selected the bald eagle as the emblem of the nation. The fierce beauty and proud independence of this great bird aptly symbolizes the strength and freedom of America.
>
> But as latter-day citizens we shall fail our trust if we permit the eagle to disappear.

An unsigned article appeared in a Los Angeles newspaper, on March 26, 1967, in which the writer declared that the bald eagle needs protection from pursuers and that its existence is threatened:

> If the bald eagle could speak, the national emblem might well complain that it is being deprived of life, liberty, and the pursuit of happiness.

Once, he stated, this bird was found all over the United States, but in recent years its numbers have declined "before the environment of civilization." On the eastern seaboard, for example, many of the bird's nesting grounds have had to give way to housing developments.

Although these birds are protected by federal law, often trigger-happy hunters kill them, thinking they are hawks. Another fact that has contributed to lessening their numbers is that they often feed on fish that have have been poisoned by the widespread use of insecticides.

The Interior Department has adopted vigorous means to protect the bald eagles' nesting places. These are closed to the public during the nesting season. The department also urges power and lumber companies to respect them.

In the *National Geographic Magazine*, a writer and naturalist, Frederick Kent Truslow, came to the defense of the bald eagle. Today some persons, like Benjamin Franklin in the early days of our country, have called the great bird "a coward and a robber of farmyards"; but Mr. Truslow stated:

> Instead of being craven, the bird is too confident of its own strength to be bullied by other species. Poultry remains are seldom found in a bald eagle's nest.

Some eagles have won for themselves a place in history, notably the bird that was named "Old Abe." He became a national hero during the Civil War. Although, as mascot of a Wisconsin regiment, Old Abe was constantly a target for enemy riflemen, he survived forty-two battle engagements and suffered the loss of only a few of his feathers.

Earlier, in July, 1818, when the original State House was finished in Concord, New Hampshire, a wooden gilded eagle was placed on top of the dome. That day there was much celebrating in the town. Stephen Winship reported that toasts were drunk to this bird:

> Those toasting were obviously equal to counting to at least 13, that one being hoisted to the newly arrived bird, thus: "The American Eagle—may the shadow of his wings protect every area of our united continent, and the lightning of his eye flash terror and defeat through the ranks of our enemies!"

6
Uncle Sam

UNCLE SAM, "the imaginary figure with stars on his hat and the stripes of the flag on his trousers," has long symbolized the United States government, just as John Bull has represented England. However, some may not realize that this "tall, bewhiskered person" who has become a national emblem actually was a real character.

Samuel Wilson, American merchant and patriot, was born on September 13, 1766, at Menotomy—now Arlington—Massachusetts. His parents, Edward and Lucy Wilson, were of Scotch-Irish origin. (Their name originally was spelled Willson.) Samuel was the seventh or eighth in a family of thirteen boys and girls.

Thomas I. Gerson, who wrote a biography of Sam Wilson, has stated that

> as a small boy . . . Sam witnessed the burial of victims of the Boston Massacre. Later he served as a messenger for the Committee of Public Safety, meeting John Hancock, Samuel Adams, and many other patriots.

Sam's father is said to have been one of the "Indians" who dumped casks of British tea into Boston harbor on the night of the celebrated Boston Tea Party. Edward Wilson took part in the Battle of Lexington; he and his two elder sons, Edward, Jr., and Joseph, served in General Washington's army.

One authority states that young Sam was left at home to help the family but that at the age of fourteen he ran away from home and

47

enlisted as a "service boy." Even in his teens, he was a hard worker and quite versatile. He was said to be "an expert bullet molder, carpenter, and bricklayer." In addition, he managed a nursery and a farm.

About the year 1780 the Wilson family moved from Massachusetts to Mason, New Hampshire. There, on January 3, 1797, Sam Wilson married Betsey, the daughter of Captain Benjamin Mann.

After the American Revolution there was a severe depression. Times were hard. Almost penniless, Sam, at the age of twenty-three, with his brother Ebenezer and several other pioneers, headed westward in 1789 to look for better opportunities of making a living.

When they reached the bustling new town of Troy, New York, they looked it over and decided it would be a good place to settle.

Since Sam was such "a jack of all trades" and not afraid of hard work, he soon took root in the community. There he was well liked for his honesty and good common sense. At first he worked as a carpenter and built houses. Soon he expanded his lines of business and managed a general store, started a distillery, operated a brickyard, and also had a number of sloops on the Hudson River. Then, with his brother Ebenezer, Sam got into the meat-packing business—"the venture that led him to enduring fame."

At the time of the War of 1812 Troy was an important point for assembling food and munitions for the American troops. Sam was a prominent citizen of the town, where he and his brother were carrying on a lucrative meat trade. The firm advertised that they could "slaughter and pack 1,000 cattle a week."

The two became the chief meat suppliers for the American Army in that region. Because of the good quality of their products and Sam Wilson's well-known integrity, he was appointed federal inspector of provisions for the army of the New York and New Jersey areas.

One of the chief customers of this meat firm was Elbert Anderson, an army contractor who always insisted that his purchases be shipped in barrels marked E.A.U.S.

On October 2, 1812, several important men visited the meat-packing plant in Troy. In the group was Daniel D. Tompkins, the governor of New York. He was curious—so it was said—and asked what the letters E.A.U.S. meant.

Then a nearby workman told him that E.A. stood for Elbert

Anderson and that the U.S. was short for Uncle Sam Wilson although, of course, it actually meant the United States. This answer amused his fellow workers, and the story soon spread.

According to one source, this story of how Uncle Sam came to be associated with our government was published in the May 12, 1830, issue of the *New York Gazette and General Advertiser*, confirmed for the benefit of later historians by Theodorous Bailey, then postmaster of New York City and a former congressman.

Another report is that Sam Wilson branded each cask of pork or beef with the large letter U.S. One day when a driver was loading some of the containers of meat for a nearby military post, he asked the meaning of the initials. Then Ebenezer Wilson replied, "Uncle Sam's beef."

"Uncle Sam who?" the man inquired.

"Why, Uncle Sam Wilson, the fellow who's giving the army its food."

That day, when the driver delivered his supplies, he told the troops what Ebenezer had said. At once the soldiers began to call their meat and "everything from canteens to cannon balls" Uncle Sam's. They also declared they were in Uncle Sam's Army, and on Uncle Sam's payroll. The horses, too, were called Uncle Sam's teams. The term spread, and soon, in Washington, employees of the federal government said that they were working for Uncle Sam.

While some historians do not give credit to the story, various sources say there is evidence to prove that the troops in the Troy-Albany district were the first to use the expression "Uncle Sam." In the spring of 1813 it appeared in a Troy newspaper, and during the same year in a political leaflet in upper New York State. Three years later, a book entitled *The Adventures of Uncle Sam* was published.

Since the man Sam Wilson was so popular in his community and seemed "to epitomize the plain American—honest, self-reliant, and devoted to his country"—the idea caught on rapidly. By the close of the War of 1812 this nickname had come "to symbolize the national character of the government." As one source has stated:

> Like the expression GI in World War II, the phrase caught the imagination of the army and soon became firmly established in American folklore as a symbol that personified the United States.

Historians have never been able to locate a picture of Uncle Sam Wilson. During the 1930's a WPA project tried to discover such a likeness, but the search was not successful. A great-nephew, Lucius E. Wilson, of New York, when asked what his uncle really looked like, stated that Sam Wilson "in form and carriage greatly resembled Abraham Lincoln." Uncle Sam was also described as "large, well-proportioned and clean-shaven, in appearance he did not resemble the usual caricatures of Uncle Sam."

Before Uncle Sam became a national emblem and the subject used by numerous cartoonists, the United States had had two other symbols of colonial America: Brother Jonathan and Yankee Doodle, "a mythical son of John Bull." However, the public didn't seem to take to these two characters. The expression Brother Jonathan is reported to have originated from a frequent remark of General George Washington: "We must consult Brother Jonathan." It is said he was referring to his good and trusted friend Governor Jonathan Trumbull, of Connecticut.

It was easy for the new symbol to replace the first two. "The idea of Uncle Sam, the genial, giant farm boy who became successful, fitted the heroic mold of the newly created United States."

One authority says that the first cartoon of Uncle Sam appeared in 1832. It was a lithograph named "Uncle Sam in Danger." In it he was depicted as "a helpless victim of politics." This cartoon was against Andrew Jackson, although Uncle Sam Wilson was a devoted Jacksonian Democrat. "The drawing showed a flag-draped Uncle Sam, seated in a chair, while President Andrew Jackson drained blood from his arm."

It is said that the Uncle Sam costume, decorated with stars and stripes, originated in the 1830's when Seba Smith, a political writer, was cartooned as Uncle Sam, wearing such an outfit. Also, a noted clown of the period named Dan Rice had a like costume that he wore continually and popularized.

In a cartoon drawn by Frank Bellow in the comic weekly *New York Lantern*, Uncle Sam was not wearing a beard. His goatee and star-studded top hat were added later by Thomas Nast and Frank Bellow for political cartoons in the magazine *Punch*. In an 1862 copy of *Punch*, Uncle Sam had been given a beard, but it was not so abundant as his present one. During the 1870's Thomas Nast made

Uncle Sam popular in *Harper's Weekly*. One writer, Warren Hall, has described the real Sam Wilson in these words:

> Sam Wilson was kindly, hard-working, shrewd, famed for wit and wisdom. He was tall and loose-jointed, but probably never wore a beard, or dressed in long, striped trousers, a frock coat, and a bespangled hat. These trimmings were added later by cartoonists.

Ever since the first Uncle Sam cartoon was created, many well-known artists have depicted this figure, and countless different versions have been drawn to suit contemporary historical happenings.

For example, during the Spanish-American War, in 1898, Uncle Sam became internationally known, along with England's John Bull.

Probably the best-known picture of Uncle Sam is the one that was used as a poster during World War I to bolster recruiting. In it, a keen-eyed Uncle Sam is pointing his finger straight at the viewer and saying: "I want YOU for the U.S. Army." The painting was done by the noted artist James Montgomery Flagg, and the original is preserved in the Smithsonian Institution in Washington, D.C.

Then, in 1926, when Charles Lindbergh made his eventful solo flight across the Atlantic, Norman Rockwell painted an unforgettable Uncle Sam as a cover for *The Saturday Evening Post*. In it is the old gentleman with an aviator's helmet on his head; "his goatee is pointed into the wind"; with flying coat tails, this Uncle Sam is heading a flight of airplanes.

During the years of World War II, thousands of billboards all over the United States carried posters with Uncle Sam's portrait, urging all Americans to help in the war effort.

In 1952 a Hollywood artist named Freedman won a prize of $2,000 in a contest sponsored by a Chicago newspaper for his Uncle Sam drawing. In his work, he modernized this national symbol. One comment about Mr. Freedman's portrayal was that his Uncle Sam "somewhat resembled Bernard Baruch in his prime."

In an article in *The Los Angeles Times* in 1952, entitled "Who Is Uncle Sam?" Robert T. Hartmann made this statement about our national emblem:

> Uncle Sam in his traditional top hat, swallowtailed coat and striped trousers, is a familiar figure on both sides of the iron curtain.

Recently in Bucharest, the Communists persuaded some poor proletarian to dress up as Uncle Sam and go around congratulating factory workers who were late, or wasted materials. He was unhappy in the role, because the workers, according to Red press accounts, poured buckets of water upon him.

While Troy, New York, was getting much glory from the fact that it was the home and burial place of the original of a national symbol, there was some opposition. Citizens of Merriam, Indiana, claimed that Uncle Sam Wilson actually had immigrated to their town and had died there, and it was their wish to erect a monument to him.

In 1959 the New York legislature passed a resolution that recognized Troy's assertion that Sam Wilson had lived and died in their city; also that he was buried in Oakwood Cemetery. A bronze plaque on a marble shaft marks his grave. The Boy Scouts of Troy see to it that flags previously flown over the White House are kept waving over his resting place. His birthday, September 13, has been proclaimed by Governor Rockefeller as "Uncle Sam Day."

In 1961, when a congressman from the Troy-Albany district had introduced a bill in Congress to make a national shrine of Sam Wilson's grave, a large delegation of citizens from Troy attended a meeting of the House Subcommittee on Public Lands. To emphasize their claims, these Trojans had brought with them "a sartorially elegant Uncle Sam," attired, of course, in the traditional outfit.

This group was headed by the author Thomas I. Gerson, who said in his speech on that occasion: "Sam Wilson not only inspired the symbol of Uncle Sam, but his own life epitomizes the spirit of American independence." And that year Congress adopted a resolution saluting Uncle Sam Wilson as "the progenitor of the American national symbol."

Although the idea of Uncle Sam has been praised and loved through the years by many Americans, in recent times there has arisen some opposition to the use of the symbolic figure. One group, in particular, believes that this "bewhiskered national symbol" should now be abolished.

The noted historian Allan Nevins says that Uncle Sam has outlived his usefulness and "should be erased from world memory." He has suggested the use of Columbia or some other dignified figure, and has asserted this opinion:

> His world is gone. He seems to carry too much Yankee "cuteness." . . . What's more, Uncle Sam lends himself too easily to ludicrous or sinister caricatures in other lands.

However, others believe that if we did eliminate Uncle Sam, there might be "a flood of foreign cartoons of the kind that Nevins dislikes the most."

Uncle Sam Wilson was uncle or great-uncle to more than one hundred nephews and nieces, although he left few direct descendants. The story goes that he was first called *Uncle* Sam Wilson to distinguish him from a younger man of the same name.

Some of his fellow townsmen reported that Sam was especially fond of good jokes; also, that to the time of his death on July 31, 1854, at the age of eighty-eight, Sam Wilson always enjoyed being reminded of his connection with the origin of our national nickname. "A man of strictest integrity and friendly," Uncle Sam Wilson no doubt would have been long remembered by fellow citizens even if he had not been the progenitor of an important national emblem.

7

The Liberty Bell
and Independence Hall

LIBERTY, or freedom, has long been the great desire of mankind, and writers and speakers in different lands have expressed their feelings about it. William Cowper, for instance, said

> Freedom hath a thousand charms to show,
> That slaves, howe'er contented, never know.

And Somerset Maugham made this significant statement:

> If a nation values anything more than freedom, it will lose its freedom. And the irony of it is that, if it is comfort or security that it values more, it will lose that, too.

Our own wise Benjamin Franklin spoke these words:

> They that can give up essential liberty to obtain a little temporary safety deserve neither liberty nor safety.

Other great Americans also have expressed their ideas about liberty:

> God grants liberty only to those who love it, and are always ready to defend it.
>
> —Daniel Webster

The God who gave us life gave us liberty at the same time.

—Thomas Jefferson

Give me liberty or give me death!

—Patrick Henry

Our reliance is in the love of liberty which God has planted in us. Our defense is in the spirit which prizes liberty as the heritage of all.

—Abraham Lincoln

Bells, it has been said, have been more intimately connected with religious and imaginative affairs, also with mankind's happiest and saddest moments, than any other instrument. Arthur Gordon has declared:

If the soul of a nation is in its flag, its voice is in its bells. For hundreds of years this has been true. Some of the same bells that were rung in England when the Magna Carta was signed, rang with equal joy when World War II ended, and with the same message: freedom gained, freedom saved. "My Country, 'Tis of Thee" recognizes the role of bells. Struggling to express the inexpressible, it does not ask that liberty merely be proclaimed; it cries, "Let freedom ring!"

Therefore, it is not surprising that the winning of American independence is closely connected with our world-famous Liberty Bell, which rang out so joyously in July, 1776, to proclaim our determination to separate from the mother country, Great Britain. Fortunately, this distinctive national symbol has been preserved in Independence Hall in Philadelphia, where each year it is seen and revered by countless Americans and visitors from other countries.

The bell, cast long before the American Revolution, had previously pealed on various historic occasions. For many years it was known as the "State House Bell" of the province of Pennsylvania.

Its name—the Liberty Bell—is attributed to Benson J. Lossing and probably appeared for the first time in print in his volume *The Field Book of the Revolutionary War*, which was published in 1852.

One writer (name not given) has said of this great American relic:

The Bell is part of our beginnings that you can actually feel and touch. It is an old bell . . . and its 2,080 pounds of darkened bronze have no resonance left in them. But its battered lip and familiar jagged crack seem to offer symbolic proof that Americans have used their freedom well.

In a booklet issued by the United States Department of the Interior is an excellent summary of the importance and meaning of this cherished Liberty Bell:

Among the famous bells of the world not one has been associated with events of so great import to humanity as the Liberty Bell. Its prophetic inscription; its appeal to the people to assemble for the redress of their grievances; its defiant clangour that memorable day of the proclamation of the Declaration of our Independence; its joyous pealings over the completed work of the American Revolution, and its last tolling over the dead of the nation, give its story an abiding interest to the nation and the world.

EARLY HISTORY

The Liberty Bell was ordered from England in 1751 to celebrate the fiftieth anniversary of the province of Pennsylvania.

William Penn had founded the city of Philadelphia in 1682, and in 1701 the province received a second charter. At first the legislative body—called the Assembly—met in rented buildings in Philadelphia. There came a period when there was much resentment, accompanied by rioting, against the manner in which the governors (who represented the Penn family and the Crown) mishandled the affairs of the colony. Many citizens begged the Assembly to meet in some other community rather than the "City of Brotherly Love."

In order for Philadelphia not to lose the distinction of being the capital, some of its leaders believed that if they would build "an impressive structure" to house the Assembly, the members would be persuaded to remain in the city. Therefore the sum of £2,000 was appropriated in 1729 to construct a State House.

The edifice was started in 1732, and in 1735 the Assembly sat in it for the first time. Originally it consisted of two stories and a small cupola. But on January 27, 1750, the Pennsylvania Assembly decreed:

. . . that the Superintendents of the State House proceed as soon, as conveniently they may, to carry up a building on the south side of said house to contain the staircase with a suitable place thereon for hanging a bell.

At first the tower terminated just a little above the main roof. Although the east room on the main floor was large enough for the business of legislation, there was need for a committee room. Then the tower was raised one story for this purpose, and also for "ye bookes."

From the time of its organization, the Assembly had had a bell for official purposes. It was said that the original one had been brought from England by William Penn. In those early days it was of great importance to have a bell at the town square to call citizens together to hear vital announcements.

The first uses were to summon members of the Assembly to the morning and afternoon sessions and to inform of the opening of the courts of justice. At the State House the original bell had been used for long years. However, many Philadelphians believed there should be a newer, much larger one. But some conservatives declared there was no justification for this added expense: their taxes were already much too high.

For several years the advocates for an improvement argued their cause to no avail. But when the time for celebrating their fiftieth anniversary as a province was approaching, the opposition ceased. The sponsors finally succeeded in getting the Assembly to vote for a new bell. They thought that this important occasion certainly called for some really loud bell-ringing. So on October 16, 1751, "a bell of such weight and dimensions as the Superintendents would think suitable, was authorized by the Assembly."

Since there were no adequate casting facilities in the American colonies at that period, the bell would have to come from England. Isaac Norris, Thomas Leech, and Edward Warner wrote on November 1, 1751, to Robert Charles, the colonial agent of the province of Philadelphia in London, as follows:

RESPECTED FRIEND, ROBERT CHARLES:
The Assembly having ordered us [the Superintendents of the State House] to procure a bell from England, to be purchased for their use, we take the liberty to apply ourselves to you to get us a good

bell, of about 2,000 pounds weight, the cost of which we presume may amount to 100 pounds sterling, or perhaps with the charges, something more.

We hope and rely on thy care and assistance in this affair and that thou wilt procure and forward it by the first good opportunity, as our workmen inform us it will be less trouble to hang the bell before their scaffolds are struck from the building where we intend to place it, which will not be done 'til the end of next summer, or the beginning of the fall.

Let the bell be cast by the best workmen, and examined carefully before it is shipped. . . .

As we have experienced thy readiness to serve this province on all occasions, we desire it may be our excuse for this additional trouble. . . .

Let the package for transportation be examined with particular care and the full value insured thereon.

On November 4, 1751, they forwarded a bill of exchange to Mr. Charles for 100 pounds.

The new province bell was first cast in London at the White-chapel Foundry late in 1751 or early in 1752, by Thomas Lester (or Lister). The bell weighed about a ton, and was modeled after the "Great Tom" of Westminster—a much larger bell cast in the thirteenth century to honor the memory of Edward the Confessor.

Completed, the Liberty Bell was shipped to Philadelphia, where it arrived in good condition during the latter part of August, 1752. The day it reached the city, many of the good people of the town went down to the dock to see the bell lifted out of the ship's hold.

The new State House building was not finished, so the Bell was suspended on heavy trusses in the yard, now part of Independence Square. Then came an unhappy day for the colonists, as reported by Isaac Norris:

> It was cracked by a stroke of the clapper, without any other violence as it was hung up to try the sound. We concluded to send it back by Captain Budden, but he would not take it on board.

Therefore, it was agreed to try to recast it in Philadelphia. Two local men were given the job. They were John Pass, a native of the island of Malta, and Charles Stow, Jr., son of the Doorkeeper of the Council.

To make the metal less brittle, the partners decided to add copper to the original metal. In recasting, Pass and Stow kept the same form of the bell and its size and lettering.

But they added their own names and the place and date of recasting. Mr. Norris in reporting on this wrote:

> . . . I am just informed that they have this day opened the mould and have got a good bell, which I confess pleases me very much that we should first venture upon, and succeed in the greatest bell cast, for aught I know, in English America.
>
> The mould was finished in a masterly manner, and the letters, I am told, are better than the old ones. When we broke up the metal, our judges were generally agreed it was too high and brittle, and cast several little bells out of it to try the sound and strength, and fixed upon a mixture of one ounce and a half of copper to one pound of the old bell, and in this proportion we now have it.

Later, in a letter to Mr. Charles in London, Norris wrote:

> After it was hung in its place, it was found to contain too much copper; and Pass and Stow were so teased with the witticisms of the town, that they asked permission to do it over.

The bell had lost its resonance; but after the second recasting the people of Philadelphia were happy that they finally had a "ringable" bell! In accomplishing this, Pass and Stow had really made an entirely new bell—of "100% American workmanship." The twice recast bell was hung in June, 1753. It weighed 2,080 pounds.

That day "the merry crew of workmen" celebrated together after hanging the bell, which was destined "to await the famous day—a quarter of a century ahead—when its tones were to bring enduring renown."

The man in charge of the work, Edward Wooley, received pay for himself and his men, at his request, not in coin but in edibles. Therefore, for "raising the bell frame and putting up the bell," his list of foods included the following items:

> Two pecks of potatoes, 44 pounds of beef, 4 gammons [hams], mustard, pepper, loaves of bread of Lacey ye baker, cooking and wood, earthenware and candles, and a barrel of beer of Anthony

Morris, the whole amounting in value to 5 pounds, 13 shillings, 10 pence [about $28].

Tables were spread in the yard, and the workmen and their friends easily disposed of all the above-mentioned victuals.

DIMENSIONS OF THE LIBERTY BELL

Circumference, lip	12 feet
Circumference, crown	7 feet, 6 inches
Lip to crown	3 feet
Height over the crown	2 feet, 3 inches
Thickness at lip	3 inches
Thickness at crown	1¼ inches
Weight	2,080 pounds
Length of clapper	3 feet, 2 inches
Cost	£60 14 s. 5d.

INSCRIPTION

The biblical inscription on the Liberty Bell is one of the strangest forecasts in all American history. It is natural that many persons have believed that the term has some relation to the gaining of our independence in 1776.

This idea is not correct. For the bell was ordered in 1751 to play a part in celebrating the fiftieth anniversary of the charter of privileges which William Penn had granted the province of Pennsylvania.

This 1701 document allowed full religious freedom to the inhabitants of Penn's colony. This was the "furthest step toward personal liberty in any of the colonies up to then."

When the sponsors of the new bell wanted an appropriate inscription for it, they selected one containing two parts. The first read: "By order of the Assembly of the Province of Pennsylvania for the State House in the city of Philadelphia."

The second section was a scriptural passage, found in Leviticus xxv:10: "Proclaim liberty throughout all the land unto all the inhabitants thereof."

Although the word "liberty" appeared on the bell, the present title was not given it until many decades later, for it was cast years before the colonists had ever dreamed of being independent of the mother country.

The Pennsylvania assemblymen realized that there was a likeness between the religious liberty they had won and the fifty-year jubilee of Bible times. But apparently no one saw how prophetic the inscription really was. One writer has remarked:

> The actors of that drama must have felt how strangely appropriate were the lines that the old Assembly decreed to cast upon the bell in 1751. None then dreamed that the inscription would prove so significant in 1776.

The prophecy was fulfilled on July 8, 1776 (not on July 4, as many erroneously believe), when the bell rang out loudly to call the citizens of Philadelphia together to hear the reading of the newly completed Declaration of Independence.

EARLY USES OF THE BELL

After the State House bell had been put in place, it is reported to have sounded officially for the first time on August 27, 1753, when it summoned the members of the Pennsylvania Assembly. The crowd was informed that the province would continue to mint coins, contrary to a recent edict of the British Parliament. During the following years it rang for numerous legislative sessions and for the openings of the courts of justice. The Bell also brought citizens together for mass meetings in the large State House yard. There, leaders gave them news of patriotic calamities or reasons for celebration. "Its reverberations," wrote Wilfred Jordan, "were often fraught with the words of prophecy, war, or woe." Therefore this "guardian of American liberty" played a vital role in the making of our nation.

Today this symbol is so revered that it is hard to believe that it was not always treated with the great respect that it is shown now. During the early years of its existence, it was rung so frequently that several complaints against the big bell were sent to the Assembly.

(The bell was not unusually big as "judged by European standards." Big Ben in London was really thirteen times as large; some Russian bells weighed more than 100 tons each. However, the State

House bell "was large enough to cause varied complaints from the citizens of Philadelphia," especially those who lived in the immediate vicinity.)

Some persons decided to try to get rid of it. A petition was signed by "divers inhabitants," who declared in their document that the bell was "a lethal object" and that they were much disturbed by its frequent sounds. In addition, they asserted that "because of its uncommon size, and unusual sound, it is extremely dangerous and may prove fatal to those afflicted with sickness."

These signers begged "to be relieved of this dangerous inconvenience, except at the time of the meeting of the Honorable Assembly and the Courts of Justice." Even though such objections were sent in from time to time, no relief was given the objectors and the matter "was laid on the table."

At the request of the Assembly, Benjamin Franklin left on February 3, 1757, for England to ask redress for the many grievances the colonists had suffered at the hands of the mother country. On that important occasion "the Bell echoed the hopes of the people's hearts as its melodious bon voyage sounded over the Delaware River as he sailed away."

The accession of King George III was proclaimed by the State House bell in February, 1761. Two years afterward, on July 8, 1763, Philadelphians answered the call of the bell and heard the welcome news that the French and Indian War had finally reached its end. That same year, on September 9, members of the Pennsylvania Assembly convened to discuss a plan for holding the first congress of representatives from the thirteen colonies.

When the Stamp Act went into effect, the bell, muffled as for a funeral, tolled slowly to summon the Assembly to consider making a protest to the King and Parliament against this unjust ruling. It sounded in similar fashion when the ship *Charlotte*, convoyed by a British man-of-war and carrying the despised stamps for Pennsylvania, New Jersey, and Maryland, came sailing up the Delaware River. That day, October 5, 1765, the bell called thousands of citizens to a meeting, at which they determined to resist this infamous act.

Then, on October 31, the colonists mourned the death of liberty and "burned publicly stamp papers at the coffee house." Fortunately, some months later the bell was "freed of its impediments; its joyous cadences resounded through the city, bespeaking the decree of Parliament, which repealed this act of tyranny."

About three years later, on April 25, 1768, citizens of Philadelphia met in the State House yard. There they made vigorous protests against the restrictions which acts of Parliament had put on American manufactures. These laws prohibited the colonists from setting up steel and planing mills and from manufacturing hats and woolen goods. The citizens also protested against the shipping of paupers to their colonies.

On July 30, 1768, the bell rang "to assemble the freemen of Philadelphia . . . to consider instructions to our representatives in the present critical situation of these colonies." Two years afterward, on September 27, 1770, the crowd in the State House yard agreed that the "claims of Parliament to tax the colonies were subversive of their constitutional rights. . . ."

The bell called the Assembly together on February 4, 1771, to petition King George III to repeal the tax that had been placed on tea. And a resolution on October 18, 1773, denounced those colonists who bought and sold the tea with its royal tax as "enemies of their country."

On December 27, 1773, at 10 A.M., the State House bell assembled the largest crowd of irate citizens ever gathered together in Philadelphia. The occasion was the arrival of the ship *Polly*, with its "odious cargo" of tea. The people resolved that they would not permit the *Polly* to land it and that Captain Ayres should return the cargo to England.

> Thus did the Bell proclaim and herald every important step toward the goal of liberty, reverberating with pugnacious, violent peals the cry of determined citizens in the largest political meeting held up to that time, in the State House Yard, that "none of the ship *Polly*'s detestable tea" that had just been brought into port "should be funneled down people's throats with the Parliament's duty mixed with it."
>
> And the vessel, the Captain and the tea sailed down the river, to return no more.

In May, 1774, many colonists were in despair at the way events were going. Once more the State House bell, "carefully muffled, tolled in a prophetic manner" and brought people together to hear of the closing of Boston harbor.

Then on June 1, 1774, a second meeting occurred; its object was to send aid to the poor in Boston who were so badly affected by the British restrictions on their trade.

> As the conflict with England approached, the Bell was rung more and more . . . its peals more inspirational as when on April 25, 1775, just after the report came to Philadelphia of the Battle of Lexington.

Unanimously the people agreed "to associate, for the purpose of defending with arms, their lives, liberty, and property against all attempts to deprive them of them."

THE BELL'S MOST IMPORTANT RINGING

After suffering many indignities at the hands of King George and the British Parliament, the American colonies decided to do something about the state of affairs. Because of their opposition to Great Britain's policies toward them, delegates from the thirteen colonies, making up the first Continental Congress, had met in Philadelphia, then the chief city of the English colonists in the new world. Their first session was held in Carpenter's Hall, not far from the State House, in September, 1774.

In May, 1775, after war had already begun in Massachusetts, the Second Continental Congress met in Philadelphia, this time in the State House, later Independence Hall. At their next meeting, in the spring of 1776, the delegates discussed the matter of complete separation from the mother country. On April 12, 1776, North Carolina had authorized her representatives to join with the other provinces in making the break with Great Britain.

However, Virginia was the first to have its delegate take the initiative. On June 7, 1776, Richard Henry Lee of that colony offered a resolution to the Congress "that these United Colonies are, and of right ought to be, free and independent States."

John Adams, the fiery patriot from Massachusetts, seconded the famous resolution. Five men were elected by ballot to draw up a document, setting forth the reasons for the desired separation from Great Britain. The committee consisted of Thomas Jefferson and

John Adams—both destined to be Presidents of the United States—Benjamin Franklin, Roger Sherman, and Robert R. Livingston.

Most of the work fell upon the chairman, Thomas Jefferson, a Virginian. He was asked to draft a statement that "out of a decent respect to the opinions of mankind" would relate the numerous grievances that were compelling the colonists to take this step. Jefferson performed most of the work in a building in Philadelphia at the corner of Seventh and High streets—now Broad. Finally, after much hard labor, he completed the task. The committee held some conferences and then presented its report to the Second Continental Congress on June 28, 1776.

On July 2, three weeks after it had been proposed to the Congress, the Lee-Adams Resolution to sever all ties with England was up for final decision. When it was passed, John Adams was overjoyed and on July 3 wrote his wife, Abigail:

> Yesterday the greatest question was decided which ever was debated in America; and a greater, perhaps, never was, nor will be, decided among men. A resolution was passed, without one dissenting colony, "that these United Colonies are, and of right ought to be, free and independent States."

After the resolution had been adopted, the Declaration of Independence, explaining the reasons for the vital break, had to be approved by the Congress. This body took up the document paragraph by paragraph. There were several days of heated debating.

It is related that young Jefferson, while his work was undergoing criticism, "sat silent and uncomfortable" as various members made 86 changes. They eliminated 480 words and left the noted document composed of 1,337 words. Jefferson—so the story goes—thought the many changes and omissions were "deplorable."

John Adams along with the other members of the Congress, was well aware what "toil and blood and treasure" it would cost them to maintain and defend this declaration. But he declared that through the gloom he could see "rays of vanishing light and glory"; also that the end was worth more than the means.

After the passing of the Lee resolution, Adams had written his wife:

The second of July will be the most memorable epoch in the history of America. I am apt to believe that it will be celebrated by successive generations as the great anniversary festival.

Two days afterward—on July 4, 1776—the Declaration of Independence was adopted in the form we know it today. And so the *Fourth* of July, instead of the second, became our national Independence Day. On that date, contrary to the belief of many, only two delegates signed the document, the president and the secretary of the Second Continental Congress.

(There was a bit of humor connected with the day. Thomas Jefferson reported later that the approval of the Declaration of Independence had been hastened because of the fact that during the extremely hot weather swarms of flies abounded; they would settle on the silk stockings of the representatives and sting them "maddingly.")

As soon as the document was adopted, it was turned over to a printer, John Dunlap, to be printed on broadsides so that copies could be sent to key places in all the colonies. At once men on swift horses left Philadelphia and carried the broadsides to all parts of the country. The original copy of the Declaration that was sent to the printer was lost, but one of the broadsides was preserved and fastened to a page in the journal of the proceedings of the Second Continental Congress. The full text first appeared on July 6, in the Pennsylvania *Evening Post*, which was sold for two coppers.

Later that summer the document was engraved on parchment with the title "The Unanimous Declaration of the Thirteen United States of America," and it had finally been signed by every member of the Congress.

John Hancock wrote his name in big letters, so King George would not have to put on his glasses to read it. Benjamin Franklin spoke those long-remembered words: "Gentlemen, now we must all hang together, or assuredly we shall hang separately."

Of this famous national document one source has asserted: "Perhaps the finest statement of democratic principles and rights ever penned, the Declaration stands today as the basis of the free government of the United States."

The State House bell, whose deep voice had been heard on important occasions in Philadelphia for about a quarter of a century before this time, was *not* rung when the Lee-Adams resolution was passed. Nor did it ring two days later—on July 4, 1776—after the Declaration was accepted.

For years countless Americans have believed the story that when the representatives of the thirteen colonies all signed the document, an old bell ringer pulled the rope and the Liberty Bell proclaimed the glad news.

This tale is said to have originated with a Philadelphia writer named George Lippard. He invented it and published it in the *Courier* in 1846. He called it "The Fourth of July, 1776," and labeled it plainly as "the inaccurate and highly colored legend of the Revolution." However, it became very popular and was widely accepted as the truth.

In this story, an aged man stood tensely in the belltower of the State House, waiting for Congress to complete its work of adopting the Declaration. Downstairs, also waiting, was "a flaxen-haired boy with eyes of summer blue," to tell the bell ringer that the deed was done. Later, in a volume entitled *Popular Patriotic Poems*, published in 1895, a poet had improved Lippard's version by having the boy call out, "Ring, Grandpa, ring!" as he rushed up the stairs with his welcome news.

Other writers acclaimed the legend and repeated it in stories and poems. Around the country it was widely believed. But research has proved that it *was* a legend.

Some time ago, Pete Martin wrote of this tale in *The Saturday Evening Post*, saying that many Americans believe that

> When a quill pen had squeaked the last signature across the parchment, a small boy rushed outside and shouted, "Ring, Grandfather, ring!" A white-haired gaffer yanked a rope while the huge crowd gathered ouside cheered. So lustily did the old gaffer pull that the Liberty Bell cracked.
>
> It's a story filled with emotional impact. Yet none of it happened. So much for the old . . . fairy tale concerning gaffer, boy, and a grimly wisecracking group of signers crowding forward on the Fourth to put their necks in a noose as they wrote their names.

Another source says: "There were on that famous Fourth no crowds around Independence Hall, no white-haired bellman, and no flaxen-haired child."

The crowning moment for the bell came on July 8, 1776, when it called together the members of the Continental Congress and citizens of Philadelphia in the State House yard. And on that important day many persons, along with the daring signers, *did* pledge "their lives, their fortunes, and their sacred honor."

At eleven o'clock that morning the Philadelphia Committee of Safety met. In this group were the signers of the Declaration and other delegates. At the same hour, the Committee of Inspection gathered at the Philosophical Hall on Fifth Street. Then they joined the Committee of Safety, and all walked to the State House yard. It had a big gateway on the south side and was enclosed by a wall. The constable, coroner, and deputies, carrying the insignia of their offices, headed the procession.

Soldiers with cannon were at the yard. In the upper room of the State House, and in the soldiers' barracks to the east and west, large quantities of munitions were stored. Near the yard stood wagons containing powder, shot, and other military stores.

Authorities differ as to the numbers that gathered that day. One said there were not more than 300 persons at the historic affair. Some citizens viewed the assembly a bit contemptuously. "I was in the Old State Yard," wrote Charles Biddle, "when the Declaration of Independence was read. There were few respectable persons present."

Miss Deborah Norris, who lived in a house on Chestnut Street, was even less complimentary: "The first audience of the Declaration was neither very numerous nor composed of the most respectable class of people."

One diarist of the era described the event as follows:

> There was a large assembly of people in the Yard who had been summoned by the tolling of the Liberty Bell, as they had been many times before on the occasion of some public event. Passing through the assembled crowd, the procession of officials, who had charge of proclaiming this state paper to the people, reached the platform at which time the Liberty Bell ceased ringing.

John Adams spoke glowingly of the day and said a great crowd had assembled: "Three cheers rended the welkin; the Battalion paraded on the Common and gave us the Feu de joie. The bells rang all day and almost all the night. Even the chimes chimed away."

At twelve noon that day Colonel John Nixon of the Committee of Safety ascended a platform about twenty feet high. It was of wood, surrounded by a balcony and railing, and was reached by a stairway.

Colonel Nixon had been selected for the reading because he was "a man of frank countenance and powerful voice." He was a descendant of an early immigrant family from Ireland, one of the founders in 1771 of the Friendly Sons of St. Patrick, and an ardent patriot. He was in command of the City Guard of Philadelphia.

Colonel Nixon stood in the bright sunshine and "in a stentorian voice" gave the public its first hearing of the famous document:

> When in the Course of human events, it becomes necessary for one people to dissolve the political bands which have connected them with another, and to assume among the powers of the earth, the separate and equal station to which the Laws of Nature and of Nature's God entitle them, a decent respect to the opinions of mankind requires that they should declare the causes which impel them to the separation.

The crowd was hushed by the impact of the introduction, but it "could not restrain its enthusiasm for the indictment of the King."

The citizens listened breathlessly as the colonel read; it is said that his reading was so clear that his words could be heard even beyond the State House yard.

Then came the greatest moment in the life of the State House bell. For a short time the crowd was silent at the end of the reading. Then from the tower of the building—afterward known as Independence Hall—came "the jubilant crashing tones of a clapper on bronze." The bell ringer was a Scotsman, Andrew McNair.

> Strong hands swung at its ropes; its tones rang out without pause, for two hours, while the city below went mad with rejoicing. . . . The Liberty Bell was speaking. . . .
> Cheers rang down the quiet streets of Philadelphia. Other bells, those of the churches, joined in. The United States had been born.

The bells in the tower of nearby Christ Church helped in the jubilation and joined in the chorus, even though its pastor, the Reverend Jacob Duche, had *not* joined in the patriotic cause.

> That worthy gentleman, however, persisted in using the public prayer for the sovereign and the Royal Family, but remained unmolested by the patriots.

Later that day, members of the crowd at the yard tore the King's arms from every public building, including the State House door, and carried them to the Common. This was the sparsely settled section west of Eighth Street, where the Continental troops had their military drills. In the evening the insignia were burned in a great bonfire made of empty casks, amid great rejoicing.

Also, on that evening, the Liberty Bell sounded again to announce the second reading of the Declaration of Independence. This was for the benefit of the soldiers. And they, no doubt, with other listeners, were thrilled to hear the immortal words:

> We hold these truths to be self-evident, that all men are created equal, that they are endowed by their Creator with certain unalienable Rights, that among these are Life, Liberty and the pursuit of Happiness.

Finally, tired but happy, everyone went home after this exciting day, on which a contemporary wrote:

> Fine, starlight evening. There were bonfires, ringing bells, and other great demonstrations of joy upon the unanimity and agreement of the Declaration.

The Pennsylvania *Evening Post* on July 9, 1776, stated that after the reading of the Declaration of Independence, three cheers were given with the cry, "God Bless the Free States of America!" So "all ties with Great Britain were severed by the Declaration."

USE OF THE BELL FROM 1777 TO 1835

After its historic and highly acclaimed ringing on July 8, 1776, the Liberty Bell sounded in Philadelphia on each succeeding Fourth of July until 1835, when it became silent.

The Pennsylvania *Gazette* on July 9, 1777, reported that after the lapse of a year, the bell pealed joyously for the first anniversary of Independence Day. Congress adjourned over the Fourth. The bell sounded even in the midst of the war to celebrate America's one year of independence and to inspire the colonists to fight on to ensure their freedom. And on this important day "the Bell led off triumphantly in the first nation-wide July Fourth celebration."

John Adams wrote his twelve-year-old granddaughter a description of the festivities:

> In the evening I . . . was surprised to find the whole city lighting up their candles at the windows. . . . I think it was the most splendid illumination I ever saw; a few surly houses were dark, but the lights were very universal. . . . Had General Howe been here in disguise, or his master, this show would have given them the heartache. . . .

A few months later, in September, 1777, came the tense night when a courier rode through the streets of Philadelphia and proclaimed the unhappy news to the stunned colonists: "Brandywine is lost! The British are marching on the city!"

After his defeat at Brandywine, General Washington knew he could not continue to hold Philadelphia; therefore, he ordered all military stores to be transferred to Bethlehem, Pennsylvania.

At once the state Assembly passed a resolution that all bells from public buildings and churches and other miscellaneous metal items should be removed from town so that his Majesty's troops could not get possession of them. For they had been seizing all the metal objects they could get hold of and melting them down into cannon and balls. They were especially eager to get possession of the State House bell, for they knew of its use and that it was "the harbinger of liberty." The patriots, for their part, were just as eager to retain their cherished bell.

On September 26 the bell called together for the final time the Pennsylvania Assembly. Messengers brought the startling news that General Howe, with his British force of 17,000 men armed with bayonets, and only 35 miles away, was heading the advance of the British and Hessian forces toward Philadelphia.

At that time the Continental Congress was in session in the city, which was serving as the capital of the newly born United States.

The leaders realized how much it would please their enemies if they could capture the members of the rebel American government. Therefore, these wise Founding Fathers acted on the old adage that "discretion is the better part of valor." Under cover of darkness they mounted their horses and rode swiftly out of town. Their rendezvous was Lancaster, Pennsylvania, which was to serve as the capital of the young nation. The route there led by way of Bethlehem.

There was much confusion during that terrifying night, but the leaders also did some good quick thinking. At once farm wagons were brought into the State House yard, and freedom-loving patriots lifted our priceless Liberty Bell down and placed it in one of the vehicles.

Then the train of 700 wagons conveying the heavy baggage and military supplies of the colonial forces started on its perilous journey. The train was guarded by 200 troops—mounted men from the North Carolina and Virginia cavalry. They were under the command of Colonel William Polk. A guard of 50 mounted soldiers and 50 infantrymen, "with sabres out and bayonets fixed," had hurried across the Delaware River into New Jersey and on to Trenton. There they placed in safekeeping precious papers and documents.

That night the Liberty Bell lay concealed in a wagon belonging to John Jacob Mickley. The owner was driving it, and with him was his eleven-year-old son, who at times would take over the reins and let his father sleep.

Unluckily, the Mickley wagon broke down on a street in the town of Bethlehem and the precious bell had to be unloaded and placed in a vehicle belonging to Frederick Leason, who took the relic on to Allentown.

> No hands more willing ever lifted the Liberty Bell than those that came to its rescue when its conveying wagon met with disaster.

Now it would be safely hidden until the time came when it could again be heard "sounding for the Continental cause."

In the records of the Moravian Church in Bethlehem is this entry:

> A continual train of Army wagons came into the place. . . . The bells from Philadelphia were brought in wagons. The wagon with

the State House Bell broke down here; so it had to be unloaded; the other bells went on.

It was indeed a real accomplishment to get the bell safely across the 50 miles of countryside "that might at any minute be turned into a battlefield."

In Allentown the Reverend Abraham Blume and his eager assistants strained with all their combined might and lifted the precious symbol from its resting place in the farm wagon. Then they carried it to the Zion Reformed Church and lowered it under the flooring, near the pulpit. Here it remained for more than one year.

During this period the minister continued to preach here, and his parishioners joined with him in singing patriotic hymns and in praying for the success of their cause and for the safety of their fighting men in the Continental Army.

Under their very feet, and silent, lay the bell, which too was quietly waiting for the tide to turn in favor of the American colonists.

Finally the course of events made a turn for the better. The British left Philadelphia. There were American victories such as the one at Saratoga. It was considered safe to return the Liberty Bell to its home in Philadelphia.

Many persons in that city who had believed the rumor (started, no doubt, to fool the British) that the bell had been sunk in the Delaware were astonished when their noted bell made a triumphant return in late September or early October 1778. It was replaced in its proper setting. The citizens were "tumultuous with joy" when its long-unheard peals again rang out over their community.

A tablet in Zion Reformed Church in Allentown bears this inscription:

> To commemorate the concealment of the Liberty Bell during the Revolutionary War in the second church built on this site. This tablet is erected by the Liberty Bell Chapter of the Daughters of the American Revolution.

One of the first important uses of the bell after its return from Allentown was to proclaim the surrender of Lord Cornwallis to General Washington at Yorktown, Virginia, in October, 1781. The

Philadelphia Council ordered this ringing, at twelve noon on October 24.

For some time the bell was not rung very much because the tower in which it hung "showed signs of decay." A local paper reported that people were afraid to ring it for fear the steeple would fall down. However, repairs were made, so the bell was able to peal forth and triumphantly proclaim the British surrender. "Four pieces of artillery sounded to the pealing of the bell and all the city bells answered."

On November 27, 1781, his Excellency, the commander-in-chief, General George Washington, and his lady arrived in town from Virginia. The old bell rang, along with the church bells, and all welcomed the chief with great demonstrations of joy.

Another day of rejoicing was September 3, 1783, when the Liberty Bell sounded to proclaim the news that the peace treaty had been signed between America and Great Britain. A writer named Keyser stated that

> . . . from this time the Bell, now world-wide known as the Bell of Independence, continued for half a century of proclaiming its announcements . . . and the tolling also at the death of our great men, and welcoming many illustrious men of our own and other nations.

In Philadelphia on July 4, 1788, there were elaborate ceremonies to recognize the anniversary and also to rejoice over the adoption of the Constitution. When General Washington died, on December 18, 1799, the bell was muffled, and it tolled late that night to announce the passing of our first President. On February 19, 1801, the bell rang when Thomas Jefferson was elected President. Three years later, in 1804, it mourned the death of Alexander Hamilton, killed in a duel by Aaron Burr.

The Marquis de Lafayette, who had helped the Americans to gain their independence, revisited the United States and Philadelphia on September 29, 1824, and was welcomed by the pealing of the Liberty Bell.

On July 4, 1826, the bell ushered in the year of jubilee—the fiftieth anniversary of the adoption of the Declaration of Independence. That day it also tolled for the deaths of two great early patriots, John Adams, aged ninety-one and Thomas Jefferson, eighty-three. By a strange coincidence, they died on the same day, and within a few hours of each other.

A great crowd gathered in the State House yard on July 26, 1826, to pay homage to the memory of Thomas Jefferson.

> The Bell of the State House was muffled; to its deep tone, the slow measure of its tolling gave a very solemn impression. . . . The Bell which had proclaimed Thomas Jefferson's immortal masterpiece and had hailed his advent to the Presidency of the Republic whose truth it had signalized, now had sounded his death knell.

The Liberty Bell on July 2, 1834, tolled once more "in solemn cadence." Ten years before, it had joyfully welcomed Lafayette. Now he had died; and on this day, people of Philadelphia first met at the State House yard. Then they went in a procession to divine services in his memory. Lafayette was the last of Washington's generals to die.

When tidings of the Catholic Emancipation Act passed by the English Parliament reached Philadelphia, the bell was sounded. July 4, 1831, is the last recorded ringing for our Independence Day. On February 22, 1832, it sounded for the last time in honor of General Washington, "Father of His Country."

After many years of continuous service it was beginning to weaken; but as one writer says, by an uncanny incidence, it lasted long enough to toll for Charles Carroll of Carrollton, the last surviving signer of the Declaration of Independence: "All the great actors in the drama for independence had passed from the mortal stage when the Bell rang for the last time."

THE CRACKING OF THE BELL

John Marshall, the eminent Chief Justice of the Supreme Court, had undergone a serious operation. Apparently he was making a good recovery, when the sudden and unexpected death of his wife proved to be such a shock that the justice died in Philadelphia on July 6, 1835.

All over the country there was deep sorrow. He had served his country well—in the Revolutionary Army and as a lawmaker, minister to France, member of Congress, and finally Chief Justice.

Therefore it was considered proper, as a token of respect to this distinguished American, that the Liberty Bell be tolled as his funeral cortege passed along the streets on July 8. The procession consisted of troops and numerous citizens out to pay their respects to him. The body was on its way to Virginia for burial in Marshall's native state.

But the great bell, always brittle, cracked while ringing for his funeral solemnities. The disaster happened on the fifty-ninth anniversary of the Liberty Bell's greatest day—July 8, 1776.

> Solemnly, and deeply the old Bell tolled. Slowly, a tiny crack, which had formed unseen, at its lower edge, widened, and ran swiftly upward. As the Bell tolled on, its note broke suddenly into a high shrill sound, and then it went silent. "Its great days of service were over; thereafter, it would be but a mute symbol of duty done."

On the silencing of this historic relic, two writers (names not given) expressed distinctive tributes to the bell in these paragraphs:

> It had lived a rich and vital life. It had tolled for a nation's weal and a nation's woe. It had tolled for the makers of the nation, for their births, their deeds, and their deaths. . . . But the spirit of the Liberty Bell will never die.

> It had lived out its life—82 years of usefulness as men live out their lives. Its active work was done; it had called the people together to preserve their rights under the British Crown; it had rung out its clamorous defiance on the great day of the Proclamation of the Declaration of Independence; it had glorified all anniversaries of that Independence. Henceforth, it remains in its ancient place, the silent symbol of not only "Liberty throughout all the land," but throughout the world.

Often it has been asked why the bell cracked in 1835. The answer has been given that the defects in it really dated back to the time of its original casting, and were caused by "cooling strains." These defects began as minute flaws; at first they were not apparent to the eye, or to the ear "by a discordant tone in ringing." The bell also had had some hard usage at times, such as the jolting and fall on the way to Allentown.

After the Liberty Bell cracked, it was really "abandoned" for the next eleven years. Then, in 1846, a plan was formulated to try to restore its sound so that it could be rung on George Washington's birthday. The crack was drilled out to separate the parted sides, and "the present large fissure was made in its side with the hope of restoring its sound." However, the experiment was not successful. Although at first it sounded "clear and loud," it suddenly "cracked further and irreparably."

In recent years some persons have maintained that, with the help of metallurgical science, the crack could be welded together so it could be heard again.

The bell is the property of Philadelphia; the National Park Service of the United States Department of the Interior, which also keeps close guard over it, and the city are both opposed to any such "tinkering." One mayor of Philadelphia, Bernard Samuel, declared that the Liberty Bell is sacred to the American people in its present condition. Often persons have said, "We like the crack."

Infinite care has been taken to preserve this historic relic. Some years ago the clapper that had been inside it for one hundred and sixty-two years was removed. As the crack spread, "a spider" of steel was installed to hold the chopped edges firmly together, It also "equalizes the weight strain, and holds the bell at all times in a safe position."

In 1915 the bell was removed from its glass case so that visitors could have the privilege of touching it.

> The cracked Liberty Bell is a cherished symbol of America's struggle for freedom. . . . The crack in the Bell helps Americans remember that their forefathers did not win liberty for this country and its people without extensive fractures.

SPECIAL USES OF THE BELL IN LATER YEARS

It has been said that no living person has actually heard the Liberty Bell; for it really has not been *rung* since it cracked in 1835.

However, on being lightly tapped, it has produced some sounds on a few important occasions. It makes "a muffled sound when struck by an especially constructed mallet." This can be done without harm to the bell.

It took part, on October 10, 1917, in a street parade in Philadelphia, on the First Liberty Loan Drive. The bell did its bit by adding emphasis to the appeal to put the Liberty Loan over. It was hailed by bare heads; and the inspiration of this symbol led to a great response to the drive. The issue of five billion dollars was oversubscribed.

In 1926 this bell sounded for the Sesquicentennial Year of our republic. On New Year's Eve, 1925, the reception usually held at City Hall in Philadelphia was transferred to Independence Hall.

Mrs. Kendrick, wife of the mayor, used a golden mallet to tap the "welcoming signals," the advent of the New Year, 1926—once, nine times, twice, then six times. The ringing was "mechanically magnified"; the sounds of the bell sped through the air to the radio audience. It was said to have sounded like "a dulled, but proud voice."

Almost two decades later, on June 6, 1944, our symbol was heard on a nationwide hookup, when its tone was broadcast to homes in every part of the United States. This was to honor the landing of the Allied forces on the beaches of Normandy; again the bell "proclaimed liberty throughout the land."

At that time, of course, it did not actually ring, but with a rubber mallet the mayor of Philadelphia was able to tell our nation that our troops had successfully landed in Europe.

> The Mayor tapped the Bell once for each letter in the word Independence. During a broadcast, later on the same day, the Bell was tapped again 7 times—once for each letter in Liberty.

Again the sound of the Liberty Bell was heard in the year 1945, when surrender occurred both in Europe and in the Pacific.

Admiral Byrd, from his location at the South Pole, once tolled it electronically by long distance. However, the guardians of the bell at Independence Hall do not care for such stunts. They fear that "an overenthusiastic tapper" might do some irreparable harm to it.

It is reported that the last time the Liberty Bell made a sound was in May, 1950, when Secretary of the Treasury Snyder "tapped it gingerly" to announce the beginning of a United States Bond Drive.

BELL RINGING ON INDEPENDENCE DAY

"Through the years," it has been said, "the sound of bells has been the sound of freedom."

John Adams was eager for a fitting celebration of the anniversary of our Declaration of Independence and asserted:

> It ought to be commemorated as the day of deliverance by solemn acts of devotion to God Almighty. It ought to be solemnized with pomp and parade, with shows, sports, guns, bells, bonfires, and illuminations, from one end of our country to the other, from this time forward and forever more.

For some decades in our country it seemed as if enthusiasm for Fourth of July celebrations was dying out. But in recent years it appears to be returning. A movement to observe Independence Day by ringing bells all over the United States was promoted.

In 1963 the bell ringing was heard around the nation. This manner of observing the important holiday was promoted by two men in Connecticut. It all started in 1962 when Eric Sloane, an artist, began the project.

Sloane asked a friend who had a daily network show to spread the idea that everyone, everywhere, should ring bells on the birthday of our country. The great response to this suggestion was so surprising that the telephones of the local studio were tied up for four hours.

Happy over the unexpected reactions, Sloane sought the aid of a neighbor, Eric Hatch, a writer, to assist in organizing a national campaign. Their slogan was "Let Freedom Ring!" The two men soon discovered that all over the nation there was a desire on the part of countless Americans for such an expression of patriotism.

Governor John N. Dempsey and United States Senator Abraham Ribicoff of Connecticut gave their wholehearted support to the movement started by Eric Sloane; they asked political officials, clubs, churches, and other groups to take part in such an observance on Independence Day.

The governor issued a special proclamation regarding the bell ringing. And the General Assembly of Connecticut passed a resolution asking that public and church bells be rung for four minutes at 2 P.M. on the coming Fourth of July, and on every such holiday thereafter.

Governor Scranton of Pennsylvania also sent out his proclamation for the bell ringing to take place for two minutes starting at 2 P.M. from "every church, school, factory, and firehouse."

Abraham Ribicoff in the Senate and Francis E. Walter of Pennsylvania in the House of Representatives introduced resolutions supporting the annual observance of bell ringing on Independence Day.

Both houses of Congress adopted these resolutions; then hundreds of patriotic organizations took up the idea. As a result, bells will ever hereafter ring on this important date, in commemoration of the gaining of our freedom. Even if the Liberty Bell cannot add its famous voice in this countrywide observance, thousands of other bells will join in the great chorus of joyful pealing from the Atlantic to the Pacific.

President John F. Kennedy endorsed this project in 1963 by saying:

> It is a worthwhile and symbolic ceremony, which should certainly renew citizen-awareness of our heritage. . . .
>
> Bells mark significant events in men's lives; birth and death, war and peace are pealed and tolled. Bells summon the community to take note of things which affect the life and destiny of its people.
>
> The Liberty Bell rang to tell the world of the birth of a new country's freedom. . . . Next Thursday, the Fourth of July, when bells will ring again, think back on those who lived and died to make our country free, and then resolve with courage and determination to keep it free and make it greater.

THE TRAVELS OF THE LIBERTY BELL

The Liberty Bell has done much traveling during its many decades of existence. In fact, it has acquired the reputation of being the most traveled bell in the entire world.

It has been displayed at several expositions in this country.

Thousands of Americans and foreign visitors saw it at the Centennial Exposition in 1876 in Philadelphia.

Then from other parts of the United States came requests that the bell be on exhibit at their expositions. The authorities in charge of it acceded to many such requests.

On July 23, 1885, the bell took its first long journey—to New Orleans and the World's Industrial and Cotton Exposition. This trip was made because of the insistent demands of southern officials that its presence "would serve powerfully to inspire the patriotism of the people and strengthen the ties of peace between the united sections."

At Philadelphia, accompanied by guards, the Liberty Bell was transported to the railway station in a truck, drawn by "six gaily caparisoned horses." On the sides of the vehicle were streamers with the words "Philadelphia—New Orleans." In the center was an emblem of clasped hands.

All along the route, the bell received great acclaim; at Beauvoir, Jefferson Davis, who had been president of the Confederacy, left his sickbed to see it. As he stood before it, he said: "Glorious old bell, the son of a revolutionary soldier bows before you."

During its stay in New Orleans the relic was seen by thousands of people, who viewed it in "a reverential manner."

On June 17, 1885, the Liberty Bell again was back at its home base. Before it left the city again, on July 25, 1893, "a continuous stream of people passed through the corridors of the ancient edifice to look upon the time-honored symbol of liberty." A large crowd gathered at the railway station to see it placed on a specially constructed car for its trip to Chicago and the World's Columbian Exposition, which celebrated the four hundredth anniversary of the discovery of the new world by Christopher Columbus.

Its progress westward was described as "one continuous inspiration to patriotism." When the train reached Oil City, Pennsylvania, "thirteen little tots in their best bibs and tuckers" presented thirteen baskets of roses to the bell. At several small towns along the way bonfires had been lighted so that the people could see the famous emblem.

On reaching Chicago, it was placed on a handsome float, with thirteen coal-black horses attached to it. A guard of 100 Chicago Hussars accompanied the relic to the Exposition grounds. At the fair, it received more homage than had ever been given kings and queens. When the procession passed the hotel where President Grover Cleveland was staying, he came out of the building and made a short address.

The bell was placed in the center of the Pennsylvania Building where it was seen by countless people during its stay of several months in Chicago. More than 25,000 persons are said to have passed by it on the opening day.

On the return to Philadelphia, the bell revisited Allentown; there it was taken by trolley car to the church where it had been hidden during the Revolution. It stayed there all night. That evening the citizens of Allentown put on "a marvelous night pageant" with all kinds of illumination. There were fireworks and a parade by civic and military groups. One truck bore the sign "Welcome Home."

In October, 1895, the bell visited Atlanta, Georgia, where the Cotton States and Atlanta Exposition was being held. Some persons had tried to prevent this second trip to the South; however, since in 1816 the City of Brotherly Love had acquired by purchase complete title to the bell, it had a right to keep it in town or send it elsewhere on visits.

When it left Philadelphia in the fall of 1895, there was "a dazzling military display" at the depot. This trip, too, was a triumphal one. At one Virginia town, a seventy-year-old great-grandson of Patrick Henry came to the train and asked to touch the bell. On October 8, in Atlanta, the symbol was given "the most cordial greeting it had ever received." There "a blind child was held up and read the inscription with his finger."

After its stay in the South, a special train carried it back to Philadelphia, where this time four iron-gray horses drew the truck that returned it to Independence Hall.

Again the Liberty Bell was on the move in January, 1902, for a trip to Charleston, South Carolina, and the Interstate and West Indian Exposition. En route great crowds met it. January 9 was "Liberty Bell Day" in Charleston; it was celebrated as a high holiday. Crowds followed it to the Pennsylvania Building. One reporter asserted:

> The significance of this relic is appreciated through the South, and the love of liberty throughout the South is as strong today as it was in the stirring times when this piece of brazen metal proclaimed freedom to the world.

On the homeward trip, the bell passed through Washington. There the Marine Band played Sousa's *Liberty Bell March* "in its very presence." Following five months' absence, it reached home again.

On June 25, 1903, it was in Boston, to take part in the Bunker Hill anniversary celebration. Even though it had rained hard all the way through Connecticut, immense crowds had gathered to see it. The mayor of New Haven remarked:

> I believe the bell is the greatest educator of patriotism we have. The gray-haired veteran and the small schoolchild are alike in their anxiety to touch this sacred old relic of Revolutionary days, and the old herald of liberty.

The Liberty Bell had the place of honor in the long procession that ended at Bunker Hill Monument, where appropriate exercises were held.

An important trip was made by the bell in 1904, when it was displayed for five months at the Louisiana Purchase Exposition in St. Louis. 75,000 schoolchildren of that city had sent an urgent appeal that it be brought there.

At the fair, June 8, 1904, was celebrated as "Liberty Bell Day," and St. Louis "turned out en masse." In the parade the bell rode majestically on a massive truck drawn by thirteen stout gray horses.

In the great rotunda multitudes saw it "lying without yoke or support, or other covering, upon an American flag as background; it was never more impressive in its simplicity."

Its next public appearance in Philadelphia was on October 23, 1913, during the Founders' Week celebration, when it was featured in the annual parade. "The sight of the old bell set throats to shrieking a thunder of applause."

The first oral message transmitted across our continent was the tone of the Liberty Bell. On February 22, 1915, it was struck three times with three wooden mallets, the sounds of the blows being carried over the wires. They were heard distinctly in San Francisco. This was the initiation of "transcontinental talking."

During this conversation, Mayor Rolph of San Francisco and others emphasized their request to have the Liberty Bell at the

Panama-Pacific International Exposition, soon to be held in that city. Names of over 200,000 schoolchildren were signed to petitions asking for its coming. Finally, after some opposition, the trip to the West Coast was agreed upon. Its departure from Philadelphia was timed with the Independence Day celebration. On July 4, 1915, the relic was placed on a train called the "Liberty Bell Special."

En route to the West Coast, the train visited Pittsburgh, Chicago (where vast throngs of people stood in the rain in order to view it), Des Moines, Topeka, Kansas City, St. Joseph, Omaha, Salt Lake City, Olympia, Portland, and other cities—about sixty altogether. Millions bared their heads as the bell sped along in its special car. "The blaze of floodlights illuminated its ancient bronze, when darkness settled over the land to which it had given its enduring message."

Several eastern officials accompanied the symbol on this long journey. It reached the city by the Golden Gate on July 15, 1915. "Liberty Bell Day" was proclaimed for its arrival, and a fine pageant was arranged. Each night it was placed in a fireproof vault.

During its four months' stay the bell was more photographed than any other object at the exposition. It was said that more than eight million persons saw it. Just before it was to leave San Francisco, representatives of foreign lands and of all of our states placed wreaths and flowers around it.

On the homeward trip, the train first went south through the state of California, stopping briefly at several cities. Reaching San Diego, the bell was displayed for three days at that city's exposition. Banks of palms and flowers surrounded it during its visit, when it was well guarded by soldiers and marines.

The Liberty Bell left San Francisco on November 11, 1915, and returned to Philadelphia on November 25. During that interval it traveled 10,000 miles through thirty states and was seen by more than 17 million people. The special train made seventy-five stops on the way back, in Arizona, Mississippi, Tennessee, Kentucky, Missouri, Illinois, Ohio, Indiana, Pennsylvania, New York, and New Jersey.

The value of these extended journeys made by the bell was well summed up by an unnamed writer in a Des Moines, Iowa, paper:

In the several trips that the bell has made since 1884, it has been of much educational value and has resulted in "edification and inspiration." Millions of people have seen it; children have kissed it, and the strip of country through which it has passed has been made more fertile for patriotism.

In one little town in North Carolina, blind children were led out to the railroad and lifted up on the Liberty Bell car so they could touch and kiss the bell they could not see. In another town, the schoolchildren came out with great armfuls of flowers with which they pelted piously the great relic. People waited for hours to see it; also whole towns turned out.

Now the bell remains quietly in Independence Hall. One former curator, Wilfred Jordon, some years ago expressed his feelings about it in these words:

> Truly the Liberty Bell has earned its final rest. Its journeys to the South served a purpose and joined the Union in stronger bonds of fellowship, after the awful break of the Civil War. But now there is no need for the balm of its presence—North, South, East, and West should join in the demand that Philadelphia keep the bell forever in trust for the nation, guard it tenderly, and grant it a lasting peace.

THE HOME OF THE LIBERTY BELL

Independence Hall, "the delight of architects and the pride of the Philadelphians," is in the heart of the city, in the square bounded by Chestnut, Walnut, Fifth, and Sixth streets. As the "outstanding Shrine of American Liberties," the hall is a most suitable home for our cherished symbol.

> It is fitting and proper that the bell rests in Philadelphia, the city of William Penn, the man of peace. For over 200 years, it has remained, by association of past events and memories, one of our most cherished and revered heritages.

The beginning of Independence Hall goes far back into our history. As we have seen, the building originally was the State House of the province of Pennsylvania. For half a century the Assembly had been compelled "to hire a house annually." Finally, in 1729, the members of the Assembly appropriated funds to build a State House.

Two prominent men, a master carpenter named Edmund Wooley and lawyer Andrew Hamilton, made the plans for this structure and supervised its construction. Because of various delays—the main one was the scarcity of skilled workmen—the building took more than twenty-five years to complete.

Designed in 1732, it was a two-story edifice, about 100 feet in length and 40 in width. Its "decked roof was balustraded between chimneys." A small cupola that resembled a watchtower rose above the center. It was designed in dignified Georgian style. One source says: "Independence Hall, with its wings, has long been considered one of the most beautiful public buildings of the colonial period."

During 1741 the cupola was removed, and a tower or steeple, to carry the new State House bell, and the stairway were added. About twenty years later this steeple had rotted and was so weak that it tottered when the bell was rung. Even though it was dangerous, it was not removed until 1781. Then a small hip roof was put on, and the bell was hung below a spire.

Independence Hall is one of our most important American historical structures, because within its walls our nation was born and several momentous decisions were made. In June, 1775, the Continental Congress chose George Washington to be the commander-in-chief of the colonial army; and here the general made his speech of acceptance.

During the winter of 1777–1778, when the British occupied Philadelphia while Washington and his troops were at Valley Forge, the British used the building as a hospital for the American soldiers who had been wounded at the Battle of Germantown. The victors had carried the injured men here "in jouncing wagons. " They also used the place as a jail for their American prisoners. It is reported that the British gave the men such short rations that some of the colonials died of starvation. After the British left Philadelphia, the Americans found Independence Hall in such a deplorable condition that they had to use many barrels of lime and other materials to recondition it.

With the British gone, the colonials returned and also brought the Liberty Bell back from Allentown. In late 1781 there was much rejoicing in the hall at the glad news of the surrender of Lord

Cornwallis to General Washington at Yorktown. The long struggle for independence was won.

In this hall Congress adopted the Articles of Confederation; later, in 1787, the same body drafted the United States Constitution "to make a weak Confederation into a strong Federal State." For four strenuous months the members had worked on the vital document.

Under the new Constitution, the federal government first met in New York City, where George Washington was inaugurated as the first President of the new nation. In 1790 the capital was again in Philadelphia, until it was moved to Washington in June, 1800.

The Pennsylvania capital was changed from Philadelphia first to Lancaster then to Harrisburg in 1816, where a new state building was erected. The Philadelphians used the old State House for varied purposes, such as a voting place and the County Courthouse.

The preservation of this important structure was not always of as much importance to the American people as it is today. Independence Hall was almost torn down at one time, for the Assembly passed an act to "slice" Independence Square into building lots and sell them at auction.

This act seemed to regard the State House as "old material": the Liberty Bell wasn't even mentioned in the plans. No provision was made for saving the building or preserving the bell. Apparently these matters "were to be left to the discretion of the wreckers."

Fortunately for later generations of Americans, the city came to the rescue and bought the square with its priceless old State House along with other worthwhile buildings, for only $70,000.

> This was a financial and spiritual investment unequalled in the history of American cities. Since then Philadelphia has protected it, performing an inestimable service in preserving the Independence Hall group for posterity.

From 1802 to 1827 a large part of the hall was leased to the eminent painter Charles Willson Peale, who used it to house his museum, which contained varied exhibits. The city bought many of the artist's historical paintings, and these formed the nucleus of the present excellent collection of Revolutionary heroes.

In 1824 Philadelphia started a movement "to lift the old State House to public attention as a national shrine." A noted American architect, William Strickland, designed a new steeple that was more ornate than the original. It also had clock faces at the 85-foot level of the building.

When in 1846 the fabricated story about the old bell ringer and the little boy was published, it called public attention once more to the Liberty Bell. But as years passed, much trash gradually accumulated in the Hall. Then, when the Centennial Year of 1876 was nearing, conditions improved. Several restorations were made; the signers' chairs were brought back and gas lamps installed. Since that time not many noticeable changes have been made.

> The Hall, a fitting home for the great Bell, has been described as "a building of serenity and symmetry, of fine amplitude, a gracious alluring building, rich in noble memories, yet touched with a living sweetness."

The bell which hangs at present in the steeple was given, along with the clock, by Henry Seibert or Seybert of Philadelphia, on July 4, 1876. It is larger than the Liberty Bell and has on it the words of the original inscription, also several patriotic and religious mottoes. It was made from metals used in five American wars: the Revolution, the War of 1812, the Mexican War, the Civil War, and the Seminole War. Each of the thirteen original states contributed 1,000 pounds of metal to be used in casting. The donor declared he had received a message from a relative in the spiritual world, telling him to purchase a bell for the Independence Hall spire.

The Liberty Bell hung in the State House steeple until July 17, 1781. While it was there, the windows of the tower were filled with sounding boards. It is said that the bell ringer slept in this room and that for some time the keeper of the tower and his family lived there.

When the symbol was taken down in 1781, it was lowered into the brick tower, where it stayed until 1846. Fearing the crack would finally destroy the historic relic, officials had it removed from the tower. It was placed on a temporary pedestal, on exhibition in the room where the Declaration was proclaimed.

In 1854 Philadelphia authorities ordered that Independence Hall be fitted up in an impressive manner. A historian named Belisle wrote in 1859:

The Bell was placed on a pedestal having 13 sides, representing the number of states that confederated for the accomplishment of Freedom, with the American Flag gracefully folded above and around it; a spread eagle sits on the Bell.

For the Centennial Year (1876) rearrangement of the hall and Liberty Bell, some changes were made:

> The old Liberty Bell, which had been taken from the cupola and placed within the Chamber, was moved to the vestibule, and suspended from the original beam and scaffolding. . . . The whole has been enclosed by a plain iron railing. . . .

In 1896, after intervening moves the bell was taken back to the base of the former tower, where it is still located. It hangs from the original hand-hewn yoke of black walnut, ordered when the bell first arrived from England. The massive beam weakened, and in 1962 the bell was carefully lowered onto a specially prepared platform. The plate that had been installed in the yoke in 1929 was replaced with a modern steel T-beam. So the ancient support, skillfully repaired, still holds up our noted Liberty Bell.

Today the bell is open to view and can be touched by visitors. It occupies the center of the south end of the vestibule. One of the first things a person notices is the gaping crack, "a zigzag fissure reaching from the rim up into the lettering."

PLANS FOR THE BELL'S SAFETY

Often questions are asked about what safety measures have been planned in case of war, fire, or an atomic attack.

After Pearl Harbor, there was some talk of sending the Liberty Bell to Fort Knox to be stored with our gold supply. Also at one time plans were drawn up for a deep bombproof shelter into which the bell could be lowered by elevator. But since some engineers believed the excavation might weaken Independence Hall itself, this idea was not carried out.

Perforated pipes have been placed under the eaves of the stately old edifice; in addition, other precautions have been taken to prevent fires.

The Liberty Bell is mounted on a mahogany truck which is fitted with steel casters for quick removal. Guards are trained to take away the panels at the bottom of the platform on which it rests; it is said it can be pushed outside in five minutes if an emergency should arise.

Also, if Call Box No. 1776 should ring in the City of Brotherly Love, it is declared that "fire equipment would boil out into the streets" from several different fire stations and that well-trained firefighters would make for Independence Hall, which they could reach in less than one minute.

REACTIONS OF VISITORS

Millions of persons visit Independence Hall yearly, especially to view the bell. It is said that a visitor usually stops involuntarily at the doorway of the place where our country was born. In speaking of the attitude of the average male visitor with his family, one writer, Saul Pett, once said: "Without being told, he quiets his kids, removes his hat, stamps out his cigarette, and quickly fastens his eyes on the Liberty Bell straight ahead."

Most tourists walk in quietly and talk in low tones. Some stand beside the bell in silence, while others take pictures of it for future enjoyment. It is said to be the only bell in the entire world in whose presence men doff their hats, and that a guard rarely has to remind anyone of this rule; headgear usually comes off spontaneously.

Though visitors have a reverent attitude toward the bell, some are a bit hazy about its history. Then the guard, or perhaps a knowledgeable child, is able to correct the misstatement that the bell cracked on July 4, 1776, because the old bell ringer rang it too vigorously. The guards encourage people—especially the children—to touch the sacred relic "to get the feel of it."

One curator reported that during his fifteen years' service at Independence Hall, only one individual ever tried to harm the symbol. However, he did succeed in making a small nick in it, when he threw a heavy paperweight in its direction. (He was soon taken away as a mental case.)

The Liberty Bell is a continuous symbol of freedom to Americans. From the very beginning of our country, immigrants came that they might have here precious liberty—to be free "to speak, to work, to govern themselves, to worship God as they pleased."

For many years travelers from all around the globe, including eminent government leaders, have visited Independence Hall to see the bell.

Emperor Dom Pedro II of Brazil, then the sole surviving monarch in South America, came to the Hall and "peered and pondered at it." Count Rochambeau, the grandson of the Marquis de Lafayette, also paid it a visit.

In 1860, when the bell was not considered so highly as it is nowadays, the Prince of Wales—later King Edward VII of England —while in the old State House asked to see the Liberty Bell. To his great surprise, the Prince and one of his hosts found it in the garret, under some debris. This neglect by our nation of the noted symbol shocked his Royal Highness. He didn't hesitate to express his resentment in these words:

> This old Bell is the greatest relic this republic has today. Instead of being here, covered with accumulated dirt, it should occupy the chief place of honor in this Hall of Independence. It is to you what the Magna Carta is to England. It is cracked, but it is an inspiration. Believe me, my friends, it affects me more than anything I have been shown.

When David Ben-Gurion of Israel entered the door of Independence Hall and saw the familiar bronze shape, he rushed toward it with open arms and exclaimed, "Oh, the Bell!"

A head guard, Michael J. Reilly, through the years watched millions of visitors and noted their reactions; he has noticed that the Liberty Bell seems to cast a spell over many of them. He especially remembered one touching incident. It was the visit of two young Japanese-American WAC's in uniform, not long after the close of World War II. Because of war injuries, both young women were blind.

When they asked Mr. Reilly to help them "read" the bell's inscription, he guided their hands over the letters. He also "showed" them the crack, while they happily chattered away. After they had left, he saw that they had taken off the roses they were wearing and had placed them in the crack of the bell.

A MODERN REPLICA
OF INDEPENDENCE HALL

Recently travelers to southern California have visited the noted Knott's Berry Farm, not far from Los Angeles. Started many years ago by Walter Knott, this is now one of the most popular recreation spots in the region. It shows old western life and times during Gold Rush days, furnishes various types of entertainment, and is popular with all who enjoy Americana.

For years Walter Knott and his wife had dreamed of constructing an exact replica of Independence Hall so that people on the West Coast could see what this "cradle of liberty" was like and learn more of our American heritage. Finally, after years of research and expenditure of much time, energy, and money, the Knotts have made their long-cherished dream a reality.

The building, externally as authentic as possible, was constructed from the original plans of the old Pennsylvania State House. More than 140,000 "custom-made" bricks were fashioned to be similar to those in the eastern edifice.

This new hall combines modern construction with stately Georgian architecture. Many tons of steel were used in the roof, floors, and tower framing. There is a fabricated steel clock tower. The lower floor has the same room arrangement as the original. On the second floor, instead of a hallway and three rooms, there is a theater seating 360 persons. This is used for showing historical, patriotic, and educational films.

One of the most interesting features of the reproduction is the Assembly chamber, in which the fiery debates took place as to whether the colonial delegates should accept the Declaration. The chamber has fifteen tables—each with a tall candle—one for each of the delegations, one for the speaker, and another for the secretary. Exact copies of the signers' chairs and other furnishings are seen here.

It is a unique experience for visitors to sit at the back of this handsome candlelit chamber and hear the voices of the men as they argue "pro and con." This is accomplished by means of an elaborate electrical sound system. As Hancock, Franklin and other members of the Continental Congress speak, listeners can almost feel they are back in Revolutionary days. There are also interesting sound effects, such as those of horses and wagons rattling over the cobblestone streets of old Philadelphia. A fife and drum corps of the Revolutionary troops adds to the sound picture.

Also on the first floor is the Supreme Court chamber. In it hangs a large colonial flag with thirteen stars; here, too, you can see an early copy of the Declaration of Independence and other outstanding historical documents and papers.

On July 4, 1966, Mr. and Mrs. Knott celebrated the one hundred and ninetieth anniversary of the signing of the Declaration of Independence by opening this reproduction to the public.

One outstanding exhibit is the fine replica of the Liberty Bell. The making of this special bell was given much thought and care.

A father and son, Ray and Bud Hurlburt, owners of the amusement company at the farm, told Walter Knott they would present a replica of the bell to his project. The son went to Philadelphia and took countless measurements and colored pictures of all the details of the original, including the yoke, base, standards, and hardware connected with it, and also the inscription.

Mr. Knott wanted to have an authentic crack in his bell; this presented a difficult problem. Finally, after several tries, the bell cracked "exactly as called for in the plans." In the Sinnissippi Forest in Illinois, a 125-year-old slippery-elm tree was found and the plank for the heavy wooden yoke was made from it. Beautifully polished cherry wood makes a perfect base for this authentic reproduction.

THE BELL IN THE NEWS

Today the Liberty Bell still makes the headlines. In April, 1967, the Beneficial Standard Life Insurance Company of Los Angeles decided to buy a replica to place in the new Liberty Park on Wilshire Boulevard in that city.

The company got in touch with the London firm that made the original bell, the Whitechapel Foundry in the East End, now called Mears and Steinbank. The cost of the Pennsylvania-province bell was about $280. In 1967 the replica cost about $3,540, plus shipping charges. The firm declared that an increase of 12 times in 215 years was really not so bad. They gave statistics to prove that the cost of the metals had gone up 20 times, and that of manufacturing about 8 times in the past fifty years alone.

The British company has been in business for over 400 years. Their representative said that if anyone should want another replica of the Liberty Bell 215 years from now, he no doubt would find the firm still doing business and could purchase an exact copy, for the specifications are still kept on file. This replica was brought to California on the *Queen Mary*'s final cruise and reached the port December 9, 1967. During the 39-day voyage it occupied the place of honor on the promenade deck.

In Forest Lawn Cemetery, in the Hollywood Hills of southern California, the owners have created the "Great Court of Liberty." Here there is a model of an early church in Maine, a monument to George Washington, and a reproduction of Old North Church in Boston and of the Liberty Bell.

At one end of the Court of Liberty is a magnificent mosaic, entitled "The Birth of Liberty." It depicts twenty-five dramatic events in American history, covering the period from 1619 to 1787. Events shown range from the coming of the *Mayflower* to the Surrender of Cornwallis. There is a picture of the Continental Congress debating, and one of the Liberty Bell. The great mosaic, 165 feet long, and about 30 feet high, contains more than 10 million pieces or tesserae of Venetian glass.

According to the founder of this cemetery, Hubert Eaton, "The Birth of Liberty" is to remind us of the ideals and sacrifices of our forefathers.

THE BELL IN LITERATURE AND ART

The Liberty Bell has long been a favorite subject in prose, poetry, and pictures. It is said that its first "graven image" was in a booklet issued in 1842. B. J. Lossing in his *Field Book of the American Revolution* (1852) reproduced a sketch in it that he had made in 1848.

A picture depicting the ancient bell ringer and the small boy appeared in *Graham's Magazine* in June, 1854, and helped perpetuate that tale. In 1856 appeared a photo by Stayman and Brother showing the interior of Independence Hall and the bell. In Belisle's *History of Independence Hall,* printed in 1859, the "Old State House Bell" is shown. This national symbol has been photographed countless times in various positions and is known around the globe. It has also been used by artists in cartoons.

The recasting of the bell was the subject of an important painting by a well-known Philadelphia artist, J. L. G. Ferris. In it the painter depicts the bell as the central figure of interest. Near it are the two partners, Pass and Stow, and also four gentlemen in colonial attire (one is Isaac Norris, who chose the inscription). There are three ladies, one of whom is just about to strike the Liberty Bell with a mallet, after its second recasting.

CONCLUSION

Through the years orators have extolled the virtues of the Liberty Bell, especially on Independence Day; one asserted:

> The life of the bell covers the most interesting periods of our history. It has rejoiced and wept with our fathers; has often sung a paean for our victories, and has silently tolled a monody for our defeats. Its tones, at times, have depressed and again inspired.

In 1893 Charles S. Keyser wrote the following on the "Significance of the Bell":

> Among the bells of the world, no one has been associated with events of such great import to humanity as the Liberty Bell. . . .
> Its prophetic inscription, its warnings through a generation to the government of Great Britain, its appeals to the people to assemble for the redress of their grievances, and its defiant clangor that memorable day of the Declaration of our Independence, its rejoicing pealings over the completed work of the Revolution, its last tolling over the dead of the nation, give the story an abiding interest to the nations of the world.

8

The White House

THE White House, official residence of our Presidents at 1600 Pennsylvania Avenue, is the oldest public building in Washington, D.C. It is almost as old as the nation itself. The main structure—170 feet wide, 85 feet deep, and 58 feet high—stands in parklike grounds of several acres.

The main entrance is through the North Portico, with its great Doric columns. Long, low galleries extend from the east and west sides; they have terraced roofs and provide promenades at the main-floor level.

All the men who have been chosen by the people to guide the affairs of our nation have lived here with the exception of George Washington. Through the many decades of its history the White House has been the scene of glittering social affairs, and on occasion, of sorrowful ones.

Originally it was "designed to avoid formal display." Today we find "it has an air of dignity and charm . . . the White House retains the simplicity of its original appearance and its rich historical associations." Because of these characteristics, Americans regard it as a symbol of our country's history and unity.

> . . . And it's the most important, exclusive piece of real estate in the world. . . . It is a symbol—the democratic image—of executive authority in a land that believes in neither crowns nor kings.
>
> —Debs Myers, *Holiday*, November, 1952

CONSTRUCTION AND RENOVATIONS

The site for our Presidents' home was chosen by Major Pierre L'Enfant, who designed the national capital. It was a ridge above a small stream that emptied into the Potomac at the present-day intersection of Constitution Avenue and 17th Street.

George Washington served his two terms as President in New York and Philadelphia; he helped to design the White House; but he died about a year before President John Adams moved into it in 1800. It is said that Washington favored a building that would combine "the sumptuousness of a palace, the convenience of a home, and the agreeableness of a countryseat."

The history of this distinctive structure goes back to the year 1792, when the Commission of the District of Columbia held a contest for the best design for it. Thomas Jefferson, who was an authority on architecture, sent in a plan anonymously, but it was rejected.

The prize of $500 went to James Hoban, an Irish-born architect. Some say his design was inspired by the home of the Duke of Leinster in Dublin. While the main facade does resemble the Leinster one, another source asserts that the "details of other faces and the interior arrangement were probably derived from contemporary houses in England and on the Continent."

> Hoban's plan called for a simple Georgian mansion in the classical Palladian style, to be built of light gray Virginia sandstone and to be balanced by two flanking wings.

(The wings were eliminated, but were added in a modified form a century later.)

The cornerstone of the White House was laid in October, 1792. The edifice was to cost $200,000, but the final figure was twice that. The John Adams family moved in during November, 1800, although the building was not completed.

On August 24, 1814, the British captured Washington and set fire to the White House in retaliation for the burning of some public buildings in Canada by American troops. The partly damaged sandstone walls and interior brickwork were still standing. James Hoban was in charge of the reconstruction; the repair work began in the spring of 1815 and was finished in time for President Monroe to move there in December, 1817. To cover the smoke-stained stone walls, the architect had applied white paint to the structure.

This building has had several different names: President's House, President's Mansion, and even President's Palace. It is said that Abraham Lincoln termed it the Executive Mansion. The British ambassador Francis James Jackson is reported to have called it the White House as early as 1811. However, this name did not become official until made so almost a century later by President Theodore Roosevelt.

Throughout its history the White House has kept pace with modern improvements. Beginning with President Monroe, who added the South Portico in 1824 (the North Portico, over the entrance and driveway, was built in 1829), almost every President has made some change at the White House.

Spring water was piped in during 1833 or 1834; gas lighting was installed in 1848, a hot-water heating system in 1853, and a single telephone line in 1880. The first elevator was put in during 1881 or 1882; electric lighting and a bell system—to call the servants—were introduced during the Benjamin Harrison administration, and it was said that some of the inmates were afraid to push the buttons.

In 1850 President Fillmore found the building in miserable condition. It was bare and dirty, and in the large room over the Blue Room was a straw carpet "made filthy by tobacco chewers." However, during the Grant administration, the tobacco problem was solved by the use of "ornate spittoons."

Chester A. Arthur, the meticulous New York–socialite President, declared after one look at the place that he would *not* live in it. He was so shocked by the clutter that he personally superintended a housecleaning, from top to bottom. At once he had twenty-four wagonloads of clothing, furniture, and miscellaneous items taken away, before he finally gave in to making the White House his residence.

On April 15, 1882, 5,000 persons attended a sale and bid for the discarded articles, which included everything from rat traps and bird cages to a pair of Abraham Lincoln's pants. This successful sale netted the U.S. Treasury the sum of $3,000. Then President Arthur commissioned decorator Louis Tiffany to refurnish the Executive Mansion in "opulent Victorian style."

By 1902, during the regime of Theodore Roosevelt, the interior had become "a conglomeration of styles and periods." The building also needed structural repairs. And for many years state business had been conducted on the upper floor. President Roosevelt advocated that this be changed; Congress appropriated $500,000 to strengthen much of the interior and to redecorate and refurnish it. The main stairway was moved; this added more space to the state dining room. A most important improvement was the addition of a west wing—the Executive Office Building—to provide a presidential office, cabinet room, and other office quarters.

In accordance with the President's ideas, the White House was refurnished in dignified eighteenth-century fashion. The work of reconstruction was begun in July, 1902, and by the end of the year was practically completed.

Between 1903 and 1948 there were changes, too; the Executive Office Building was enlarged; guest rooms were made in the attic; and the third story was remodeled in 1927. Early in the Franklin D. Roosevelt administration, a fund for a swimming pool was raised by public subscription. A few years afterward a modern electric kitchen was added, as were the east wing, an atomic-bomb shelter, a small gymnasium, and other features. In 1948, on the second floor behind the columns of the South Portico, a balcony was constructed.

RENOVATION, 1948–1952

In 1948 a thorough inspection revealed alarming structural conditions. For example, one leg of Margaret Truman's piano had made a hole in the ceiling of the family dining room. The President's bathtub was sinking into the floor above a reception room. Some ceilings had dropped several inches, and the foundations were discovered to be too weak to support the walls. The entire place was in grave danger of collapse.

Soon Congress authorized a Commission on the Renovation of the White House. Some experts stated it would be much cheaper to erect an entirely new building. However, national sentiment was for keeping the original. After much deliberation, the commission decided to adhere to the historic floor plan and retain the exterior sandstone walls, thus preserving the basic architectural design.

The Truman family moved across the street to Blair House. Late in 1948 all furnishings were removed from the White House and put into storage. Workmen completely dismantled the structure, except for the outer walls. Concrete foundations were put in, and the wooden beams and brick supporting walls were replaced by a steel framework.

Excavation provided a much-needed basement for various service facilities. The building was air-conditioned; dentist's and doctor's offices were added; the solarium over the South Portico was enlarged; and a modern broadcasting and television room was constructed.

All the historic rooms were rebuilt exactly as before, and more rooms added. Before the renovation there were 62 rooms and 14 baths; afterward there were 132 rooms and 20 baths. Now the White House has a 2-story basement and 4 floors.

In the renovation, efforts were made to retain or restore the original atmosphere, while providing a more livable home for the President and his family. While the work was in progress, one writer said: "America's most famous residence is being converted from a death trap to a permanent fireproof structure."

Congress had appropriated the sum of $5.4 million for the work, but when the restoration was finished in 1952, the bill came to almost $5.8 million.

The Truman family moved back across the street, after an absence of three years, in March, 1952. Reporters noted that President Truman, who had spent three weeks in Florida, successfully dodged what most men dislike—moving day. When he returned that evening from the South, he found all his belongings had been moved back to his former residence.

Newspapers featured pictures of the smiling President with Mrs. Truman, entering the renovated mansion. He was holding up a key, just given him by a White House official.

On March 29, 1952, Mrs. Truman personally escorted newspaper-women around the shining new home; and on May 3, President Truman conducted a forty-eight-minute tour with men reporters. After giving an informal history of the building, he was asked to perform on the piano in the East Room. He played a part of Mozart's Ninth Sonata. The chief executive fairly beamed on this occasion, for he was thrilled by the beautifully restored home. He declared to the reporters: "The revamped White House should be good for a thousand years."

THE WHITE HOUSE GROUNDS

The "President's Park" is divided into two sections. Eighteen acres are enclosed within the iron fence that surrounds the White House and the grounds proper. The other, containing 52 acres, includes the Ellipse, which is bordered by beautiful American elms.

The south side of the White House has a semicircular portico, which overlooks a broad lawn with flower gardens and groves of trees. This is the private park of the President and his family. The public is admitted to it only on Easter Monday, the day when the youngsters arrive to roll eggs down the sloping lawn.

The custom of egg rolling started when Dolly Madison was the First Lady. John Payne Todd, a son by her first husband, told his mother that centuries before, children in Egypt had rolled eggs against the pyramids.

So rolling Easter eggs began in our national capital on the grounds of the Capitol Building. However, during President Hayes's administration, officials at the Capitol protested against the custom, declaring that this yearly event was ruining the grass; they stated they would place guards there to keep the crowds out on Easter Monday.

Then kindhearted Lucy Webb Hayes (whose youngest children were aged nine and six) intervened in 1878 for the children of the city. She invited them to come to the White House lawn instead. Everyone had a grand time that day, with the two Hayes children romping with Washington boys and girls.

This colorful event was perpetuated, and it continued until

World War I. After peace came, President Warren G. Harding renewed the custom. It was not observed during World War II. But in 1953 the Eisenhowers invited children of twelve years or under to come with their parents, to bring their own eggs, and to take part in the fun. This interesting Washington happening always attracts many spectators and countless avid camera fans.

John Quincy Adams was a keen student of botany. During his era at the White House, he spent much of his leisure time making a garden on the grounds. In addition, he succeeded in getting an appropriation through Congress for a fence around them.

In 1850 there was a serious attempt at landscaping around the mansion. Andrew Jackson Downing, considered the outstanding American horticulturist of his period, supervised the work, which was done in "the popular romantic style." And today the beauty of the front lawn is enhanced in the spring by colorful beds of flowers around the large pool with its fountain.

There are interesting and historic trees planted on the White House grounds. Among them is the "Russo-American Oak," or "Friendship Tree." According to Marjorie C. Peacock, many years ago Senator Charles Sumner of Massachusetts visited the tomb of George Washington at Mount Vernon. He noticed there an American oak that overshadows the burial place.

The senator picked up some of the acorns under the oak and sent one of them to his friend the Czar of Russia. It was planted on the grounds of one of the imperial palaces.

In 1898, when E. A. Hitchcock was our ambassador at the court in Saint Petersburg, he inquired about this oak tree. Later he visited the sturdy oak and saw an inscription near it. Translated into English, it said:

> The acorn planted here, taken from an oak which shaded the tomb of the celebrated and never-to-be-forgotten George Washington, is presented to his Majesty, the Emperor of all the Russias, as a sign of the greatest respect, by an American.

Ambassador Hitchcock gathered some of the acorns, planted them, and sent one of the saplings to President Theodore Roosevelt, who planted it near the West Terrace on April 6, 1904. Mr. Hitchcock said of this young tree:

I hope it will reach such an age and strength as will, for years to come, typify the continued friendship of the governments and people, respectively, of the United States and Russia.

Thus, through many decades, the White House grounds have been carefully and beautifully landscaped with a great variety of trees, shrubs, and flowers, which have made the surroundings of the mansion so attractive.

The simple dignity of the White House is enhanced by the natural beauty of its informal, carefully landscaped grounds. Many of the trees are of historical interest, such as the magnolias planted by President Andrew Jackson. New trees have been selected for their variety. Flower gardens and well-kept lawns form an appropriate setting for the President's home.

—White House Brochure, United States Department of the Interior

THE EXECUTIVE MANSION TODAY

Soon after John F. Kennedy became President, his wife began a program to redecorate some of the White House rooms. In 1961 she appointed a Fine Arts Committee to help her acquire authentic historical furnishings. There was also a special committee for obtaining a permanent collection of American paintings.

The First Lady's efforts and those of her committee members have resulted in numerous notable changes in the historic public rooms. The famous Red and Blue rooms, for instance, were the first ones to be refurbished and redecorated.

Mrs. Kennedy and the committee made a plea for the return to the White House of objects that had belonged to presidential families. The results were amazing; many persons sent in outstanding gifts and loans. These included such diverse things as a chair from Lincoln's bedroom, Dolly Madison's tufted sofa, James Madison's medicine chest, James Monroe's armchair and pier table, a bust of Martin Van Buren, brass andirons that had belonged to Zachary Taylor, and a rocking chair similar to the one President Lincoln sat in that fatal night at Ford's Theater.

Among the outstanding items Mrs. Kennedy rediscovered in the building were rugs woven especially for Theodore Roosevelt; a desk that Queen Victoria had presented to President Hayes; the gold and silver flatware that James Monroe had ordered from France in 1812; and "a set of lavender-bordered Lincoln plates, which, although slightly chipped, are now used at White House dinners."

In February, 1962, Mrs. Kennedy made an hour-long appearance on television, during which she gave a tour around the newly furnished White House rooms. There was a historical narrative of the executive mansion, filled with interesting anecdotes. Mrs. Kennedy's idea of taking on this project came from the feeling that the building should display those things which Americans have produced so well, such as furniture and pictures.

Near the close of her television tour, President Kennedy joined his wife and praised her refurbishing, which he said would bring more Americans into contact with the men who had lived in the White House. He declared that "history is people" and asserted that seeing President Grant's table, Abraham Lincoln's bed, or the Monroe gold dinner set makes these men seem more alive. He added: "Every President gets stimulus from the knowledge of living in close proximity to the people who are legendary, but who actually were alive and were in these rooms."

President Kennedy stated that the White House is becoming of more importance each year and that the structure dramatizes the great story of America. In the year 1961 more than 1.3 million persons had visited the building. The President expressed the hope that other First Ladies would continue trying to make this home "the center . . . of a sense of American historical life."

An important by-product of Mrs. Kennedy's project was the publication of the first official guide to the White House. It is a 132-page booklet with historic accounts and many color photographs among the 206 illustrations. Sixteen of the famous rooms are shown. The text is by Mrs. John N. Pearce, a registrar-historian at the Smithsonian Institution.

The Kennedys invited former President Truman and his wife and daughter for dinner and to stay overnight at the White House. The three were delighted with the decor and the interesting changes made by the First Lady. This was in November, 1961.

Since Mrs. Lyndon B. Johnson has become mistress of the White House, she also has taken much interest in adding American art to the building. She has acquired paintings by such noted American artists as Thomas Sully, John Singer Sargent, and Winslow Homer.

She also obtained for the west wing a loan of more than sixty works from the Smithsonian Institution.

Six classic columns separate the White House lobby from the main corridor. The columns and pilasters along the wall are of Vermont marble, while the floors are of Tennessee marble. High ceilings and the ornamental stairway give a feeling of spaciousness to the main floor landing. The seals of the thirteen original states are carved in the marble-faced opening of the staircase.

On the first floor the furnishings and decor are mainly late-eighteenth-century style. Articles of historic interest have been retained and others added by generous donors. Many portraits of former Presidents and First Ladies hang on walls on the main floor. In the China Room are examples of wares used by families in different administrations.

The library, redecorated in 1961–1962, has a suite of rare Duncan Phyfe furniture. In 1952 the original kitchen, with its old fireplaces, was restored, but adjoining it is a modern all-electric kitchen.

The important public rooms on the main floor are the East Room, State Dining Room, and three salons, named for their distinctive colors: the Blue, Red, and Green rooms.

The Blue Room, noted for its oval shape, is considered by many critics the most beautiful one in the White House. Its walls are covered with blue silk which has a spectacular gold pattern. Encircling the room, below the cornice, is a blue-draped valance. Window valances are of the same material as the wall covering. An American eagle surmounts each curtain rod. There are three original gilt Monroe chairs and eleven reproductions; their blue backs have eagles embroidered on them.

The Blue Room was redecorated to represent the Monroe period. On the mantel are gilt candlesticks brought from France. The Monroe pier table was restored and placed in its original location. Lights come from four wall sconces and two large Empire candelabra. On the walls are portraits of early Presidents. In this charming room the President receives guests before state dinners and at teas and receptions. Sometimes as many as seventeen hundred persons are invited to receptions for the judiciary, the Senate, House, and armed forces.

The Green Room, used for informal receptions, has been restored as a Federal parlor of about 1800. The walls are covered with moss-green silk, and the long curtains are of the same material and have tassels of green and silver.

The furniture is of American design based on English styles. Pictures by American artists are on the walls. On the dark-stained oak floor is a pale-green rug with the seal of the President of the United States woven in it.

On the white mantel are gilt vases and a Hannibal clock. In 1847 an anonymous donor presented the handsome crystal chandelier.

The striking Red Room was completely redecorated as an American Empire parlor. The walls are covered with red silk brocade with a scroll border of gold. Draperies and upholstery are of matching fabrics.

Among the furnishings in the Red Room are sofas that once belonged to Nelly Custis and Dolly Madison. An Empire gilt chandelier with electic candles hangs from the ceiling; on the white-marble mantel is a musical clock, presented in 1952 by the French president. The floor of the Red Room is covered by an antique Savonnerie.

This salon serves as a reception room before small dinners. Here, too, the First Lady receives guests. (On March 3, 1877, Rutherford B. Hayes took the oath of office in this room.)

On the main floor is also the oval Diplomatic Reception Room, which was designed and refurnished by the National Society of Interior Decorators. It has classical furniture and a rug containing the seals of all fifty states. In 1961 its most striking feature—scenic wallpaper, printed in France in the 1800's—was put on the walls. It shows Berlin, New York Harbor, West Point, Niagara Falls, and Natural Bridge, Virginia.

The largest room in the building is the famous East Room, which is 87½ by 45 feet and is decorated in white and gold. The window draperies are of gold and ivory-white silk damask. On the white mantels are gilt candelabra of the Monroe era. The walls are covered with white-enameled paneling.

Large crystal chandeliers, dating from 1902, hang from the elaborately decorated ceiling. There is an oak parquet floor. Although it is a large room, the East Room is a gracious one. On its east wall hangs the most notable portrait of George Washington, by Gilbert Stuart.

The concert grand piano, a Steinway, has decorations of folk-dancing scenes. At one end of the room is a specially built stage where plays and operas are presented.

In this noted room many gala events have taken place: large receptions, balls, and musicals. Here daughters of Presidents U. S. Grant, Theodore Roosevelt, Woodrow Wilson and Lyndon Johnson were married.

The East Room has also witnessed several sorrowful affairs—the funeral services of William Henry Harrison, Zachary Taylor, Abraham Lincoln, and Warren G. Harding. In addition, the bodies of William McKinley, Franklin D. Roosevelt, and John F. Kennedy lay in state here.

The State Dining Room serves for all large dinners and luncheons; it can comfortably seat 100 guests. Paneling of English oak extends from the floor to the ceiling. Originally installed in 1902, it was painted off-white in 1961, making a good background for the gold-damask window draperies.

"The splendor of the setting has been enhanced by the gilding of the central chandelier," which also dates from 1902 and hangs from the decorative stucco ceiling. The effect is strengthened by the use of gold-rimmed chinaware and of gold-covered sterling flatware (vermeil). In the center of the room is an antique mahogany table. A portrait of Abraham Lincoln is over the mantelpiece.

At least five state dinners are given each year by the President, for the Cabinet, Supreme Court, the Speaker of the House, Vice-President, and foreign diplomats. Other banquets are staged in honor of visiting dignitaries. The seating at such meals is strictly by protocol; where each guest is placed depends on his rank in the government or in the diplomatic corps.

Adjoining the State Dining Room is the presidential-family dining room, which in 1961 was refurnished in late-eighteenth-century style. There is a crystal chandelier with candles. To the west is the butler's pantry; this opens into the State Dining Room and is connected with a kitchen on the ground floor by a servants' elevator, dumbwaiter, and a stairway.

The public is not admitted to the second or third floor, which are reserved for the presidential family and their guests. Until the reconstruction in 1902, the second floor also housed the executive offices, with not much room left for the family. The story goes that four of Theodore Roosevelt's sons slept crosswise on Lincoln's bed. Now there are several suites for the family and friends on the upper floors.

The Rose Room (or Queen's Room) is furnished as an "elegant" lady's bedchamber of the early nineteenth century; it is always assigned to the "top" feminine guest. It has already housed five queens: Elizabeth, the Queen Mother, and Elizabeth II of England; Wilhelmina and Juliana of The Netherlands; and Queen Mother Frederika of Greece. The chief-ranking male guest sleeps in the Lincoln Room. The first distinguished guests in the White House after the latest renovation were Queen Juliana and her husband, Prince Bernhard.

The White House is open from 10 A.M. to 2 P.M., Tuesday through Friday, except on holidays, and on Saturdays from 10 A.M. to 2 P.M., April 1 through Labor Day, and 10 A.M. to noon, Labor Day through March 31.

Visitors are admitted at the east entrance. After entering the ground-floor corridor, they ascend the stairway to view the public rooms on the main floor.

Often people must wait in line for some time, especially during summer vacations. In April, 1967, an innovation was added to make the waiting less tiresome. Along 125 feet of the fence, small black boxes were placed; from these come a 5-minute message. Thus "the talking fence" gives tourists a recorded history of the White House, highlighting the historic events that have occurred in it and telling of individuals who have "slept there." Those waiting in line are given an idea of what they will see on their conducted tour through the interior.

UPKEEP OF THE WHITE HOUSE

While the United States government pays most of the bills, the chief executive is responsible for feeding the household servants. When Harry S. Truman became President, he cut down on the number of employees, saying he could not afford to pay as large a "tab" as the Roosevelts had.

Each year Congress appropriates about $528,000 for the upkeep of the building and grounds. This amount covers supplies, repairs, utilities, and employees' salaries. About 100 persons are employed, including chauffeurs, cooks, butlers, maids, housekeeper, engineers, and gardeners.

Police also guard the mansion, and Secret Service men are on hand to protect the President and his family at all times. These men are hand-picked, after a minimum of two years in the Washington metropolitan police. Several of them are excellent linguists; altogether, they make up one of the most efficient police systems in the world. As combination diplomats, psychologists, and crack shots, they simultaneously fend off habitués of what reporters call the "nut corner," while treating all visitors with smoothness, dispatch, and courtesy.

SOME WHITE HOUSE "INMATES"

Once someone remarked that the White House "bears the imprints of successive Chief Executives" just as the nation does.

> Through the years the White House has been a mirror of the people. Not only the character of the Presidents, but the times themselves left their imprint.
> And through it all—the shenanigans and the sacrifice, the gab, and the gallantry—the White House echoed to the jigtime of history.

Here are some of the "bits and pieces" that are remembered about several of the heads of our government.

When President John Adams bought a $50 billiard table, he was accused of corrupting the youth of the nation.

Thomas Jefferson, sensing the mood of the people, discouraged all aristocratic practices. In his own social life, he practiced democratic simplicity. It was his custom to open the White House each morning to all visitors. When George Washington and John Adams were in office, they merely bowed to their callers; however, Jefferson started the custom of shaking hands with them.

James Madison, with the help of his versatile wife, Dolly, was noted for his fashionable soirees. John Quincy Adams went to bed punctually at 11 P.M. each evening; he rose at 5 A.M. and walked 4 miles each day before eating breakfast.

When "Old Hickory"—Andrew Jackson—came to the White House, he had recently lost his beloved wife, Rachel. Their love, it was said, was one of the great romances of all time—"a profound attachment between two remarkable human beings."

One source states that the White House atmosphere under Jackson was "earthy"; "stilted" under Martin Van Buren; and "impeccably respectable" under James K. Polk.

Chester Arthur loved to entertain lavishly; once he spent $1,500 for floral decorations for a single dinner party, even though the White House had its own hot house. And the cigar makers are reported to have idolized William McKinley, as he was a devotee of cigar smoking.

Calvin Coolidge was proud of his wife—in his own way—for she had social graces he did not possess. But it is said that he scolded her for taking riding lessons, also for going on hikes with just a Secret Service man.

If it, of course, a high honor to be the First Lady of our great country. But the position demands much self-sacrifice, for she has little privacy and practically no time to herself. Jack Anderson once asserted: "First Lady is not an elected office and draws no salary. But it is a full-time job that goes with being married to a President."

Harry S. Truman once summed up the matter in this fine fashion: "A President needs many things, but brains, ability, and a loyal following mean nothing, unless by his side there is an intelligent and understanding wife."

The first First Lady to live in the Executive Mansion, Abigail Adams, wrote that the place was on a grand scale, but it would need thirty servants to care for it. She also commented on "the damp plaster, the lack of bell pulls, and the dearth of firewood that left the large rooms cold and drafty."

Dolly Madison was noted for her "bespangled and feathered turbans." We have long heard the story that in 1814, when the British burned the White House, Dolly cut Washington's portrait from the frame, rolled it up, hid it under her skirt, and fled from town. However, Dolly herself, in a letter written "while the enemy was at the gates," told the true version of this episode:

I insist on waiting until the . . . picture . . . is secured, and it requires to be unscrewed from the wall. The process is found too tedious for these perilous moments; I have ordered the frame to be broken and the canvas taken out. It is done, and the precious portrait placed in the hands of two gentlemen of New York for safekeeping.

In after years Dolly Madison was still a prominent figure in the national capital. She took part in the dedication of the Washington Monument, and it was her privilege to send the first personal message over Samuel F. B. Morse's newly invented telegraph.

During the French Revolution, while Elizabeth Monroe was living in Paris, the wife of the Marquis de Lafayette was in prison awaiting her execution. Mrs. Monroe went to see her. As a result, the captors spared her life, for they wanted to maintain friendly relations between France and the United States.

Many tributes were paid Elizabeth Monroe; here is what President John Quincy Adams once said of her:

> This lady, of whose personal attractions and accomplishments it were impossible to speak in terms of exaggeration, was . . . the cherished, affectionate partner of his [the President's] life. . . .

Louisa Adams, John Quincy Adams's wife, was the daughter of an American businessman who resided for years in London. She met her future husband at her home in England. After their marriage, Adams represented our country abroad in several places including Russia. Later it was said that in spite of her long residence in foreign lands, Louisa's tastes were "not worldly, but literary and artistic."

Because Martin Van Buren was a widower, fashionable Angelica Van Buren, wife of his eldest son, served as his hostess. The young couple had gone to Europe on their wedding journey. It was reported that the southern bride there "picked up some royal notions" which later offended the Americans. For example, at her receptions she decided to receive her friends seated in an elevated chair; this "caused a democratic ruckus."

The first wife of President John Tyler (first chief executive to become President because of the death of a President) started the custom of having the Marine Band play *Hail to the Chief* when the President was coming. (She was also the first First Lady to die in the White House.)

Harriet Lane, niece of our only bachelor President, James Buchanan, acted as his hostess. She had traveled abroad, was quite sophisticated, and wore "low-necked dresses, lace berthas, and voluminous skirts." She was noted for her tact; during the troublesome, tense period just before the Civil War, at the opening of a reception she had the band play *Dixie* and at the close *Yankee Doodle*.

The life of Mary Todd Lincoln in the White House was not a happy one, with the death of her son Willie and the shadow of the Civil War hanging heavily over the place. She was the subject of much criticism for various things, including extravagance. However, she declared she had to wear clothes of costly materials, for the public scrutinized closely everything she wore.

Although Lucy Webb Hayes (the first hostess who was a college graduate) was quite religious and held family prayers each morning and also had hymn-singing sessions for members of the Cabinet and Congress, there was a happy domestic life in the White House during her regime. Her receptions ended with the band playing *Home, Sweet Home*. Mrs. Hayes was the first presidential wife to make a trip to the West Coast.

Mrs. Benjamin Harrison is given credit for saving the White House china and starting this valuable collection, which can be seen today. (She was the second President's wife to die there.)

Mrs. Taft had lived in the Philippines, Italy, and France, as her husband's duties for the United States had taken him to those places. Therefore, she was well fitted for life in Washington. A great lover of music, Mrs. Taft organized the Cincinnati Symphony Orchestra.

No White House hostess, it is said, was ever more popular than Mrs. Calvin Coolidge. One day, before her marriage, she was taking the White House tour as a tourist. She then had the "nerve" to tinkle the keys of the piano in the East Room, never dreaming that someday she would be mistress there.

Mrs. Herbert Hoover had had much experience living in different countries around the globe because of her husband's engineering projects. At the executive mansion she was an efficient housekeeper and saw to it that historical furnishings were restored. She also bought fifty "comfortable" chairs for the White House.

The varied events of the period (the longest one in its history) when Eleanor Roosevelt was its mistress are well-known history.

She traveled more miles and met more people than any other President's wife. On these trips she was Franklin D. Roosevelt's "eyes and ears" and brought back to him much valuable information from the grass roots.

Mrs. Roosevelt also made more speeches and "got into more hot water" than any other First Lady. She was quite independent and had decided ideas of her own, one of which was the right of her five children to lead their own lives.

In striking contrast to Eleanor Roosevelt was Bess Truman, who enjoyed entertaining small groups at the White House, such as her bridge club from Independence, Missouri. Mrs. Truman did not try to mix in political affairs. One person described her as "a quiet, kindly person, and always a lady."

Mamie Eisenhower was widely known for her love of pink flowers and her "ever-present bangs." She enjoyed settling in the White House for eight years, after having lived in so many different houses and apartments during her husband's long army service.

Jacqueline Kennedy, one of the youngest of our First Ladies, will always be remembered for her bouffant hair-do and pillbox hats (both started far-reaching fads). Her parties with "the younger set" were quite different from former ones, as was the music played at them. Lester Lanin often led his orchestra at such parties. When the band leader thought the hour was growing late, he asked an aide whether he should play *Good Night, Ladies*. Usually he would be told, "Don't stop now; the boss is having a good time." There was always much fun at the Kennedy parties; White House butlers and others said there hadn't been such good times for forty years.

With the coming of the Johnson teen-agers, the gay life at the executive mansion continued. The new First Lady made a great hit with her many guests. Someone remarked of her: "She has a charm that would wilt the most starchy guest."

Mrs. Johnson's favorite color is "sunshine gold." In showing some newswomen around the White House, she told them Dolly Madison had been the first President's wife to paint any of the walls yellow. Mrs. Johnson declared she was delighted that Mrs. Kennedy had redecorated the oval drawing room (above the Blue Room) in yellow, with the furniture covered in gold brocade and the curtains of similar material.

Unlike some of her predecessors, Lady Bird Johnson is keenly interested in politics and social problems. One reporter recently wrote of her:

> This lady's idea of a delightful day is a "women-doers'" talk-fest over the luncheon table, a visit to an antipoverty project, and a tea to promote American beautification, same afternoon.

WHITE HOUSE CHILDREN

Ever since the White House was built, presidential youngsters and their varied doings have made news and have been an important part of the executive-mansion scene.

Six of our chief executives had no children of their own: George Washington, James Madison, Andrew Jackson, James K. Polk, James Buchanan, and Warren G. Harding. However, some of them managed to have children around them.

President Washington married a young widow, Martha Custis, with two small children, Patsy (or Patty) and Jack Custis. It is said that the "Father of His Country" treated them as if they were his own. But none of this family ever lived in the White House, completed after Washington had finished his two terms in office.

Only one of the first five United States Presidents had a son—John Adams, our second chief executive. His daughter Abigail married William Smith, who served as her father's secretary. This couple's son was the first child to visit at the White House. There he had fun playing with his grandfather and also watched his grandmother hang clothes to dry in the East Room.

When Thomas Jefferson became President, he was a widower. One of his daughters and her family lived with him during the winter of 1805–1806. On January 17, 1806, her second son, James Madison Randolph, was born—the first baby boy to arrive in the famous mansion.

Dolly Madison's son, Payne Todd, was in college when his mother became the First Lady and his stepfather was President. Maria Monroe went to live in the White House when she was fourteen, and she has the honor of being the first presidential daughter to be wed there.

John Quincy Adams's son married Mary Heller in 1828, and their daughter was born the following year—the first baby girl born at the White House.

Andrew Jackson, mourning the death of his wife, Rachel, asked her nephew Major A. J. Donelson and his wife, Emily, to live with him in the Executive Mansion. Three daughters were born to the Donelsons there. Once the President gave a large party for his seven "grandchildren"; on that occasion, it is said, he served them "substantial" food; afterward he enjoyed seeing them all romp around the East Room.

Twelve-year-old Betsy Blair was a great favorite of Andrew Jackson. She lived across the street in Blair House (in late years used by the government as a guest house for distinguished visitors). The President asked Betsy to stay with them, as she liked to play with the Donelson youngsters. (When the cornerstone for the great Treasury Building was laid, Andrew Jackson put a lock of Betsy's hair in it.)

Also a widower, President Martin Van Buren moved into the White House with his four grown sons. He married again in 1838, but a son born in the executive mansion lived only a few hours.

When he took office, William Henry Harrison (who died one month later) brought with him the widow of his eldest son and her two young boys.

After President Harrison's death, Vice-President John Tyler moved in with his first wife. All of their seven children were grown except two. His first wife died at the White House; during her illness, Alice, who was fourteen, took charge of her brother, Tazewell, two years younger, often taking him to church and elsewhere. When President Tyler's little granddaughter became three years old, he gave an unusual party for her. The East Room was beautifully decorated with flowers and lights, as fairyland, and the honored little girl was dressed as a fairy.

Zachary Taylor's youngest daughter was her father's hostess (another daughter married Jefferson Davis, later president of the Confederacy).

Millard Fillmore's daughter also assisted the President in his entertaining, while her brother was the presidential secretary. The young Fillmores both loved reading and books; during their father's administration Congress made an appropriation of $5,000 to start a White House library.

The Franklin Pierces were a sad couple when they entered the White House. Two children had died in infancy, and just before the inauguration, their third child had died in a railway wreck. Outside the required official entertaining, the Pierces did not indulge in much social life. However, at times they did entertain young members of their Sunday-school class.

When Abraham and Mary Todd Lincoln took up their residence at the White House, Robert, their eldest son, was at Harvard; the younger boys, Willie and Tad, were aged eleven and eight. These two "romped all over the place," as one contemporary reported. Sometimes they put on shows in the attic, dressed up in their mother's old clothes.

Early in 1862 both boys became ill with fever, and Willie died. Mrs. Lincoln was so grief-stricken that she never again entered the room in which her son had passed away.

Tad often got into mischief. It was said that the President was too indulgent with him. Tad's pranks enraged White House officials, but they amused the public. He often would walk into a Cabinet or other meeting and crawl under his father's desk. Or he would break in to intercede for someone waiting in the corridor, with whom he had talked.

Tad was popular with some persons around the executive mansion, especially the Secretary of War, who made him a Lieutenant of Volunteers. Soon the youngster was busy drilling a company of boys and posting them at strategic points to guard his father and the White House.

There was a large family in the mansion when Andrew Johnson came to live in it; besides his own children (one son was his secretary), grandchildren and other relatives lived there. The President often took the boys and girls for picnics in Rock Creek Park. He also enjoyed having them roll eggs on Easter Monday. On his sixtieth birthday the chief executive gave a children's party for hundreds of Washington youngsters.

There were four children in the Ulysses S. Grant family: three boys (one was at Harvard) and Nellie, a typical teen-ager of her day. She liked to drive her phaeton through the Washington streets and lead all-night cotillions. Her brother Jesse enjoyed astronomy; he had a telescope on the White House roof. His father often joined him there during his study of the stars.

When the Garfields moved into the mansion they had four boys, aged eighteen, sixteen, eleven, and nine, and one girl, Mollie, fourteen. One of the boys—so a story tells—once rode his bicycle down the main staircase, while another went swimming in the White House fountain.

Once these Garfield children were neglecting their school studies. The tutor complained to the President, who instituted a program of studies at mealtimes and each day quizzed the youngsters thoroughly in regard to their lessons.

President Arthur was a widower when elected to the presidency, with a ten-year-old daughter, Ellen (or Nelly). Each day she took a carriage ride around Washington with her father. By the end of his term, when she was fourteen, she was permitted to attend official receptions with a cousin whose mother, Mrs. McElroy, was the White House hostess.

Grover Cleveland was the first and only President to be married in the mansion. When he and his wife moved in for the second time (after his failure to be reelected following his first one), they had a seventeen-month-old daughter, Ruth. A second child, Esther, was born in 1893; and their third girl also arrived during Cleveland's second stay in the White House.

President Cleveland used to carve boats for the children to play with in the bath tub. He also enjoyed "showing off" the three little girls; often when important people called at his office, he would ask his wife to bring in the youngsters, no matter how they were dressed.

It was an unusual household when President Benjamin Harrison lived at the White House. Four generations were represented there: Mrs. Harrison's father, the Reverend Mr. Scott; and a married daughter, Mary Harrison McKee, her husband, J. R. McKee, and their two small children. The younger, Benjamin, was called "Baby" McKee and was a great favorite with President Harrison and newspapermen. The child was baptized in the executive mansion by the Reverend Mr. Scott with water brought from the River Jordan, in Palestine.

President Theodore Roosevelt's first wife died when Alice was born. By his second wife he had four boys: Theodore, Jr., Kermit, Archie, and Quentin, and one girl, Ethel. When the family reached the White House, Theodore, Jr., was at Groton; but the younger boys and Ethel made themselves at home, brought in all sorts of animals, and "followed their instincts completely."

The Roosevelt boys walked on stilts through the corridors and also roller-skated and rode bicycles on the second floor. It was reported that at times Ethel and Kermit would shinny up a lamp post and put out the light after the lamplighter had been on his evening round.

When the Taft family reached the White House after the father had taken the oath of office, they found young Charles Taft waiting there to take them up to the family quarters in the elevator. He had learned to operate it when playing there with his pals, the Roosevelt boys. And at age eleven Charles was sometimes put in charge of the switchboard when the operator went to lunch. He and Quentin Roosevelt always went together to their public school in Washington.

The three daughters of President Woodrow Wilson were much loved by the entire nation. Once they decided to hide their identity; they donned old clothes and wore veils, then got in line outside the White House, joined other Washington citizens and tourists, and took the conducted tour through their home. When they asked the guide if they could see the room where the Wilson girls slept, the request was refused. During World War I Jessie sang at camps for our soldiers in Europe.

Sadness came to the Coolidge family after they moved to the executive mansion. One of their two sons, Calvin, Jr., died from an infected foot after he had been playing tennis. (President Coolidge did not allow his sons to entertain their friends at the White House, as he feared someone would gossip about them.)

When Herbert Hoover was elected President, he had two grown sons. But while Herbert Hoover, Jr., was recovering from tuberculosis at Asheville, North Carolina, his wife and their children lived at the White House with his parents. These Hoover youngsters met some important visitors during their stay, including the King and Queen of Siam.

Things were lively at the mansion during the long regime of Franklin D. Roosevelt. Often four generations would be staying there. At the time of his first inauguration, three of the five sons were married. At the first-term ceremonies only two grandchildren were present, but thirteen attended the fourth inaugural.

James Roosevelt loved to tell of a happening on the day his father was inaugurated in March, 1933. Late that night, his brother John and two others drove up to the White House gate in a battered jalopy. The guard refused to let them in declaring that no President's son would ride in such a junk heap. So John had to spend the night in a hotel lobby. (The car really belonged to James Roosevelt.)

On another occasion, when John came home and wanted a snack, he found the refrigerator was locked. He also disliked the idea that often, when he wanted to talk with his father, he had to contact him through a secretary.

Margaret Truman, an only child, attended college while at the White House. Then she embarked on her singing and acting career. She naturally had many Washington friends, as she had lived in the city while her father was United States senator and Vice-President.

One night she and two girl friends had a slumber party and slept in the 9-foot Lincoln bed. But she reported later that since the mattress was so "lumpy," the girls ended the night by sleeping crosswise.

She also admitted that dating lost much of its allure for her when she had to be accompanied by Secret Service men. So she decided she'd wait to marry until her father was out of the White House (which she did).

General and Mrs. Eisenhower lost one son in infancy. At the time of their residence in the mansion, their second son, John, was a graduate of West Point and in army service. He and his wife had four children. The Eisenhowers often entertained these grandchildren at the White House; there, on April 22, 1956, Mary, aged four months, was baptized.

The White House child who probably rated more headlines and newspaper space than any other youthful occupant at 1600 Pennsylvania Avenue was Caroline Kennedy. She was three and her brother, John, not a year old when they moved in, the youngest children to reside there since the days of the Clevelands.

There's the classic story about her on Inauguration Day: she burst into a room where her father's staff was assembled and delivered this important piece of news: "Daddy's upstairs with his shoes and socks off, doing nothing!"

Often she would delight and surprise guests by popping into a room to see her father. Caroline attended school on the third floor with eight playmates. When lessons were over, the children played on swings or on a jungle gym, or rolled small barrels on the White House grounds. There too she rode her pony, Macaroni, or climbed up into her own secret tree house.

In order that Caroline would not miss one of the most popular joys of childhood, her mother, on Halloween in 1961, allowed her, dressed in a Halloween costume, with a mask, to go out with a Secret Service man.

Lynda Bird Johnson, nineteen, and Lucy, sixteen, were the first teen-aged girls in the White House since the Taft administration. (In 1964 Lucy changed the spelling of her name to "Luci.") Both graduated from the Cathedral School in Washington, D.C.

For a time Lynda attended her mother's alma mater, the University of Texas in Austin; then she graduated from George Washington University. Luci was a student at the school of nursing there but married Patrick Nugent in 1966. In December of the following year, Lynda was married to Marine Captain Charles Robb. Naturally, the Johnson girls' social life was closely scrutinized, and both received much newspaper publicity.

At times the former "White House children" have been asked to return to their old home. For instance, in May, 1959, the Eisenhowers invited the twenty living offspring of former Presidents back to see their old home. However, only eight could accept.

Mrs. Eisenhower took the group on a tour of the interior, from top to bottom. Some of them had not been back since their fathers had left office. They were delighted with the renovation made during the Truman era.

Since the Lyndon B. Johnsons have lived at the White House, there was another interesting meeting of "Ex-Inmates," as Margaret Truman Daniel termed them. In the Queen's Bedroom, Mrs. Daniel and others made up a panel moderated by Lynda Bird Johnson. The President's wife introduced the members by saying that "Unlike George Washington, all of the panel slept here; but they're going to talk about their waking moments in this house."

They agreed that living in the White House was not much fun, but according to Mrs. Daniel, "It has some compensating memories."

ANIMALS AT THE WHITE HOUSE

Animals have long been associated with our Presidents. Although Washington did not live at the White House, he was an animal lover; he had his pack of hunting dogs and fine horses, and there are many equestrian portraits and statues of him. Martha Custis Washington had a canary; and one grandchild, Nelly Custis, was devoted to her pet dog.

When Thomas Jefferson lived at the White House, he kept on the grounds the grizzly bear which Meriwether Lewis had brought back with him from his famous expedition to the Northwest. Jefferson also had a tame mockingbird, and it is said that his chicken coops were located on the site of the presentday swimming pool.

Dolly Madison's macaw used to scream at her guests. When doughty old General Zachary Taylor was head of the executive mansion, his prize possession was his horse, Whitey.

The two younger Lincoln boys during the Civil War had many pets, including goats, ponies, dogs, cats, and white rabbits. Once Tad was caught driving his team of goats around the East Room. One year some friends sent the Lincolns a large turkey for their Thanksgiving dinner. Tad named it Jack, made a pet of it, and became quite attached to it. He deeply resented the idea of its being killed for their holiday dinner. He begged his father to spare it. The President tried to reason with him; finally he gave in and signed— for the happy Tad—a reprieve for the lucky bird.

Once President Benjamin Harrison had to rescue his favorite grandchild, "Baby" McKee, from a runaway as the child was driving his little goat wagon on Pennsylvania Avenue.

When the Theodore Roosevelts occupied the White House, the boys had "a whole menagerie, including snakes and a bear." Other pets were dogs, cats, parrots, guinea pigs, turtles, and kangaroo rats. Someone said that about the only thing they didn't bring in was an elephant.

Once when Archie was confined to bed with the measles, he wanted to see his pony. Quentin managed to get the animal into the elevator from the basement and then to the sickroom to visit the invalid. President Roosevelt had a pet bulldog, which fell into disfavor when he bit a foreign ambassador and almost caused an international incident.

During the William Howard Taft regime a cow named Pauline Wayne used to graze peacefully on the White House grounds.

The Coolidges had a canary, and the First Lady owned a pet raccoon named Rebecca. Both Coolidges were strongly attached to two handsome collies named Rob Roy and Prudence Prim. The former was noted for "food begging." Senator Morris Sheppard told a story of what happened to him one morning when he was breakfasting with President Coolidge. Rob Roy came up to the senator's chair and barked loudly. "He wants your sausage, senator," said the usually taciturn President. Senator Sheppard gave the animal *his* sausage, but he reported later that he did *not* get another in its place.

President McKinley had a pet parrot; he would whistle the first part of *Yankee Doodle* and the bird would complete the tune.

That noted Scottie, Fala, the close companion of his master, Franklin D. Roosevelt, will always have a place in White House history.

Caroline Kennedy was a great lover of pets when at the executive mansion; she had several hamsters, her pony, a canary, parakeets, and Tom Kitten. She also loved to watch the ducks and goldfish at the White Pool.

When she was only one year old she got her Welsh terrier, Charlie, to whom she was devoted. She received an unusual present from Russia, when Nikita Khrushchev sent Mrs. Kennedy a famous dog, Pushinka, daughter of the much-publicized Russian muttnik Laika that went on the long space trip. The two dogs, Charlie and Pushinka, played happily together at the White House and went on trips with the family.

WHITE HOUSE WEDDINGS

Although the first President's daughter to be married in the mansion was Maria Monroe, the first actual wedding there was that of Dolly Madison's widowed sister, Lucy Payne Washington—not related to the general. She married Supreme Court Justice Thomas Todd on March 29, 1812, before the British burned the White House.

The seventeen-year-old Maria Monroe was "the petite, shy daughter" of President James Monroe. Her bridegroom was her first cousin, Samuel Lawrence Gouverneur, who served as presidential secretary.

The wedding day, March 9, 1820, was "a stormy, rain-lashed Thursday." Only 42 guests—relatives and friends—witnessed the ceremony, performed by the Reverend William Hawley of St. John's Church.

Eight years later, in 1828, John Adams, son of John Quincy Adams, was married in the Oval Room to his cousin Mary Heller.

Mary E. Lewis (daughter of the presidential adviser and chief crony of President Andrew Jackson) wed a young French diplomat, from the French Legation, Alphonse Pageot, in the executive mansion.

Abraham Van Buren, oldest son of the President, married Angelica Singleton. She was related to Dolly Madison, who was reported to have been the matchmaker in this marriage.

Elizabeth Tyler, daughter of President John Tyler, married William Waller at the White House in the East Room on January 31, 1842. (It was during this same year that the British novelist Charles Dickens was entertained here.) Elizabeth was just nineteen at the time of the wedding.

When Nellie Grant was returning from England after being presented to Queen Victoria, she met on shipboard a young Englishman named Algernon Sartoris. He was a nephew of the famous British actress Fanny Kemble.

Nellie was only eighteen, but President Grant and his wife consented, and in 1874 gave the young couple the finest, most elaborate wedding that had ever taken place in the White House. There were 200 guests in the East Room to see the ceremony. Nellie had eight bridesmaids, and her brother, Colonel Fred Grant, was best man. On the tables, laden with delicacies, there were flags of both nations as decorations. The young couple received gifts valued at more than sixty thousand dollars.

However, the most lavish nuptial affair staged in the White House is said to have been that of President Grover Cleveland and his 22-year-old ward, daughter of his former law partner. (His sister had been his hostess until his wedding.)

In the fall of 1885 the chief executive proposed and urged her to take a year to think it over. But Miss Folsom gave him her answer the following spring. She and her mother went to Europe, after her graduation from college, and came back with a White House trousseau. On the day of the wedding, President Cleveland walked into the elaborately decorated Blue Room hand in hand with his bride, while the Marine Band on the lawn outside played a wedding march. The guns at the Navy Yard fired a salute, and church bells pealed.

Mrs. Cleveland was quite popular and had much influence at the White House. Two years later her husband was defeated for reelection. But both he and his wife were determined to return in four years.

Therefore, when Frances Cleveland left the mansion, she surprised a servant by telling him to take good care of all the furniture and ornaments. "For," she said, "I want to find everything just as it is now, when we come back." She added, "We are coming back four years from today." Mrs. Cleveland's words came true; her husband was the only President in American history to return for another term after being defeated for reelection.

Four other White House weddings followed the never-to-be-forgotten Cleveland-Folsom one. In the East Room in 1906, Alice Roosevelt, daughter of Theodore Roosevelt, who had been "the darling of Washington society for years," married Nicholas Longworth, a congressman and member of a prominent Cincinnati family.

There was much excitement and splendor about this wedding. It was the first marriage of a President's daughter since the Grant-Sartoris event thirty-two years before. Alice was "witty and prank-loving," but her wedding was quite formal. A thousand American and European diplomats and other dignitaries were invited. The Republic of Cuba sent her sixty-three pearls with a diamond clasp, while the Empress of China gave her rich silks and ivory carvings. The Pope sent her a mosaic of a famous Vatican painting.

At the wedding supper, when the bride tried to cut the cake, she declared the knife was too dull. So she borrowed a sword from one of the guests and "proceeded to slash the cake with great gusto."

Two of Woodrow Wilson's daughters were married in the White House. In 1913 there was a 140-pound cake when Jessie Wilson became Mrs. Francis Sayre. The groom was a Harvard graduate who served as Assistant Secretary of State and later as United States high commissioner to the Philippines. The Marine Band played as the wedding party went to the Blue Room. Government dignitaries, diplomats, navy and army officers, and other distinguished persons made up the guest list. The "elegant collation" was served in the State Dining Room.

Eleanor Wilson, the youngest of the three Wilson daughters, was married on May 7, 1914, to William Gibbs McAdoo, Secretary of the Treasury and later United States senator from California. Because of Mrs. Wilson's illness, the affair was much simpler than Jessie's wedding had been. Only members of the President's Cabinet and a few friends were present. Mr. McAdoo's daughter by a previous marriage acted as flower girl.

Fifty-three years later, December 9, 1967, Lynda Bird Johnson, daughter of President Lyndon B. Johnson, was married in the famous East Room to Marine Captain Charles Robb, "in the beauty of the White House agleam with the lights and garlands of the Christmas season."

> Lynda, in the traditional long white gown of a bride, and Robb in his dress blue Marine uniform, stood before a white altar on a low platform in the center wall of the East Room.

The seven bridesmaids were gowned in ruby-red velvet, in keeping with the White House decor of Christmas garlands, evergreens, and red and white flowers. The 500 guests, including relatives, friends, and members of the Cabinet and the Supreme Court, watched the ceremony and the departure of the bride and groom under an arch of swords.

President Johnson, on this memorable occasion, admitted that "as you might expect, the father of the bride is quite nervous."

WHITE HOUSE FOODS AND ENTERTAINING

From the earliest days presidential foods and entertaining have been news.

The day after Martha Washington reached New York, she presided at a formal dinner for twenty guests. No doubt that menu included some of the favorite dishes of the period, such as baked fowls with oyster dressing, roast ham, assorted preserves, pickles, desserts, raisins, and nuts. Washington is said to have been especially fond of hickory nuts.

Our first First Lady entertained lavishly, using the personal silver decorated with the Washington coat of arms. (It had been made from Martha's own melted-down pieces.) She started the noted presidential breakfasts. One British visitor stated that such a meal with the Washingtons included "sliced tongue, dry toast, bread and butter."

John and Abigail Adams managed to hold a public reception in the incomplete White House on New Year's Day, 1800. During their regime they entertained at weekly state dinners, served at 2 P.M. Often, too, after six-o'clock tea, they had music and dancing for their guests. The First Lady, although a semi-invalid, "held sprightly levees in the half-finished, barren White House."

Since President Jefferson had lived in France, he was partial to French cooking and imported a chef from that country. Both American and French dishes were served, including beef, ducks, turkeys, "the new foreign dish, macaroni," and fancy desserts. Jefferson claimed that he had brought from France the original recipe for ice cream.

He liked intimate dinners of just four persons so that there would be good conversation. The servants were dismissed after they had placed before each guest a tray containing the entire meal.

President Jefferson also gave two public receptions each year. On July 4, 1801, for example, he received guests in the Blue Room, where they helped themselves to cake and wine from sideboards, while the Marine Band furnished background music.

Once Thomas Jefferson received an extraordinary gift—a 1,325-pound cheese. It reached the White House on a wagon drawn by six horses. The vehicle bore a sign reading, "THE GREATEST CHEESE IN AMERICA FOR THE GREATEST MAN IN AMERICA." Since he did not approve of presidential presents, he paid two hundred dollars for the cheese and served it at an Independence Day dinner.

"Queen" Dolly Madison, although from a Quaker family, loved

gay social life and was an outstanding hostess. After she married James Madison she "embarked on the social career for which her vivacious nature was so well fitted." She was not only the famed hostess who "introduced some of the brilliance and glitter of Old World courts into the social life of the White House," but she was "an expert and industrious housewife, who rose at dawn and set the White House machinery in motion." At her husband's inaugural ball, Dolly Madison sat between the French and British ambassadors at a beautifully appointed crescent-shaped table.

The great variety and abundance of food at the Madison dinners became the talk of the town. However, at that time, turkeys cost only 75 cents, potatoes 40 cents a bushel, shad 2 for a quarter, and a young porker just $3. At the Georgetown Market, the Madison steward often bought provisions costing $50 for one day, a large sum for that era.

Frequently for breakfast the Madisons ate fish, bread, and tea; their midafternoon dinner consisted of soup, several meats, pudding, and pastry; at "high tea" the main dish often was baked oysters.

At formal state dinners this First Lady did not follow the continental method of serving one course at a time. Since she had everything put on the table, someone remarked that the board had the appearance of "a Harvest Home supper."

Back of each guest stood a servant to see that he had plenty of the various meats, preserves, cakes, almonds, and raisins. After the ladies had left the dining room, Dolly served them tea in the drawing room. She also started "Dove" dinners for the wives of Cabinet members, when the latter were being entertained by the President.

When Elizabeth Monroe took over, she added French furniture to the White House, as she had lived in Paris for several years. (This did not appeal to some Americans.) For the executive mansion the Monroes ordered the famous gold service, a handsome glass "plateau," and elegant bisque ornaments from France. Using the finest linens and silverware, Mrs. Monroe served dinners of French cookery, in formal continental style.

Under John Quincy Adams and his wife, Louisa (both of whom had spent several years in Europe), there was gay social activity at the White House. Each week they invited thirty persons for dinner; they held a "drawing room" every other Tuesday and gave frequent evening parties from 8 to 10 P.M. At these affairs guests chatted together, promenaded, and drank coffee or wine, the latter often costing President Adams as much as fifty dollars per evening.

During the height of the season, the Adamses presided at "Assemblies," where both young and old danced to the music of a small orchestra. At 10 P.M. supper was served at a table that "fairly groaned" with good edibles, including baked ham, venison, poultry, cakes, puddings, wines, and punch.

It is said that Andrew Jackson's favorite breakfast was turkey hash on waffles, with biscuits and blackberry jam. At his inaugural reception, because he believed the White House belonged to the people, he allowed the great crowd to roam over the grounds. Punch and lemonade were served to 20,000 persons on the lawn. Then the servants were mobbed by the overeager visitors, who swarmed into the mansion and ruined some of the expensive curtains, draperies, and carpets.

President Jackson gave carefully planned dinners, ending with nuts, Madeira wine, and ice cream. He had been introduced to this dessert by Dolly Madison and was immensely fond of it. Once during his term of office he gave a supper for 1,000 guests; the crescent-shaped table was loaded with everything the chef's imagination could conceive. Jackson also enjoyed giving parties—with plenty of ice cream—for his grandchildren.

Like Thomas Jefferson, President Jackson received a great cheese, 1,400 pounds, with a diameter of 4 feet. It bore the sign "FOR THE GREATEST AND BEST." On Washington's birthday, 1837, he invited the public to attend his farewell reception and to sample the enormous cheese.

As the crowds thronged through the executive mansion and frantically cut off pieces of the cheese, they smeared rugs and furniture with it. The odor lingered—so the story goes—long after Jackson had left the White House. President-elect Van Buren was so disgusted over this affair that he swore he would have *no* food served at *his* receptions.

Van Buren's daughter-in-law was his official hostess. He had been abroad as one of our ministers and had brought a French chef back with him. He was criticized for ordering expensive silverware and for serving such elegant dinners to his friends and no food to the public.

However, Washington socialites were much pleased with the way the new President reestablished formal social customs, and they praised the well-cooked and beautifully served dinners. During intermissions at White House balls, guests enjoyed refreshments of cakes and ices. Later in the evening, "collations" with cold meats, oysters, chicken, and intricate desserts were served.

The first Mrs. John Tyler, at her weekly dinner parties of about forty guests, kept to her Virginia fashion of feeding them. The President and his second wife, the attractive Julia Tyler, served cake and wine at their levees. The last Tyler party, with 2,000 guests, was long remembered because of its unusual decorations, excellent food, and delightful hospitality.

As Sarah Polk was very strict in regard to her religious views, there was no dancing while she was our First Lady, and no refreshments were served at receptions. However, as she was so friendly to all, the public forgave her for the lack of food at such affairs.

Until the time of the Fillmores, all meals were cooked in the kitchen on open hearths; when cook stoves were installed, the cook was displeased. President and Mrs. Fillmore entertained such celebrities as Louis Kossuth, Washington Irving, and William M. Thackeray.

Harriet Lane, hostess for James Buchanan, had spent some time in Europe and was influenced by its customs. At the White House she, like Elizabeth Monroe, was accused of trying to force foreign ways on our capital.

But Miss Lane presided gracefully over Cabinet dinners and on state occasions, notably when the Prince of Wales, later King Edward VII, was entertained at a dinner.

One of the most elaborate Buchanan banquets featured a cake 4 feet high, with a flag containing the coat of arms of each state. On that occasion, it is said that the guests consumed 400 gallons of oysters, 500 quarts of chicken salad, 60 saddles of mutton, 75 hams, plus 1,200 quarts of ice cream.

At an early Lincoln reception, a New York caterer furnished the refreshments. The famous Monroe "plateau" with "ornate devices in spun sugar" centered the festive table. The numerous delicacies included terrapin, oysters, game, fowls, pâtés, jellies, and assorted desserts. (No doubt Abraham Lincoln was amused by all these fancy foods, since he enjoyed munching on a piece of gingerbread.)

At President Lincoln's second inaugural banquet, the menu consisted of beef, veal, poultry, game, and smoked meats, and ended with cakes, tarts, jellied creams, ice cream, fruit ices, coffee, and chocolate.

Because of ill health, Eliza Johnson (Mrs. Andrew Johnson), usually let her daughter play the part of hostess. However, on Johnson's sixtieth birthday, when he honored his five grandchildren by giving a party for them (300 guests were invited), Mrs. Johnson did appear. There was dancing in the East Room, followed by refreshments.

The gracious Julia Dent Grant often entertained the Cabinet ladies at luncheons before her afternoon receptions. Sometimes the Grants had twenty-nine courses at their state dinners; these often featured a special rice pudding, created by their Italian chef. One meal, costing $1,500, was served when Queen Victoria's third son was entertained. At the wedding breakfast for Nellie Grant and her bridegroom, the famous gold table service was used. The menu for the elaborate affair was printed on white satin, and the wedding cake was "a magnificent creation."

During the Rutherford B. Hayes administration, a 1,500-piece set of fine Haviland china with assorted floral decorations was purchased for the White House. Mrs. Hayes, called "Lemonade Lucy" because of her temperance beliefs, broke her rule of no liquor just once— when two Russian Grand Dukes were visitors. Some guests called the Hayes era "the cold-water regime," declaring that at Lucy's parties "water flowed like wine." Only coffee was served with the fancy French dishes when President and Mrs. Hayes entertained one hundred friends on their twenty-fifth wedding anniversary.

At President Garfield's inaugural dinner, the guests consumed 1,500 pounds of turkey, 200 gallons of chicken salad, 3,000 biscuits, and 200 gallons of coffee.

The Arthurs did things in elegant style and entertained such noted singers as Christine Nielsen and Adelina Patti. They gave a banquet to welcome former President and Mrs. Grant on their return from a round-the-world tour. At this dinner there were 14 courses, and 8 different wines were served.

After the Cleveland-Folsom marriage in the Blue Room, the fifty guests sat down to a bounteous "collation." The floral centerpiece was in the form of the ship *Hymen* and bore a flag with the initials

"C" and "F." Later Mrs. Cleveland presided at a memorable dinner honoring the Infanta Eulalia of Spain.

President Benjamin Harrison gave a long-remembered dinner for the small fry on "Baby" McKee's birthday. Fifteen high chairs were filled with excited little guests. There were biscuits in the shape of baby chicks with spread wings, and bonbons were at each place.

The Theodore Roosevelts presided at more than 200 social events during their White House stay, including an outstanding one for Prince Henry, brother of Kaiser Wilhelm.

President Taft ate beefsteak for breakfast. However, his lunch was merely an apple and a glass of milk. To celebrate their silver wedding anniversary the Tafts gave a garden party with refreshments served inside.

The first Mrs. Wilson dispensed southern hospitality; Mrs. Harding, like Mrs. Wilson, enjoyed using the handsome table services in the executive mansion. For official parties Mrs. Harding served "high-class" food, but her husband liked to entertain his "old cronies" with hearty breakfasts or suppers of wieners and sauerkraut. He also insisted on having toothpicks on the table.

President Coolidge was noted for his pancake-and-sausage breakfasts, during which meals he was often completely silent. Once, when the Prince of Wales was a dinner guest, everyone was surprised to hear the President talking to him. Mrs. Coolidge, a charming hostess, often planned outstanding musicales, with refreshments, after her dinner parties. This First Lady had "egg-eating" parties instead of the customary "egg-rolling."

When the King of the Sandwich (Hawaiian) Islands visited the executive mansion, he insisted on having three personal attendants behind him. And at dinners he ate only foods handed him by his chief valet.

The Franklin D. Roosevelts, in addition to their formal affairs, enjoyed Sunday evening chafing-dish dinners, with such items as scrambled eggs. Mrs. Roosevelt "dignified" the hot dog by serving it at an inaugural-day luncheon. And at a long-talked-about characteristic American party for King George VI and the Queen, at the Roosevelt home at Hyde Park, she introduced the royal pair to this same food.

As years have passed, White House meals, in many cases, have become simpler, in this era of calorie-counting. However, on state occasions, recent occupants—the Trumans and the Eisenhowers—have served distinctive banquets, using the Monroe gold set and the handsome Lenox dishes purchased while Mrs. Truman was First Lady.

When President and Mrs. Eisenhower entertained President Rhee of Korea, they brought out the Monroe "plateau" again. François Rysavy, their Czech-born chef, once described the dinner, with more than sixty notable persons present, which was given in the State Dining Room to honor the President of Vietnam, Ngo Dinh Diem. On that occasion all-pink flowers, including snapdragons and carnations, in gold vases, furnished the decorations.

The menu included *mousse de fois gras*, green-pea soup, celery, olives, crabmeat Mornay, Long Island duckling, apple rings, wild rice with mushrooms, buttered asparagus, lettuce with green-goddess dressing, and for dessert frosted mint delight with petit fours.

Another outstanding and long-remembered dinner, with one hundred guests, occurred in 1959, during the Eisenhower administration. This banquet was given to honor Premier and Mrs. Khrushchev and their two daughters.

That evening, in the colorful State Dining Room, the E-shaped table was artistically adorned with golden-yellow chrysanthemums and smilax, while yellow candles added to the beauty of the scene. Again the famous *surtout de table* of the Monroes was in front of the honored guests. Crystal goblets stood at each place, the plates were the Eisenhower white china with gold edges, and the cutlery was gold forks, spoons, and pearl-handled knives.

Among the items served on this occasion were roast turkey with cornbread stuffing, cranberry sauce, escalloped sweet potatoes, Boston brown bread, and coleslaw in tomato baskets.

When Jacqueline Kennedy became our First Lady, she gave the White House "an entrancing Old World flavor" with dinners featuring superb French cuisine.

In France she had been so impressed by the dinner given her and President Kennedy at the Palace of Versailles that she set a delightful precedent by staging a gala lawn party and dinner at historic Mount Vernon. This affair was to honor the President of Pakistan, Mohammed Ayub Khan, and his daughter.

The guests were conveyed along the Potomac River in two

yachts. Before the banquet, the visitors wandered through the rooms of President Washington's famous home. A fife and drum corps in Colonial attire played; some Revolutionary War maneuvers were reenacted by men in cocked hats, scarlet coats, and white breeches for the enjoyment of the visiting president. The National Symphony was on hand to play for this distinctive event.

The dinner, by candlelight, was served in a pavilion; the food included such dishes as avocado and crabmeat mimosa, chicken and rice, raspberries with cream, and petit fours. This successful occasion will no doubt go down in White House annals as a unique and delightful departure from the usual culinary fashion of the executive mansion.

With the tragic death of John F. Kennedy and the coming of a new President, Lyndon B. Johnson, there have been varied changes at the White House in the way of foods and entertaining. Since the family was so addicted to ranch living, their new home took on a Texan flavor. No Johnson reception was considered complete without a massive ship-round of beef on the groaning buffet table, along with buttered bread slices, a bowl of Fritos, and a chafing dish of the inevitable chili-con-ceso dip.

President Johnson has entertained several international guests at his ranch in Texas, where they learn something about southwestern foods and hospitality.

In February, 1964, when the Johnsons honored the diplomatic corps, the menu was unusual and included one of the President's favorite dishes from the Southwest—chili con queso.

> Mrs. Johnson had ordered dishes from each area of the United States: a giant roast of beef from the West; shrimp creole from the South; beef ragout from New England; salmon from the Northwest; roast turkeys, hams, and many other tempting dishes.

When the Johnsons were hosts to the Shah of Iran and Empress Fara, the dessert Strawberries Romanoff became Strawberries Fara; and it is said she was "entranced."

Before the time of the Kennedys, there was a receiving line; however, they enjoyed walking around among their guests and chatting with them. The Johnsons went back to the receiving line.

A most unusual dinner of the Johnson regime feted the legislators.

For the first time in White House history, a portable charcoal broiler was wheeled out onto the West Terrace, on the roof of the swimming pool. There distinguished guests hungrily lined up for sizzling steaks and other "man-filling" dishes.

Mrs. Johnson further displayed her flair for innovations when she gave a gala dinner dance on the East Terrace, on the roof of the movie theater. Borrowed shrubbery screened the terrace from "oglers" along Pennsylvania Avenue, and tables were set up in cabaret style around the dance floor.

No doubt as long as we continue to elect and send Presidents to the White House, the foods they, their families, and guests enjoy will attract national attention.

CHRISTMAS AT THE WHITE HOUSE

The John Quincy Adams family enjoyed having young people around, and at the Christmas holidays put on "assemblies" or balls for them, with an orchestra consisting of a piano and two violins. "Daniel Webster punch" was much in vogue at that time. It is reported, too, that carols (lately revived) were sung in the streets by young Negroes; also that yule logs were quite popular.

The Tyler family enjoyed yuletide festivities; they once gave a long-remembered fancy-dress ball at this season. The James K. Polks staged a "Christmas gala" at the executive mansion. And the two youngest Hayes children are said to have played Santa Claus and distributed presents to White House employees.

Sources seem to differ as to when the first Christmas tree was actually set up in the mansion. One writer says it was during the Franklin Pierce administration (1853–1857). On that occasion the President and Mrs. Pierce entertained the entire Sunday school of the New York Avenue Presbyterian Church, at which distribution of gifts around a Christmas tree was featured.

Another authority asserts that in 1891 President Benjamin Harrison had a tree, to which he referred as "an old-fashioned Christmas tree." At that time the chief executive declared that each American family should follow his example and decorate a tree. This particular one is said to have been set up to delight his namesake and favorite grandchild, "Baby" McKee.

As Christmas trees became more popular in the United States, some Americans got the idea that if the cutting weren't stopped, our national forests would be depleted. President Theodore Roosevelt was noted for his strong belief in the preservation of our national reservations. He carried on a vigorous campaign and declared there would be *no* holiday trees in the White House during his term of office.

Not long afterward, President Roosevelt was surprised and quite angry to discover that two of his young sons, Archie and Quentin, had managed to smuggle a small tree up into the former's room. After a severe scolding, the youngsters went to talk with a good friend of their father, Gifford Pinchot, noted for his work as a professional forester, and begged him to help them.

Mr. Pinchot finally succeeded in convincing Theodore Roosevelt that the cutting of young evergreens actually was a good thing for the forests, rather than a harmful practice. The two youngsters were allowed to keep their Christmas tree; and ever since that episode, such trees have been set up in the executive mansion.

The story goes that Christmas caroling outside the White House began when William Howard Taft was in office. At midnight on Christmas Eve, a group of singers appeared on the lawn and sang *Adeste Fideles*. Suddenly a light shone in an upper window; then the carolers saw a big man clad in a dressing robe, beaming down happily on them. After they had completed their singing, President Taft called out, "Merry Christmas! Thank you so much!"

Things were humming around the old mansion at yuletide when the Franklin D. Roosevelts were the occupants, and the young folks, home from school, spent a gay week there.

The First Lady loved Christmas giving, and all year on her extensive travels was busy picking up gifts. At 5 P.M. on Christmas Eve, President Roosevelt lighted the giant community Christmas tree. After the family dinner, each member hung a stocking on the mantel in the President's bedroom.

Next morning, there was much excitement as each looked in his stocking. Church services, the reading by the President of Dickens' *Christmas Carol*, and a family dinner made up more of the celebration.

When the Trumans lived at the Executive Mansion, there was one especially beautiful tree, just after Margaret had sung her first concert in Washington. In her book of memories, entitled *Souvenir*, she described the tree:

> The White House was decorated with a huge tree against the French doors in the East Room. It was an evergreen tree, trimmed entirely in silver and white, with fragile silver baubles and tinsel and icicles. Of course there was also a decorated tree on the lawn, lighted with a myriad glimmering lights. The switch was thrown by the President with due ceremony.

During the Eisenhower era the White House was always handsomely decorated, with the decor varying from year to year. Several times they had their son, his wife, and the grandchildren with them for the holidays. On such occasions the "family" tree (under which the children found their presents) was in the west hall, on the second floor, which the President and his wife used as a sitting room.

There, in accordance with an old family custom, all members gathered around this tree and sang carols together. Mrs. Eisenhower played the organ, while all the others "let go with full-throated renditions of old favorites."

During their two terms in the executive mansion, the "big" trees in the Blue Room varied; one had blue and silver bells, while pots of white poinsettias made an effective contrast.

When the Kennedys came to the White House, Caroline had a special 3-foot tree of her own. It had been sent her by the forester who had also cut down the 18-foot one that was set up in the center of the oval-shaped Blue Room. It was a perfectly shaped balsam, topped by a many-pointed star placed just a foot below the ceiling.

Mrs. Kennedy developed the idea of having "a real children's tree," patterned on Tchaikovsky's *Nutcracker Suite*. The lights were in the form of small candles, and blue-velvet ribbons were wound around the boughs.

Tin animals, real ginger cookies, and candy canes, alphabet blocks, small Christmas packages, toy musical instruments, baskets, and other decorations woven of straw dangled from the branches.

Many of these ornaments had been made by elderly and blind workers in different parts of the United States. The holiday decorations all through the White House that year carried out the theme of "a typical country home, with emphasis on holly, mistletoe, and other evergreens."

Because Caroline and the rest of the family were going to Florida, she was especially eager to have a preview of this special tree before leaving. So, while a party was in progress for White House employees, Caroline was allowed to view the distinctive tree. Also, for the first time in many years, the "Great Tree" would be seen by the general public, for the mansion was to be open to visitors that Christmas week.

The Johnson family spent Christmas at the ranch in Texas during the early years of the Johnson regime. But before they left Washington there were many parties and the chance to see the decor, which was quite different from that of the Kennedys.

Once there was a dazzling 18-foot, ceiling-high tree in the Blue Room. It was decorated with an early-American scene and had 3,000 ornaments, including nuts, popcorn, cranberry chains, candied fruits, wood roses from Hawaii, straw stars, toy-soldier drums, and pine cones. Other decorations were petticoat lace, seed pods, geranium bunches, and gingerbread cookies made in the shape of Santa Claus, dolls, snowmen, camels, teddy bears, and milkmaids.

> The top ornament is what the White House described as "a federal empire angel," made especially for this tree out of burlap. Wooden figures, including a rocking chair, a soldier and a bugle, are displayed at the base of the tree, which was planned and decorated by Mrs. Johnson and her staff. . . .

A manger scene with forty-three porcelain figures of eighteenth-century manufacture was placed near the tree, against a backdrop of light-gold antique satin.

That year, in the Johnson family quarters, a small, long-needle pine, decorated in much the same fashion as the tree in the Blue Room, was placed on a table in the west hall. It was adorned with popcorn chains, cranberry garlands, and small ceramic figurines.

In 1965 the Johnsons added a Spanish-Indian touch to the White House decor—a piñata—in the front hall. This red, green, and gold ornament, in the tradition of Latin-American lands, was displayed to visitors. The piñata—"a smiling sunburst"—was used as an ornament only, and was not the usual container filled with sweets for the children.

GHOSTS IN THE WHITE HOUSE

Perhaps it is only natural that a building which has housed so many famous personalities and within whose walls so many important events have occurred should have some ghost stories associated with it.

During the time of the Tafts some of the staff said they had seen Abigail Adams walk, with outstretched arms, through the closed door into the East Room, where she used to hang her wash.

It was told, too, that Mrs. Taft one day asked a gardener to transplant some rose bushes. He did so, and soon afterward the rumor spread that Dolly Madison (who had originally planted them) was seen hovering around the garden, trying to find her lost rose bushes.

There was a recurring story that a picture would fall from the wall whenever the death of a President was imminent. There were reports, too, of strange noises in some of the bedrooms. And it was said that once loud laughter came from the bed on which Andrew Johnson had slept.

However, most of the ghost stories related to the White House had to do with the spirit of Abraham Lincoln. His ghost was most often seen—so it was asserted—when the country was going through perilous times. Some maintained they had heard Lincoln's boots going back and forth in the halls, while others told of seeing his tall, gaunt figure standing at the window in the Oval Room, from where he used to gaze out during the dark war days.

A former valet of Franklin D. Roosevelt declared he had seen Lincoln's ghost. Also one evening a maid went upstairs to do some work; soon her screams were heard; she rushed down the stairs and said she'd seen Lincoln sitting on his bed, pulling on his boots.

One evening at dinner in the White House a prominent woman guest told Franklin D. Roosevelt that she had fainted dead away the evening before. She had opened her door, in answer to a knock, and there stood Abraham Lincoln.

President Harry Truman admitted that he himself had experienced two "creepy incidents." At two different times he was awakened by a knock at his bedroom door. He thought it was someone to tell him that Winston Churchill was calling from London. When he answered the rap and opened the door, there was no one in sight.

Once as reporter Deb Myers was chatting with Eleanor Roosevelt in the garden at Hyde Park, Mrs. Roosevelt summed up the reactions of our chief executives to life in the White House in these words:

> I am convinced that every President comes to believe he is guided by a spiritual force that is beyond his understanding. During the terrible anxiety of D-Day, when the President read over the air the prayer which he had written, I had the feeling that he was reading it, not only to sustain others, but to sustain himself.
>
> I expect that almost every President, alone in his White House study at night, facing a great decision, looks over his shoulder now and then, and wonders if Washington, Jefferson, Jackson, Lincoln, and other great Presidents, who have experienced this awful loneliness, aren't somehow standing by.
>
> —*Holiday*, November, 1952

9

Our National Capitol

WHEN you visit Washington and view the Capitol, which for many decades has served as the meeting place of our law-making body, you will no doubt agree with these writers:

> Here is a shrine, marking the highest point yet reached by man in his eternal quest for free government, imperfect, perhaps, but unparalleled in history; and the public appeal is boundless.

> The towering landmark that stands on the hill is the most important and historic structure in the United States, and one of the world's greatest examples of architecture.

More than a century ago—in 1862—when the New England novelist Nathaniel Hawthorne saw the structure, he declared:

> It is natural enough to suppose that the center and heart of America is the Capitol, and certainly in its outward aspect, the world has not many statelier or more beautiful edifices. . . .

Allan Nevins, a distinguished present-day historian, has asserted:

> . . . our proudest boast is that no Capitol in all the world has done more to safeguard free democratic debate, the privileges of minorities, and the fundamental civil liberties of man.
> The Capitol is History; it is the Major Symbol of the Nation, full of minor symbols.

THE BUILDING

Our national Capitol is one of the most imposing buildings in the entire world. On its great dome is a statue of Freedom, whose head is 304 feet above the ground. The structure is 751 feet long, is 350 feet wide, and has 540 rooms, "all humming with activity." These include restaurants, post offices, railway and airline offices, and haberdashery and tailor shops.

Set in a park consisting of about 130 acres in the center of Washington, the building covers nearly 4 acres. Two wings constructed of white marble house the Senate and the House of Representatives. The center contains the Rotunda, Statuary Hall, and the old Supreme Court chamber.

At the front entrance of the Capitol are huge flights of steps "that seem to flow" from beneath the great columns of three large porticoes. The central entrance has two big bronze doors with panels that depict scenes in the life of Christopher Columbus. They include his discovery of America and other important episodes. These doors were modeled in the 1850's by Randolph Rogers and are considered by critics as fine as any in the world.

The doors open into the great Rotunda, which is in the exact center of the building. Just underneath the dome, it is an immense circular room, 96 feet in diameter and more than 180 feet from the floor to the highest point of the dome. A spiral staircase leads to the top, from which there is a magnificent view of the city of Washington.

THE SITE

An act of Congress, of July 16, 1790, gave President Washington the power to choose the specific location for the new capital, or Federal City, as it was known.

At first the President wanted to locate it near his own estate of Mount Vernon; he talked to his neighbors about donating land for the new project. However, some were violently opposed to the idea, even though Washington tried to show them that the value of their holdings would be increased by their nearness to the national capital.

When the decision was finally made to locate it on the Potomac River, many Americans were displeased with the site. Some termed it "the Indian place," while others called it a "howling malarious wilderness."

In spite of opposition, President Washington went ahead with plans and selected Major Pierre Charles L'Enfant, a French engineer who had served with him during the American Revolution, to design the new capital.

L'Enfant completed his work, which was on a grand scale, in about one year. In laying out the streets and avenues in his magnificent plan of 1791, he chose the location for various public buildings, including the Capitol, the most important of all our national structures.

Our Capitol is the first one planned by any nation exclusively for such a purpose. (The name "Capitol" comes from the Capitoline hill in Rome, the highest and most important of the seven hills on which the city is located.)

Before 1800 the American Congress had met in eight different places: Philadelphia, Baltimore, New York, Lancaster, York, Princeton, Annapolis, and Trenton.

Major L'Enfant was especially eager to place the "Congress House" in the best possible situation. Therefore, for its site he chose a commanding position on an 88-foot-high hill, heavily wooded at the time and known as Jenkins Hill. He wrote of the site:

> I could discover no one [situation] so advantageously to greet the congressional building as is that on the west end of Jenkins Height. . . . It stands as a pedestal waiting for a monument.

From this spot there is a splendid view of the entire city. While the Capitol is not in the exact center of the city, it is the center for the street-numbering system. Major L'Enfant in his plan designed many streets at right angles to each other, forming a "grid." There were also broad avenues, which sweep diagonally across this grid. He wanted the Capitol to face east, for at that time it was thought that most of the growth of Washington would be in that direction. However, this did not come to pass; many of the finest homes were located in the other direction.

CONSTRUCTION

With the site chosen, three commissioners for the District of Columbia were selected: Thomas Johnson, David Stuart, and Daniel Carroll. Their first problem was to get a design for the important structure.

At that time, in 1792, there was no architect in the country who had ever conceived of a building of such grandeur. Jefferson said he wished the structure to be "simple, noble and beautiful," while "Washington wanted a Capitol that would reflect the free spirit of the new republic, the surging strength of her people, and their wish to express national pride."

In March, 1792, Jefferson suggested to the commissioners that they put on a competition to get plans. At that time he was Secretary of State and also the first superintendent of public buildings. The men decided that instead of asking a foreigner to come over, they would try to find an American who could submit a suitable design. To the winner they offered $500 and a lot in the new city.

Of the fourteen designs received before the deadline, none came up to Washington's expectations. Finally, he and the others accepted one submitted by Stephen Hallet, a Frenchman who had fled the Revolution in France.

Three months later the commissioners received a request from Dr. William Thornton, an amateur architect, for permission to submit a plan. When his work arrived in the latter part of January, 1793, both Washington and Jefferson were well pleased with it. The former wrote Dr. Thornton that "grandeur, simplicity, and convenience appear to be well combined in this plan," and the latter said: "Thornton's plan has captivated the eyes and judgment of all. It is simple, noble, beautiful, and modern in size."

Strange to say, Dr. Thornton had never studied architecture, and he knew little of blueprints. (He had been born in the Virgin Islands and had studied medicine in Scotland.)

The commissioners were in a dilemma. They had already accepted Hallet's idea, but they decided to change to Thornton's design. He was so informed in a letter on April 5, 1793, and received the prize money. Then, in order to appease Stephen Hallet, they made him superintendent of construction of the Capitol building.

Dr. Thornton's plan called for a central structure, with a rotunda surmounted by a low dome and with smaller buildings or wings on each side. The edifice was in classic Roman style, "with Renaissance accents." In front was a portico with a pediment, and on the west side there was a semicircular portico. (Thornton's original design has been lost, but prints made from it are available.)

After construction had started, plans were formulated for the cornerstone-laying, which took place on September 18, 1793.

The Alexandria *Gazette* for September 25, 1793, has left an interesting, detailed account of the rites at this cornerstone-laying. In his chief role that day, Washington was supported by the Alexandria Volunteer Infantry and his fellow Masons from Maryland, Virginia, and the District of Columbia.

The long parade began when the President arrived on the Virginia bank of the Potomac; then it crossed to the Maryland side and proceeded to Presidential Square. "The procession marched two abreast in the greatest solemn dignity, with music playing, drums beating, colours flying, and spectators rejoicing."

However, when the marchers reached Tiber Creek, they had to break ranks to step from stone to stone over the small stream, then on to the foot of Capitol Hill and the site of the proposed building.

That day George Washington wore a Masonic apron said to have been fashioned by the Marquise de Lafayette. He used a marble-headed gavel to call the assembly to order and a silver trowel for laying the stone. On it he placed a silver plate with the date, marking the thirteenth year of American independence. (Today the exact situation of the original cornerstone is not known; however, it may be in the southeast area of the original north wing of the Capitol.)

It was a very festive occasion; bands played; soldiers paraded; and the American flag waved proudly over the proceedings. There were the customary long orations, interspersed with prayers; and artillery volleys roared. Altogether, it was a noisy occasion, but a jubilant one.

The formal ceremonies ended that day with prayer, "Masonic Chanting Honours," and a fifteen-volley salute from the artillery. Then

The entire company retired to an extensive booth where an ox of 500 pounds was barbecued, of which the company generally partook, with every abundance of other recreation.

In spite of the "ostentatious" beginning, the work on the Capitol went slowly at first. For some time Jenkins Hill was "a place of confusion, scattered materials, brick kilns, and squalid huts for laborers."

Stephen Hallet tried to find as many defects as possible in Dr. Thornton's design. For a year he made changes and also kept submitting designs to the commissioners, hoping they would approve one that he could claim as his own.

Finally, after he had disregarded Washington's orders, Hallet was dismissed on November 15, 1794. Dr. Thornton was appointed to the commission and, with Washington's approval, tried to obliterate Hallet's changes. Later, for some time, the work on the Capitol was under the supervision of James Hoban and George Hadfield.

At last, the first unit—the north wing—was completed. It was built of sandstone from Aquaia Creek, in Virginia. This was the part of the building used by the United States Senate and was also occupied by the Supreme Court until 1835. This section was the first of a grand architectural plan which Thomas Jefferson declared "captivated the eyes and judgment of men."

Late in the fall of 1800, the national government moved from Philadelphia to the new Federal City. On November 22 Congress convened here for the first time.

Washington was not much to speak of in those early days; Pennsylvania Avenue was just a mud road covered with weeds and bushes. Houses were scarce, and the 32 senators and 105 representatives had a difficult time finding accommodations. Often 10 or 20 of them were crowded into one small dwelling.

On March 6, 1803, by appointment from President Jefferson, a Britisher, Benjamin H. Latrobe, was put in charge of the Capitol construction as surveyor of public buildings. He continued in this work until 1818. Latrobe was a trained architect and civil engineer. In 1795 he had been offered the position—at £1,000 per year—of surveyor of public offices in London. But he refused it, as he preferred to come to America and seek advancement in the young republic.

When Latrobe took his position here, he found flaws in Dr. Thornton's design, and in spite of the latter's objection, made some structural changes. In 1807, under his supervision, the south wing was completed. (At first the central part was not built; the two wings were connected by a wooden walkway.)

When the War of 1812 broke out, most of the action was far away from the new capital city. But in the late summer of 1814, Rear Admiral Sir George Cockburn landed British troops in Maryland, marched on Washington, and captured it on August 24, 1814. His main idea was to destroy completely the original Capitol building, "then, as now, one of the principal symbols of the American way of life."

Rear Admiral Cockburn himself took part in burning the structure. This was done in retaliation for the earlier destruction of some public buildings in Canada by American troops. The officer is said to have stood on the chair of the Speaker of the House and called out, "Shall this harbor of Yankee democracy be burned?"

At once the British soldiers set fire to desks, chairs and other furniture. The entire interior was destroyed, as was the walkway between the wings.

(During the period of rebuilding and completion of the Capitol, Congress met in a brick building, Blodgett's Hotel, at First Street and Maryland Avenue.)

After the fire, the work of reconstruction was started by President Madison. The original design was adhered to; the cornerstone was laid on August 24, 1818, just four years to a day after the burning. Fortunately, Latrobe and Hoban were available for the work, and the Rotunda and interior were completed. Since Benjamin Latrobe was "the first great Greek revival architect," the interiors of the Senate and House of Representatives "took on the Greek theater form."

From 1818 to 1829 Charles Bulfinch, an eminent architect appointed by President Monroe, built the central part. He is credited with finishing the edifice as Dr. Thornton and Benjamin Latrobe had planned it.

By 1843 the House chamber was becoming too crowded, because new states were being added to the Union. Therefore President Fillmore appointed Thomas U. Walter as the fourth Capitol architect and asked him to design new wings for the structure.

On July 4, 1851, there was another cornerstone-laying; at this celebration Daniel Webster was the orator of the day. In the cornerstone box a copy of his speech describing the state of the Union and other historical documents were placed.

Walter added the new wings to the Capitol; they were built of marble from Massachusetts and Maryland. The House occupied its new chamber on December 16, 1857, and the Senate on January 4, 1859.

During the past century more changes have been made at the Capitol. One source states that just as our form of government was not meant to be "as fixed and unchangeable as the pyramids," so our Capitol has also been subject to change and modification. And an article states:

> Change, remodeling, alteration, always with profound regard for the basic integrity of the original structure, have been the order of the times for the Capitol.

Steam heat was added in 1865, elevators in 1874, and electric lights in 1882.

When Thomas U. Walter resigned in 1865, he was succeeded as Capitol architect by Edward Clark (1865–1902). The latter was followed by Elliott Woods, who died in 1923. During his time the House and Senate office buildings were constructed.

Today the Capitol has in its south wing the largest legislative hall in the world—the House of Representatives, with 444 seats and a visitors' gallery. There the Democrats sit on the Speaker's right, and the Republicans on his left. In the north wing is the Senate chamber, with 100 desks; a center aisle divides it, as in the House.

In addition, the Capitol has an art gallery and a school for the pages. An electric subway of open cars runs between the senators' old and new offices and the Capitol.

Even though visitors today may not actually see the same Capitol that Washington and Lincoln did, this "complex" will remain, as it always has been, "a place of awe and great majesty."

One of the most important changes, made between 1955 and 1962, was extending—by 32½ feet—the east wall, the portico, and the two immediately joining wings. This wall was faced with white marble, but "the indented appearance" was retained and "the original facade appears as if unchanged." (President Eisenhower presided at the cornerstone-laying for this change.)

This improvement—at a cost of $11.4 million—added 100,000 square feet of space and made room for 54 offices, 8 rooms for Senate and House documents, and House and Senate dining rooms.

On June 14, 1966, the Commission for the Extension of the United States Capitol announced a $34 million plan to extend the west front by 44 to 88 feet.

This project, according to Representative S. S. Stratton, would largely destroy the last visible portion of the original building. "In its place would be added 4.5 acres of extra space for 2 new restaurants, 2 auditoriums, and 115 hideaway offices for favored congressmen and senators."

It was reported by Representative Stratton that the commission meets behind closed doors, invites no open debate, and keeps no records of its proceedings. Since 1955 this group has had the power to make all Capitol changes. The only check on their authority is the power of Congress to deny them funds.

According to a newspaper report in May, 1967, a team of architects "prowled" the Capitol from top to bottom. Afterward they agreed that it needed repairs but that it was not yet falling down. Although there is some settling, the building is *not* sliding downhill.

This inspection was made by the American Institute of Architects, which is opposed to the idea of extending the west front to create more office space. Charles W. News, of Baltimore, president of the institute, declared that this west front is all that remains of the original exterior and that to cover it up would be "a great mistake."

THE DOME

No matter how many times you visit Washington, you are thrilled to see the great dome of the Capitol illuminated and dominating other capital lighting. By daylight it gleams in the sunlight and can be seen from all parts of the city and the outlying countryside.

The United States Capitol stands today, a great stately and monumental building, linked with the history of the nation. The great Dome has an impressive dignity, visible for miles distant as one approaches the capital city.

This hemispherical dome is one of the greatest in the entire world. It weighs 8,909,200 pounds and consists of 2 cast-iron shells with a stairway in between them. The 36 columns around its drum represent the number of states of our nation when it was built. The dome at its outside exterior is 135½ feet in diameter and has 108 windows.

The present structure was not included in the design for the Capitol drawn by Dr. Thornton. The original one—wood covered with copper—was patterned, according to one source, after that of the ancient Pantheon in Rome. However, another writer gives credit to the Russian Cathedral of St. Isaac.

The dome has gone through a series of changes. In 1850 it was described as "a squatty, black-topped inverted bowl." The newer one is the creation of Thomas U. Walter, who recommended that a new wrought-iron dome be placed over the old one.

Construction of the massive replacement began in 1855. Since the Capitol was considered "the dauntless symbol of the Union's strength and purpose," the work on it was continued during the Civil War. When some persons wondered about this, President Lincoln is reported to have said, "If people see the Capitol going on, it is a sign we intend the Union to go on."

The new dome was finished in 1863, when a huge bronze statue of Freedom, created by Thomas Crawford, was swung into place over it. Through the years, this Capitol dome has been influential in molding the architecture of state capitols, for many of them have similar domes.

THE FREEDOM STATUE

When the decision was made to place a new dome over the old one, the question arose as to what should top it. Finally it was decided that a statue, symbolic of the liberty which the United States had won, would be most fitting. The figure of Freedom is "a magnificent lady who seems entirely at ease on the top of a marble 'lantern,' hundreds of feet in the air."

The majestic figure is 19½ feet high, weighs 15,000 pounds, and cost over $23,000. As one source says, it may be somewhat too large for the supporting structure; but "it has become in the eyes of most Americans the outward symbol for legislative bodies." And according to an official brochure, "The Capitol, Symbol of Freedom":

> The statue of Freedom . . . may not be artistically the greatest statue ever sculptured, but you notice it holds the highest place on the Capitol structure. This is because its significance is holy.

Thirteen columns, representing the original states, support the pedestal on which the figure rests. And on this base are the words "E Pluribus Unum."

When the sponsors of the idea were looking for an artist to create the desired figure, they contacted the American sculptor Thomas Crawford, then living and working in Rome.

He was born in New York City in 1814 and died in Rome in 1857. At the age of fourteen he was working as a woodcutter. A few years later he was an apprentice in stonecutting in the studios of Frazee and Launitz, in New York.

In 1835 the young artist was accepted as a pupil by Bertel Thorvaldsen, noted Danish sculptor. During a period of poverty and overwork, the American consul at Rome befriended Crawford and helped him through his convalescence.

Then he began to get commissions; in 1840 the Boston Atheneum bought his Orpheus group, and his success was assured. He also created a statue of Beethoven for that same city. In 1844 Crawford married Louise Ward (sister of Julia Ward Howe, composer of *The Battle Hymn of the Republic*). Five years later the sculptor won in a competition to design a statue of George Washington, to be erected in Richmond, Virginia. At his death, he was considered a leading American sculptor.

Thomas Crawford was thrilled to be asked to do this figure of Freedom for the United States Capitol. It was the crowning work of his entire career.

He was suffering from a malignancy in his eyes, which doctors told him was incurable. However, in spite of this, he was determined to finish the model for the statue.

The sculptor at first planned his statue as "Armed Liberty," wearing the soft freedom cap used by former Roman slaves, but in Washington there was quite an argument about this headdress. It was also considered suggestive of the caps worn in the French Revolution.

Secretary of War Jefferson Davis believed that since our fight for independence had been won, the cap was not suitable. After this argument, the artist changed the figure to "Freedom." He added a helmet, with a great crest of eagle feathers to indicate the Indian origin of our land. "Thus Freedom came to represent the ideal of not one man, but of many men, willing to compromise their differences for her sake."

At first the figure was unclothed, but as there were many protests about the undraped statue, Crawford went to the opposite extreme and wrapped her completely in a buffalo robe. "He molded a long flowing robe around her ample waist and up over her shoulder—a simple, serviceable robe."

The sculptor shows Freedom as having just won a battle. One hand is on a sword, while the other holds a wreath (or olive branch) and rests on a shield. As one authority has said, Crawford modeled this majestic figure in full maturity.

> No weak woman, Freedom, big-bosomed, big-hipped, the kind of woman who would move with calm, unhurried, undeviating step toward her goal. She would always know her goal, too. So he put wisdom in her brow.

Finally the sculptor finished the plaster model, for which he received $3,000. It was to be sent to the United States to be cast in bronze. Unfortunately, the artist died before the work was shipped, so he never knew of the "perils on the sea" which it encountered before it reached America and its permanent place on the Capitol dome.

The model was consigned for shipment to the *Emily Taylor*, "a leaky old bark." On the evening of April 19, 1858, she left Leghorn, Italy, for New York. The model of the figure, in five sections, lay in the hold of the ship.

They had not proceeded very far before the vessel began to take on water alarmingly. At once the captain ordered her to put into

Gibraltar for repairs. An entire month was spent there; on June 26 the *Emily Taylor* again started on her westward journey. Only a short way out, a heavy storm hit them; the ship pitched and tossed; and by July 12 she was again taking on water.

The captain ordered some of the cargo thrown overboard to save his ship. It helped somewhat, but next day water was pouring into her bottom. Some of the sailors, knowing their lives were in danger, begged him to throw the statue out, but the staunch American skipper refused to give up his precious cargo and defiantly declared to the crew: "No, we'll founder before we throw Freedom away!"

The *Emily Taylor* almost did founder; but after changing their course, they were able to make it to a port in Bermuda, with their lives and the model.

The sections were put ashore there, where they remained until December, 1858, when the *G. W. Horton* took them aboard and carried them to New York. The schooner *Statesman* took the figure down the coast and up the Potomac River; it reached Washington on December 30, 1858. At once Congress commissioned Clark Mills to cast the model in bronze at his foundry in Bladensburg, Maryland.

By October, 1862, the bronze figure was ready to be placed in its permanent position. (The plaster model was given to the Smithsonian Institution.) However, "the intrigues, jealousies, quarrels of men" were still to keep Freedom from her high place, for the Civil War was in progress.

But President Abraham Lincoln did not forget the statue and asked that the work on the dome be continued. Late in 1863, when the tide of battle was beginning to turn in favor of the union, he felt the people needed something to assure them that all the bloodshed had not been in vain.

At last everything was set for the celebration at noon on December 2, 1863, when the last section of the figure of Freedom would be placed. Under the direction of General Montgomery C. Meigs, superintendent of installation, four pieces had already been put in position on the high pinnacle and bolted together. Below in the square a great crowd had gathered. They waited breathlessly as the last part—the head and shoulders of the huge figure—was swung into the position of honor, where it took about thirty minutes to secure it.

Loud cheers went up from the crowd; soon a flag was waving

over the statue; and from the Field Battery on Capitol Hill came a proud salute, followed by answering volleys from forts around the city. It is said that when President Lincoln heard the thunderous salutes, he smiled happily. His dream of having Freedom in her proper place on the Capitol had become a reality at last.

The statue faces east; as someone has said, there she stands, "facing each hopeful dawn, sometimes clouded in mist, sometimes shining in the flood lights."

> Ever since, every day, she has boldly affirmed her faith in the United States and its freedom. And ever since, too, she has been honored by thousands who have come from every corner of America to look up and gain courage from this revered symbol of their way of life.

This statue of Freedom is included in the "freshening up" of the Capitol which is given each part of the building every three or four years. The figure is recalked and painted. For protection from lightning, there are ten bronze points tipped with platinum, and at times these must be retipped and sharpened.

The statue was dark during World War II, but when peace came a great crowd gathered there to see lights on it again. And one person made this wish: "May the time come when the bronze lady on the Capitol will be the symbol for the whole world."

THE CONGRESSIONAL PRAYER ROOM

In accordance with our national motto, "In God We Trust," in April, 1955, the Eighty-third Congress of the United States provided, for the first time in American history, a nondenominational room that can be used for prayer and meditation by members of the Senate and House of Representatives.

There are no persons in the world who have such momentous decisions to make, not only for our own country but also in matters of world concern; therefore, it is most fitting that our congressional men and women have a place where they "can be alone with God."

The Prayer Room, noted for its simplicity, is decorated in blue and has two kneeling benches and ten seats. On the altar, made of white oak, is an open Bible. At each side of the altar is a tall candlestick with the traditional seven lights, and at the right is an American flag.

Above the altar is a distinctive stained-glass window that shows George Washington kneeling in prayer. The background is clear, ruby imported glass. Two panels depict the front and back of the Great Seal of the United States. Under the upper panel is a phrase from Lincoln's Gettysburg Address: "This Nation under God." This window was a gift from a number of designers and craftsmen in the Twenty-first Congressional District of California as "a thank offering to this country."

Behind the figure of General Washington is etched the first verse of Psalm 16: "Preserve me, O God, for in Thee do I put my trust."

In the two lower corners of the window, each section shows an open Bible with a candle and this sentence from Psalm 119: "Thy word is a lamp unto my feet and a light unto my path."

ART IN THE CAPITOL

The Capitol is not only the seat of our democratic government and a noted shrine; in 1864 it began a career as a museum.

In April, 1864, Representative Rice of Maine introduced a resolution that a "National Statuary Hall" be created out of the old semi-circular room, formerly the House of Representatives chamber. The congressman declared that the hall was worse than useless and that it had become "a place of storage and traffic." It was his belief that if the great room were lined with heroic figures from our history it would be an inspiration to visiting Americans.

The Rice resolution, which became a law on July 2, 1864, authorized the President to begin a museum collection of statuary. He was

> . . . to invite all States to provide and furnish statues, in marble or bronze, not exceeding two in number for each state, of deceased persons who have been citizens thereof, and illustrious for their historic renown, or for distinguished civic, or military services, such as each State may deem to be worthy of this national commemoration. . . .

The room is today decorated with paintings and statues showing important scenes and prominent figures in American history.

Statuary Hall is 96 feet in diameter and served the House of Representatives for many years. The Supreme Court used it from 1857 to 1935.

By 1933 there were 68 statues in the hall. Finally, because of the weight, it was decided to relocate some of them and to permit each state to have only one here, their second choice to be placed elsewhere in the Capitol. So far 87 favorite sons and 4 daughters have been so honored; besides full-length statues, there are 73 marble and bronze busts. Three states, Hawaii, Alaska, and New Mexico, have not yet made any contributions.

The first woman to have her replica in Statuary Hall was Frances E. Willard of Illinois, leader of the temperance movement. Next was Esther H. Morse, who helped Wyoming become the first state in the Union to have woman suffrage. The other honored women are Dr. Florence R. Sabin of Colorado, a scientist, and Maria L. Sanford, an educator from Minnesota.

Among the men represented in the sculpture are Ethan Allen, Robert Fulton, Charles Carroll of Carrollton, Henry Clay, John C. Calhoun, Daniel Webster, John Winthrop, Will Rogers, William E. Borah, Benjamin Franklin, John Hancock, Thomas Crawford, Charles Sumner, Abraham Lincoln, John Paul Jones, Thomas Starr King, Lew Wallace, Jefferson Davis, Thomas H. Benton, Roger Williams, Robert E. Lee, and Robert La Follette.

Under the dome in the Rotunda are statues and busts of Washington, Lincoln, Jefferson, Hamilton, Jackson, Lafayette, Grant, and Garfield.

Most of the sculpture inside the Capitol and on the building dates from the nineteenth century. One critic speaks of it as "artistically undistinguished, although of considerable interest because of its patriotic subject matter."

When it became known that the Capitol was starting a museum,

Objects of art and paintings of great artistic merit or sentimental significance, or both, and that have become national heirlooms, poured in and took space in many parts of the Capitol Building.

Now there are more requests for display room than there is space available.

Today the Capitol has about 375 works of art, among them 119 portraits—Presidents, 2 Vice-Presidents, 48 Speakers of the House, and other important Americans, including some Indian chiefs. There are 52 paintings other than portraits.

In the collection of seven paintings of George Washington, the one considered most valuable is the work of Rembrandt Peale, which hangs in the Vice-President's Room. There are several excellent pictures by such distinguished artists as Gilbert Stuart, John Vanderlyn, and Thomas Sully.

The Discovery of the Hudson River, the work of the noted American landscape painter Albert Bierstadt, can be seen at the head of a private stairway in the Speaker's Lobby.

In 1817 Congress made arrangements to secure from John Trumbull four priceless historic paintings for the Capitol. This artist had fought in the American Revolution, and his works are noted for their accuracy of detail. Each 18-by-12-foot painting cost $8,000. These "priceless links" with our struggle for independence include these subjects: *The Signing of the Declaration of Independence, The Surrender of Burgoyne, The Surrender of Cornwallis at Yorktown,* and *General Washington Resigning His Commission as Commander-in-Chief of the Army.*

Another well-known painting, *The Emancipation Proclamation,* by Francis Bicknell Carpenter, shows Abraham Lincoln in a historic setting—the first reading of the document "advancing man's march to freedom." This picture hangs in the Senate wing of the Capitol.

A painting with a rather modern look by Howard Chandler Christy, *The Signing of the Constitution,* is to be seen in the House of Representatives wing. It is described as "a fine graphic, like a scene caught at a high point of drama."

Two other important historical paintings are *The Embarkation of the Pilgrims,* by Robert W. Weir, and *The Baptism of Pocohontas,* by John Chapman.

The artists who decorated the Capitol used much symbolism in their varied works. The architect Benjamin Latrobe had columns topped "with purely New World products," such as Indian corn and tobacco leaves. He once told President Jefferson that the corn-ear motif, for example, had given him more approval from Congress "than all the Works of Magnitude, of Difficulty, and of Splendor that surround them."

Several varied objects of art in the Capitol collection have been presented by foreign artists. These valuable contributions include a bronze bust of Washington by David D'Angiers which was received from France in 1905, and a bronze bust of James Viscount Bryce, British ambassador to the United States and author of *The American Commonwealth*. The bust was a gift from the Sulgrave Institute.

The French nation in 1918 presented huge 6-foot Sevres vases, which may be seen at each end of the Senate and House reception rooms. In the Senate wing is a painting by Krohg which depicts Leif Ericson discovering America in the year 1000, a gift from the Norwegian Friends of America.

Without doubt the greatest artistic glory of the Capitol is the outstanding 300-foot frieze which encircles the Rotunda, just below the great dome and 58 feet above the floor.

Countless visitors have craned their necks to view this sweeping piece of art; for "the thrill of the nation's history, from Columbus to the Wright Brothers, lives in the Rotunda."

Much of this gigantic work of art was done by the "Michelangelo of the Capitol"—Constantino Brumidi, a man with a most unusual and remarkable career. He was born in Italy of Greek descent in 1805, studied at the Academy of Arts, and then gained quite a reputation by restoring the frescoes in the Vatican. But as he longed for real freedom and wanted to escape political persecution, Brumidi came to the United States when he was forty-eight years old.

At a salary of about $3,000 per year, and often under severe criticism, the artist spent the years from 1855 to 1880 working on varied decorations in the Capitol. He filled the building with an astounding number of "monumental murals, medallions, and decorations"; he enjoyed laboring to cover the interior "with vivid patriotic designs." Nothing was too much trouble for him to do for his beloved adopted country. Once he signed a painting. "C. Brumidi, Citizen of the United States." This was the mural *The Surrender at Yorktown* that now hangs in the House restaurant.

One critic states that Brumidi's masterpiece is the giant fresco *The Apotheosis of Washington*. He painted this in the "eye" of the Capitol dome, where it covered 4,664 feet of concave surface. The forms in the inner circle represent the thirteen original states and the Union. George Washington is seated between Liberty and laureled Victory. In doing this great work, Brumidi often had to lie on his back on the scaffolding. He completed this in eleven months, when he was sixty years old.

For five years he labored on the intricate decorations in the President's Room. In addition to portraits of Christopher Columbus, Benjamin Franklin, and the members of Washington's first Cabinet, Brumidi created, both in oil and fresco, unusual designs of animals, birds, flowers, fruits, scrollwork, symbolic figures, and "pensive Madonnas and happy cherubs." He also depicted landscapes showing American farming and industry.

In the Brumidi Corridor in the Capitol, on the ground floor of the Senate wing, this artist covered the walls and ceiling with paintings of birds, medallion portraits, and drawings of important inventions.

Constantino Brumidi was master of one of the most difficult of all art techniques—that of true fresco. It is believed that this craft began in ancient Egypt. It flourished in Italy at the time of Michelangelo and was used on the Sistine Chapel in the Vatican. Brumidi's Rotunda frieze is an excellent example of it.

This type of painting requires that the artist apply pigments to fresh plaster, laid one-half inch thick. Often lying on his back, he must paint quickly before the plaster dries. If it does, he has to tear out the complete section and redo it.

Since the work is done in parts, hairline cracks are left. These must be filled in and touched up with a paint made of cottage cheese, lime, and pigment. Once dry, the strange mixture holds like iron.

When the fresco hardens, it becomes light and sparkling, as the lime and sand shine through in the plaster. The colors take on brilliance and hardness and will last for centuries. Brumidi's skillful shading of light and dark in his great frieze makes the figures look like bas-relief sculpture, whereas the painting is of course perfectly flat.

In the frieze we see the supreme talent of this Italian artist. Brumidi was seventy-two years old when he set up the scaffolding to begin the long-dreamed-of circular work to depict important episodes from American history.

He was working on a scene of William Penn and the Indians when his chair slipped from the scaffolding. Desperately he grabbed for a hold on the platform. There he hung by his arms for about fifteen minutes until helpers rescued him. This terrifying experience took Brumidi's last strength. His working days were over, a few months later he was dead.

He was so poor that Congress had to appropriate funds for his burial. For some time he lay in an unmarked grave. Then, more than sixty years later, the grave was rediscovered. Myrtle Cheney Murdock wrote a biography of Brumidi, and it was mainly through her efforts that a marker was placed on his grave. It bore the artist's own words as his epitaph. (He had written them after he had become well known and was asked to do other commissions):

> My one ambition and my daily prayer is that I may live long enough to make beautiful the Capitol of the one country on earth in which there is liberty.

When Constantino Brumidi died, the great frieze was less than half completed. Congress commissioned his pupil, Filippo Costaggini, to complete the panels. It took the latter eight years to translate to full scale eight small drawings which Brumidi had left. When Costaggini died in 1880, there was a 30-foot gap remaining in the frieze.

It was not until 1953 that this space was filled in by a third fresco artist, Allyn Cox of New York. So the work begun in 1877 took about three-quarters of a century to complete. Fortunately, because of Cox's exquisite craftsmanship, his work is in complete harmony with that of Brumidi and Costaggini. Congress ordered the entire frieze cleaned and three new scenes to be added by the third painter.

The frieze tells the story of the development of our country in these vivid scenes: "The Landing of Columbus, 1492"; "Cortez Entering Montezuma's Mexico, 1521"; "Pizarro's Conquest of Peru, 1533"; "The Midnight Burial of De Soto in the Mississippi, 1541"; "Pocohontas Rescuing Captain Smith, 1606"; "The Pilgrims' Landing, 1620"; "William Penn Meeting the Indians, 1682"; "Oglethorpe Reaching a Peace Treaty with the Indians, 1732"; "The Battle of Lexington, 1775"; "Reading of the Declaration of Independence, 1776"; "The Surrender of Cornwallis, at Yorktown, 1781"; "Tecumseh's Death, 1813"; "General Scott's Entry into Mexico City, 1847"; and "The Discovery of Gold in California, 1848."

The three last scenes, by Cox, were added to memorialize the ending of the Civil War in 1865, the Spanish-American War of 1898, and the first powered flight of the Wright Brothers in 1903.

GREAT EVENTS IN THE CAPITOL

As the visitor views the statues and pictures of distinguished Americans who have played vital roles in molding our history, he is reminded of the dramatic events that have happened here, and gets "the feeling of fateful decisions made within its walls that have rendered triumphant and immortal man's march to freedom."

Among the early incidents was the vote by the House of Representatives that gave Thomas Jefferson the presidency over Aaron Burr when there was an electoral tie in 1801. In 1803 Congress ratified Jefferson's Louisiana Purchase, which added much territory to our country. Funds were voted the Lewis and Clark expedition to the Northwest; also money was appropriated to strengthen our young navy against the Barbary pirates that were preying on Mediterranean shipping.

From the 1820's to the Civil War the Capitol was the scene of much spirited oratory and bitter discussion over the slavery and states'-rights problems.

After the Monroe Doctrine had been promulgated, there was growing national pride; the feeling of "manifest destiny" swept through the Capitol and over the country. A treaty with Mexico ended our conflict there; another, with Great Britain, settled problems of the Northwest.

The sectional division brought many difficulties. In the old Senate chamber the noted orator Daniel Webster made his famous "Reply to Hayne" speech. Henry Clay and John C. Calhoun battled over the Compromise of 1850. Daniel Webster, in his never-to-be-forgotten "Seventh of March" speech, pleaded with the Senate to pass the compromise. Because of this, Webster was denounced by his friends and lost his chance for the coveted presidency.

With the outbreak of the Civil War the enlarged Capitol had a new use—as barracks. When President Lincoln called for seventy-five thousand volunteers, many of these troops were housed there. They called it the "big tent" and boasted of their "portrait-hung parlors, comfortable sofas, and desks for writing letters." For some time as many as three thousand soldiers slept in the building.

The hungry men lined up to get a chance to cook bacon, bake

biscuits, or make coffee at fires in the basement. The vaults were used to store flour, beef, and pork when Washington feared a siege. Bakeries, too, were set up in the basement, where bread for men at nearby forts was baked.

Soon the Capitol was used for sadder purposes. As hundreds of wounded men were brought into the city, it served as one of the hospitals. Among those who came to nurse the injured, to visit them and bring them some comfort, was the kindly poet Walt Whitman.

Finally, when the long struggle was over, the Capitol again was used for its primary purpose—that of lawmaking.

After his impeachment trial, Andrew Johnson completed his term of office; later he returned as a senator. During his trial he had been humiliated, but when he entered the Senate that day, he received congratulations and flowers. Then the former President shook hands with men who had voted for his conviction.

After the war came the trying Reconstruction period, then the rise of "big finance," the Spanish-American War, and the U.S. renewal of interest in world affairs. On April 2, 1917, President Woodrow Wilson appeared before a joint session of Congress and asked for a declaration of war against Germany, "to make the world safe for democracy." Two other important measures were settled in the Capitol when woman suffrage became law in 1920, and Social Security in 1935.

Franklin D. Roosevelt, on December 8, 1941, stood before Congress with another war message: "Yesterday, December 7, 1941, a date which will live in infamy. . . ."

And in February, 1962, Colonel John Glenn addressed Congress after he had made American history in outer space by his "three-times-around-the-world whirl."

The Capitol has heard eloquence equaling that of the British Parliament, and it has seen written such "immortal charters of idealism as the Fourteenth Amendment." Also, when the Supreme Court of the United States held its sessions here (until 1935, when it went into its own building), the justices made many momentous decisions.

Here, in the Rotunda, our nation has paid high tribute to sixteen Americans, among then four slain Presidents: Abraham Lincoln, James Garfield, William McKinley, and John F. Kennedy.

Others who have lain here in state include Representative Thaddeus Stevens and Senator Charles Sumner, both opponents of slavery; Major Pierre C. L'Enfant, designer of Washington; Admiral George Dewey, of Spanish-American War fame; the Unknown Soldiers of World Wars I and II and the Korean War; President Warren G. Harding; Chief Justice and former President William H. Taft; General John J. Pershing; and Senator Robert Taft.

INAUGURALS AT THE CAPITOL

Thomas Jefferson was the first chief executive to be inaugurated at the new federal Capitol. He is said to have strolled from his boardinghouse and was sworn in in the Senate chamber. James Madison took the oath of office in the House of Representatives, then went outdoors to address the assembled crowd.

In 1817 James Monroe had the first outdoor inauguration ceremony. Since the British had burned the Capitol, the lawmakers were using a temporary structure. Because some believed this was not safe, the event was held outside. Since that time it has been the tradition for our Presidents to be inaugurated on a special platform built over the great steps at the east front. (Because of inclement weather, Taft took the oath in the Senate chamber.)

The Chief Justice of the Supreme Court administers the oath; then the new President gives his inaugural address and leads a great parade of the various branches of the armed forces along Pennsylvania Avenue to the White House. For many years the event took place on March 4; but in 1933, by the Twentieth Amendment to the Constitution, the date was set as January 20.

At Abraham Lincoln's first inaugural, in 1861, "a tall, gangling figure stood on the wind-raked stand, built over the front steps." There were sharpshooters stationed on the roof, for a rumor had gone around that the platform might be blown up. The ceremonies occurred "beneath the hoists and scaffolds on the Capitol dome."

It was on this long-remembered day—when the Civil War was threatening—that President Lincoln made his stirring appeal for conciliation by declaring, "In Your hands, my dissatisfied countrymen, and not in Mine, is the momentous issue of Civil War."

Four years later, when the end of the conflict was in sight, the

Civil War President delivered his impressive second inaugural address: "With malice toward none . . . let us strive on to finish the work we are in, to bind up the nation's wounds . . ."

Many years afterward, during another period of stress, Franklin D. Roosevelt came to the presidency. At his first inauguration, our country was trying to lift itself out of a great economic depression, so Roosevelt encouraged the nation "to pull out of it" and spoke these inspiring words: "The only thing we have to fear is fear itself."

By inauguration day, January 20, 1961, a change had been made in the east front of the Capitol that was not approved by all Americans. Some thought it changed the character of the great building. This work had been completed just in time for the inauguration of John F. Kennedy as thirty-fifth President.

On this occasion that dynamic young man made a speech that aroused his countrymen, ending with the words that will go ringing down the ages:

> Let both sides join in . . . creating . . . a new world of law, where the strong are just and the weak secure, and the peace preserved.
>
> Ask not what your country can do for you—ask what you can do for your country.

SOME OUTSTANDING CONGRESSMEN

The men who have served the United States, both in the Senate and the House of Representatives in our Capitol, have been of different religions, racial origins, occupations, and outlooks on life. One source made this statement:

> The typical Representative . . . is so much the typical American— and so indistinguishable from the tens of millions of his fellow Americans—that he can qualify for the composite American citizen.

On the pediment of the new Senate Office Building are these words: "The Senate Is the Living Symbol of Our Union of States." And during the years since we won our independence, many of the nation's outstanding leaders have been heard in the Senate chamber. In addition, fourteen of them have gone on to become Presidents. A few women have served here; for example, Margaret Chase Smith has been in the Senate for more than a quarter of a century.

In 1959 a committee headed by Senator John F. Kennedy was chosen to select the five most distinguished senators since that body began functioning. Those named—after much deliberation—were Henry Clay, Daniel Webster, John C. Calhoun, Robert La Follette, and Robert Taft.

Some of the greatest debates in our history have been heard here. The members of this body, although of "remarkable individuality" (some have been controversial figures), have long been respected for the high quality of their characters. In his book *Citadel,* William Allen White made this statement in regard to the Senate:

> For a long time I have felt that the one touch of authentic genius in the American political system, apart of course, from the incomparable majesty and decency and felicity of the Constitution itself, is the Senate of the United States.

An early outstanding member of the House of Representatives was John Quincy Adams, often called "Old Man Eloquent" by his associates. Two years after he had finished his presidential term, he was elected from Massachusetts to the House of Representatives. In this capacity he served for seventeen years, which some people believe to have been the most distinguished of his career.

Then, on February 2, 1848, John Quincy Adams "was cut down by an attack of paralysis that killed him, ending a half-century of service to his country." He was stricken on the floor of the House; he died later in the office of the Speaker of the House. No statue in the Capitol commemorates him, but a small bronze plate in Statuary Hall marks the place where he fell.

Another chief executive, James Madison, spent four terms in the House and introduced legislation that later formed the Bill of Rights. When he became President in 1809, he was the first of sixteen chief executives who had served in this branch of Congress.

Several unusual and colorful figures have played roles here, among them Davy Crockett, the noted frontiersman, "as untamed as the woods he roamed." Sam Houston served two terms in the House before going to Texas and winning fame there. Once he was tried for assaulting a fellow member.

During the first part of the nineteenth century the House of Representatives frequently was the scene of wild brawls. Often members' tempers rose and there was violence on the floor. In 1858 angry debates over the Kansas Statehood Bill occurred. "Because of its frenzied partisanship, brawls, and duels, some called the House the 'Bear Garden.' "

Another striking Representative was Thaddeus Stevens, who is reported to have engineered the only impeachment trial of a U.S. President—that of Andrew Johnson. He has been described as "able, bold, unscrupulous," and is said to have dominated the House during the 1860's.

Jeanette Rankin, an ardent suffragette, was elected a representative from Wyoming in 1916. She was the first woman so honored. In addition, Miss Rankin was one of five members who could not bring themselves to vote to send the nation into World War I.

A colorful personality from New York was Fiorello La Guardia, the "Little Flower," as he often was called. He was as popular a character as ever served in the House, especially noted for his "vibrant wit and social progressiveness."

The Rayburn Room, in the House of Representatives wing, is used as a reception room for members of the House and honors the memory of Sam Rayburn; he was first elected to the House in 1913 and served here until his death on November 16, 1961. No other record in the House can compare with his. Here is the code of leadership Sam Rayburn laid down for himself:

> I shall be just. I shall be fair, and lead as the lights are given to me, as I have in the past, being proud to be a member of this House. As I have said to you so often, the House of Representatives has been my life, and it is today, and always has been, my love.

President Lyndon B. Johnson is the ninth chief executive to have served both in the House and the Senate. When he made his first presidential address to a joint session of Congress on November 27, 1963, he set the tone of his future relations with Congress in these words:

> For thirty-two years Capitol Hill has been my home. I have shared many moments of pride with you, pride in the ability of the Congress of the United States to act, to meet any crisis, to distill from our

differences strong programs of national action. . . . I firmly believe in the independence and integrity of the legislative branch. And I promise you I shall always respect this.

CAPITOL VISITORS

In the *Capitol Dome Newsletter*, published by the U.S. Capitol Historical Society, the editor states:

> The United States Capitol is a giant complex of rooms and corridors —a magnificent building of massive and beautiful architecture, which, as the legislative center of our Federal government, is one of the most visited buildings in the country.

And another writer made this statement:

> The Capitol of the United States serves the people not only as the seat of living democratic government, but also as a national shrine.

On a record day—April 22, 1965—almost 34,000 persons visited the structure. From 900,000 to 1.5 million people come here each year.

Visitors may go through the Capitol from 9 A.M. until 4 P.M. The only exceptions are Christmas, New Year's Day, and Thanksgiving. The galleries of the House and Senate are open during the sessions of Congress. If either the House or Senate remains in session beyond 4:30 P.M., the wing of the Capitol in use will stay open until the session closes. Tours are conducted through the building from 9 A.M. to 3:55 P.M.

During the summer months (through Labor Day), the Capitol is open until 10 P.M. Generally during this period Congress is not in session, but the Rotunda, Statuary Hall, and the Crypt may be inspected. During the summer it is an advantage to visit the edifice at night, for one of the military services' bands gives a concert on the East Front Plaza at 8 P.M. on Monday, Tuesday, Wednesday, and Friday.

In addition to the great throngs of Americans who make their way to the Capitol—many with their children—there are numerous visitors from other lands who go away inspired by the historic surroundings.

The first notable foreign visitor was the Marquis de Lafayette, who as a young man had crossed the Atlantic from France to aid General Washington during the American Revolution.

Lafayette, the "Pride of Two Countries," revisited America in 1824. The Capitol Rotunda had recently been finished; here a civic reception was given him, and he was warmly welcomed as a "Symbol of Alliance." On December 10, 1824, the Marquis was the first foreign visitor to address the Congress of the United States.

Britain's most distinguished son—Sir Winston Churchill—spoke to a joint session of the House and Senate on May 19, 1943. Later Congress gave him honorary United States citizenship. And Emperor Haile Selassie, the "Lion of Judah," in an impressive address invited American technicians to come to Ethiopia to assist in its development.

On May 4, 1961, both branches of Congress listened to a speech against colonialism in which President Habib Bourguiba told of the problems affecting his new republic, Tunisia. And Japan's Minister Hayata Ikeda (whose wife and daughters, in colorful native dress, were also present) spoke to our lawmaking bodies on June 22, 1961.

Another notable foreign speaker here was Mohammed Reza Pahlavi of Iran, who appeared before Congress on April 12, 1962.

Both houses met on May 28, 1964, to hear the eminent Irish patriot Eamon de Valera as he thanked the United States for aid to his native Ireland.

As time goes on, countless thousands, both from our country and abroad, will continue to visit our Capitol. Many will wonder at its beauty and dignity and recognize the fact that it is truly one of our most distinctive national symbols. No doubt they will agree with the writer of these words:

> To the American his Capitol is a part of himself. It is the living symbol of his freedom, the basis for his political self-respect, and the proof of one of the greatest historical phenomena of all time: more than 195,000,000 people actually governed by themselves.

10

The Statue of Liberty

===

On Liberty Island, New York Harbor, in "the foremost place of its country's showplace," stands the statue of "Liberty Enlighting the World." Although the United States contains countless monuments, this colossal statue is unique in that it represents two ideas: the continued friendship of the French and American peoples and the spirit of liberty that gave birth to our country.

The great copper lady has now stood for more than eighty years at the chief entrance to "the land of the free." She is shown as a proud woman, whose loose robe falls in graceful folds to the base of the image. Under her foot, broken chains typify the winning of liberty by a free people. Her huge crown has spikes like the rays of the sun; in her left arm is a book inscribed with the date of American independence—July 4, 1776. The most striking feature is the great torch that Liberty holds in her right hand, high above her head—the light that has welcomed millions of freedom-loving peoples to our shores.

ORIGIN OF THE STATUE

The idea for the Statue of Liberty originated when a small group, including several young artists, met at a dinner party in 1865 at Glatigny, near Versailles, just outside Paris.

The host was Edouard de Laboulaye, a journalist, a historian of the American Civil War, and a great admirer of American political institutions. That evening he suggested that the two countries join in a memorial to be finished in time for the centennial of the Declaration of Independence, in 1876. This would be a symbol cementing the friendship of the two nations since the American Revolution, "when, supported by the French with sinews of war, it helped turn the tide of victory to the side of the Colonies."

However, because of the Franco-Prussian War (1870–1871), the project had to be postponed. Ten years after the idea had first been suggested, on November 6, 1875, 200 Frenchmen and Americans dined together. At this meeting they founded the Franco-American Union, with Laboulaye as president.

BARTHOLDI CHOSEN AS THE SCULPTOR

When the union definitely decided to present a memorial to the United States, they wisely chose the Alsatian scupltor Frédéric Auguste Bartholdi to do the work. This was most fitting, for one source has said: "To Bartholdi, America was the great pioneer that had shown the whole world the pathway to liberty."

Frédéric Auguste Bartholdi, born on April 2, 1834, died in Paris, October 4, 1904. The son of wealthy parents in Colmar, Alsace-Lorraine, he lost his father when he was only nine years old. Later the mother sent young Bartholdi to study law in Paris. As the youth preferred to wander around and visit art studios, the law instructors finally wrote his mother that since he would not work at his law studies it was simply wasted time to try to keep him there.

Next Bartholdi studied art at Colmar and also at the Beaux Arts School in Paris. He at first devoted much time to painting; he also studied architecture. (Later this training served him well, for through it he learned how to handle with much success difficult problems of structure and materials.)

The boy was just seventeen years old, during the cold winter of 1851, when the Parisians were discontented under the rule of Louis Napoleon. As he walked to and from his sculpture workshop he encountered many angry rioters. However, he was too engrossed in his work to take part in the revolts.

But he did witness a distressing scene that stayed in his memory. For Bartholdi saw a woman with a torch attempting to set fire to a barricade. She had a dedicated look on her face. The young student was horrified when she was shot and fell to the ground near him. One authority has stated that it is no wonder that when, years later, he was commissioned to design the Statue of Liberty, the sculptor made a sketch showing a woman holding high a torch of liberty.

At the age of twenty-one Bartholdi traveled to the Middle East with a painter friend, J. L. Gérôme. Apparently the trip was a beneficial one, as it showed him that painting was not his forte. After that the young artist wisely turned to the medium in which he would become world famous, that of sculpture. His early statues were portrait busts.

While a student at the Beaux Arts, he won acclaim for his great statue of the French General Rapp; and in 1864, at the early age of thirty, Bartholdi received from the Emperor the Order of Chevalier in the Legion of Honor. This was given the sculptor for his distinctive statue of Admiral Bruat.

The young Alsatian served in the French Army during the Franco-Prussian War and helped defend his native town of Colmar when the Prussians overran it.

After his military service, Bartholdi turned his attention to creating patriotic and symbolic statues, some of which were quite gigantic. These monumental pieces of sculpture glorified "heroic ideas, personalities, and events."

His masterpiece along this order was the Lion of Belfort, "best of a number of patriotic sculptures inspired by the French defeat." This work commemorated the siege of Belfort, France, in 1871 and the French defense there in opposing the Prussians. Bartholdi carved this in the red rock of a hill towering above the town of Belfort. Thus, by the time the sculptor was thirty years old his "heroic works were famous throughout France."

France's aid to America in the Revolution inspired some of Bartholdi's best works. In Paris there is his statue of Washington and Lafayette; and in the same city is a small replica of the Statue of Liberty, which was sent there from the United States. It is mounted on the Pont de Grenelle, one of the many bridges crossing the Seine. In Union Square, New York City, is a Bartholdi statue of Lafayette arriving in America; this was presented in 1876 by French residents in that city. Also in the Botanical Garden in Washington, D.C. is a fountain designed by the illustrious artist.

THE DESIGN OF THE STATUE
OF LIBERTY

When Bartholdi was selected for the important undertaking, the Franco-American Union sent him to New York to investigate matters and to confer with the American authorities regarding it. The story goes that as he sailed into New York harbor, he was inspired and

> . . . conceived the idea of a colossal statue to stand at the very gateway of the New World to represent the one thing man finds most precious—Liberty.

At once he drew a rough sketch showing a woman with a crown of rays and holding on high the torch of freedom. Under her left arm was "a blurred object" later inscribed with the date July 4, 1776. The woman was depicted as striding forward, after breaking the shackles that bound her ankles. The Franco-American Union accepted Bartholdi's design, and it is said that the artist made no major change in his original conception.

The big question was where to place the gigantic gift. Finally, after much deliberation, the site was designated, on Washington's birthday, 1877, as Bedloe's Island in New York Bay. The French sculptor, on a visit in June, 1871, had suggested this location instead of Governor's Island so that the people of New York would not have to look at her back. Also he wanted the statue to welcome the immigrants coming here to start a new life.

BEDLOE'S ISLAND

The oval-shaped piece of land—Bedloe's Island, now Liberty Island—in upper New York harbor is about 1.6 miles southwest of Manhattan Island, with the Battery its nearest shore point. Although it is in New Jersey waters, it is part of New York State and has a New York City post-office address.

This island, containing about 12½ acres, has had an interesting history and has been under varied ownership. Of course it originally belonged to the Indians. At first it was called Oyster Island, then Love Island. Governor Lovelace made it an "exempted" island and granted it to Isaac Bedloe. He was a Dutchman who reached the New World from Calais in 1639, while still in his teens. Following his death, in 1673, his wife sold the land for £80. During the American Revolution its name was Kennedy Island.

The star-shaped wall around the base of the statue is that of an old military installation, Fort Wood, named for Colonel Eleazer Wood, a hero of the War of 1812. Constructed between 1808 and 1811, Fort Wood was an Army post until abandoned in 1837. It originally had twenty-four heavy guns; the number of troops stationed at Fort Wood ranged from about 50 to 600. One authority has declared that Fort Wood had never surrendered, nor had it ever been shelled or attacked.

The uses of this historic island have been varied. They include the following: as a farm, pesthouse, gallows, dump, military prison, quarantine station, harbor defense, Signal Corps radio station, and military police post.

On October 15, 1924, the Statue of Liberty was declared a National Monument by President Calvin Coolidge. After the army abandoned Fort Wood, the rest of the land was added to the monument.

Then the work of landscaping the island began. As years passed, there was some deterioration, and during World War II the work of improving it came to a halt. Afterward the task was resumed, and the island became somewhat closer to Bartholdi's dream of a "pleasure ground for the soul of the American people."

In 1956 Congress passed a resolution to change the name from Bedloe's Island to Liberty Island, and on August 3, 1956, President Eisenhower approved the change. This was done to recognize the symbolic significance of the Statue of Liberty.

An unsigned article in the Paris edition of the New York *Herald Tribune* (July 4, 1960) contained these paragraphs:

> Generations of schoolchildren learned that the Statue of Liberty stood on Bedloe's Island; no one ever lost his way looking for the island; no one ever mistook the great monument for a statue of

Bedloe; no one ever was shipwrecked, stranded, or eaten by cannibals there.

We're sure, of course, that the same beneficent conditions will prevail on Liberty Island; and that Bartholdi's famous Statue will continue to stir the heart and pride of all who visit it. Just the same, we mourn the passing of a stubborn and rugged old name in a sea of uniformity and obviousness. And is that poor old Isaac Bedloe we hear, muttering along with Madame Roland: "Liberty, what crimes are committed in thy name!"

CREATION OF THE STATUE

When Bartholdi returned to France, he made several models of the proposed statue. At last the sculptor completed the original clay model, for which his mother posed.

It was she who inspired her son, and kept the idea of the statue alive in his mind, through difficulties and disappointments. Today her features are immortalized in . . . the Statue of Liberty, the symbol of a great faith and a great dream.

The sculptor signed 200 small terra-cotta replicas, each 4 feet in height, which sold for 1,000 francs each. This money went toward the general fund. Bartholdi spent ten years of his life in planning, promoting, and completing the gigantic work.

It was not easy for Bartholdi and those in charge of construction to select the proper materials. They had to be able to withstand the strong, salty winds. In addition, because of its great size, the figure must be made of comparatively light material. Finally it was decided to use copper, as it was not so costly as bronze and was lighter than stone.

At first the artist made a 9-foot model, which was then increased to one of 36 feet, divided into sections. Next each part was enlarged to full size. Patterns were made over which the 300 copper plates cut into numbered pieces were to be hammered on by hand. Two-hundred thousand pounds of copper were used. This metal was hammered to a thickness of only 3/32 of an inch, "just a bit thicker than an American cent." It is said that this is the world's most celebrated example of repoussé work, the process of shaping metal by hammering it over a mold.

The iron framework of the statue (which is firmly anchored into the foundation of the pedestal) was designed by Gustav Eiffel. One source declared that the creation of this colossal image "was more than an artistic undertaking. Its construction was an architectural and engineering feat."

Young Eiffel did such an excellent job on the statue that the terrific Black Tom explosions in nearby Jersey City in 1916 did not damage the structure. This catastrophe took place at the munitions docks in Jersey City on July 30. Two persons were killed and damages amounted to $40 million. The explosion was traced to German saboteurs. Later Eiffel achieved much fame for "his amazing Eiffel Tower, a landmark of which the French are justly proud."

THE RAISING OF FRENCH FUNDS

Naturally, in carrying out the important project, the matter of funds was paramount. In cementing the friendship of the two countries, the French were to furnish the statue, the United States the site and base.

The proposition—so it is said—met with mixed reactions in both countries. An important French newspaper was skeptical that it could actually be accomplished. On this side of the Atlantic, the *New York Times* "whimsically" suggested that the monument be placed at the Battery so people would not have to take a boat to reach it.

In France, Edouard de Laboulaye, as president of the Franco-American Union, had the job of making plans, collecting funds, and carrying out the great project. In 1875, at the first dinner of the union, the sum of 40,000 francs was collected.

Next an appeal was made to the French people themselves to send in contributions, for this memorial was to be the gift of the population, and not of the French government. The response was "warm and quick"; the city of Paris donated $2,000; a lottery was held; and all over France varied public entertainments were given to raise money. One writer has stated:

Small amounts were given by workmen, tradesmen, peasants, schoolchildren, scrubwomen, and hundreds of persons with limited resources.

However, it was not easy to raise the great sum of $250,000 by personal gifts. The collection of the funds slowed down in France, and it took ten years to obtain the complete amount. But: "Every cent of this amount was contributed by popular subscription, and governmental assistance was not needed."

RAISING OF FUNDS IN THE UNITED STATES

As the money for the pedestal was to be raised in our country, a committee of prominent men began the collection in 1877.

When the estimated cost of $125,000 was raised and the pedestal had been built to the height of 15 feet, it was found that the original amount would not be enough to finish the base. It was reported that there was not too much interest in this undertaking in New York itself, also that elsewhere in the United States most of the people were "even more apathetic."

Months went by and interest waned. Things looked serious for the completion of the pedestal, which had been started in 1883. A miracle happened when Joseph Pulitzer, owner and editor of the New York *World*, entered the picture. A Hungarian by birth, Mr. Pulitzer reached our shores in time to serve in the Union Army in 1864.

When this distinguished publisher realized the position the United States was in, he decided to devote all his energies to finish the collection of enough money to complete the base. Since France was giving us the statue, he insisted that the American people come across with the funds to finish the pedestal. His *World* "daily hammered away with publicity in the form of news, cartoons, and editorials."

Many benefits for the fund were staged; small replicas of the statue and sheet music about it were sold. The names of the donors—no matter how small the amounts given, even pennies presented by schoolchildren—were listed in the *World*. After an intensive campaign of a few months, Mr. Pulitzer was able to announce, on August 11, 1885, months after the statue had arrived in New York, that that enough money had been collected to complete our obligation.

COMPLETION AND DEDICATION

The lack of money, as has been stated, caused delay in completing both the statue and its base. In 1876, at the Centennial Exposition in Philadelphia, "the truncated right hand, holding the torch," was exhibited; it was also shown in Madison Square Garden in New York City. Two years later the head and shoulders were displayed at the Paris World's Fair, where spectators were astonished at the gigantic proportions of these parts.

After the framework had been put together in Paris, the American minister Levi P. Morton drove in the first rivet. This ceremony occurred on October 25, 1881, and honored the victory at Yorktown, where the French troops and American colonials had been allied.

The statue was completed by May 21, 1884. Then, on July 4, 1884, in Paris, the French people "in a great outpouring of friendship and francs . . . gave this staunch symbol of liberty to the United States." The formal presentation was made by Count Ferdinand de Lesseps, the head of the Franco-American Union after the death of Laboulaye, and later connected with the construction of the Panama Canal.

Following the ceremony, the statue was taken apart; the sections were numbered and packed in more than 200 cases. These were shipped on May 21, 1885, from Rouen, France, on the steamer *Isere*.

They reached our shores on June 17, 1885, and were kept in hastily built sheds on the island until the base could be completed. The great task of reassembling the statue began. Bartholdi came to New York to direct the work. The "skeleton" was set up and the hammered copper sections were attached and bolted firmly to the central framework. More than 300,000 copper rivets were used in the process. On October 23, 1886, the last one was driven in, and the colossal work was ready for dedication.

The unveiling took place in the presence of distinguished representatives of both France and the United States. There was much pomp and ceremony, even though the weather was cold, with a heavy mist and intermittent showers. About 2,500 persons gathered at the base. They included members of Congress and noted personalities. New York harbor was full of tugboats, barges, and other vessels, all filled with people who wanted to see something, at least, of the dedication. Many persons lined the shores; and it was estimated that more than a million spectators saw part of the ceremonies.

Edouard de Laboulaye did not live to see the completion of the great project. But the creator of the statue, Bartholdi, was present.

President Cleveland accepted the mammoth memorial as "a friendship gift to mark the 100th United States Independence anniversary" and declared: "We will not forget that liberty has made here her home."

SIZE OF THE STATUE OF LIBERTY

The Statue of Liberty stands 151 feet high from base to torch and weighs 450,000 pounds, or 225 tons. The torch rises 305 feet above the bottom of the pedestal. As a piece of sculpture, the statue is "dramatically unique." As far as is known, this image is the largest one man has ever created, and "it dwarfs such masterpieces as Michelangelo's David in Florence." The statue is said to be 46 feet higher than the Colossus of Rhodes. Here are a few of the majestic dimensions: her mouth is 3 feet wide; the head from chin to cranium, 17 feet, 3 inches; and the length of her index finger is 8 feet. There are 168 steps from the top of the pedestal to the head.

THE PEDESTAL

The pedestal, almost 150 feet in height, is "one of the heaviest pieces of masonry ever built," and cost about $280,000. It rests on a 23,500-ton concrete foundation. Four large steel girders inside it connect with the framework of the statue. In this way the image has been able to withstand, through the years, the high winds blowing across the harbor. There are 167 steps from the land level to the top of the pedestal; also an elevator runs to its top.

THE EMMA LAZARUS QUOTATION

Within the pedestal the last five lines of the poem *The New Colossus*, by Emma Lazarus, are engraved on a plaque:

> Give me your tired, your poor,
> Your huddled masses yearning to breathe free,
> The wretched refuse of your teeming shore,
> Send these, the homeless, tempest-tossed, to me:
> I lift my lamp beside the golden door.

Emma Lazarus, born in New York City on July 22, 1849, of Spanish-Jewish origin, was a talented American essayist and poet. A member of a wealthy family, she was educated by private tutors and passed a pleasant youth, showing much literary promise at an early age. Her volume *Poems and Translations*, published in 1867, attracted the notice of Ralph Waldo Emerson, the great American poet and philosopher. They became good friends and kept up a lifetime correspondence.

In 1879 the Russians began their persecution of the Jews and continued it through 1883. The tragic happenings stirred Emma Lazarus and made her much more aware than she had been of her Jewish heritage. She changed from "her purely artistic, literary pursuits to an impassioned defense of Judaism." In 1881, when many Jewish refugees began to come to New York, Emma Lazarus was moved to action; soon she was noted for her efforts to organize relief for them, both here and in Russia. She became their leading American exponent and devoted her remaining years to the cause of Jewish freedom.

When an auction of literary works was held at the Academy of Design in New York, Miss Lazarus contributed a sonnet called *The New Colossus*. The poem, addressed to the Statue of Liberty, revealed her strong belief in America as a refuge for the persecuted peoples of the earth. Its title was suggested by the Colossus of Rhodes, one of the Seven Wonders of the Ancient World, a gigantic bronze statue of Apollo set up about 280 B.C. at the harbor of Rhodes. The poem revealed the Statue of Liberty as "a mighty woman with a torch" and "the mother of exiles," welcoming the lowly and oppressed.

Emma Lazarus died of cancer at the age of thirty-eight in 1887.

During her lifetime not much notice was given to the poem. However, in 1903, sixteen years after her death, a bronze tablet containing the now-famous last five lines was placed within the pedestal. This was just about the time the large immigration from southern Europe began.

LIGHTING THE STATUE

The lighting of this colossal figure to best advantage has been a difficult problem. The original system of electric lights has been replaced at different times by more modern equipment. The present system almost doubles that of the former installation and is equivalent to 2,500 times full moonlight.

At night the torch in Liberty's right hand gleams with powerful fluorescent lights and can be seen 15 miles out at sea.

At first the illumination of the torch was maintained by the Lighthouse Service. In 1916 funds were raised by subscriptions through the New York *World* for the permanent lighting of the figure and for floodlights at the base. On December 2, 1916, President Woodrow Wilson turned on the new system.

During World War II the Statue of Liberty was blacked out for the duration. Then on V-E Day, May 8, 1945, "The lights were turned on again, in all their brilliance." And it is a thrilling sight to see it at night from a passing steamer or the Staten Island ferry. Then her true self is revealed, and you realize she is correctly named "Liberty, Enlightening the World."

ADMINISTRATION

At first the Statue of Liberty served as a lighthouse. It was considered an important aid to navigation and was under the jurisdiction of the Lighthouse Board. In 1901 it was placed under control of the War Department, which maintained Fort Wood on the island.

On October 15, 1924, President Coolidge proclaimed the Statue of Liberty a national monument. In 1933 it was transferred to the National Park System, United States Department of the Interior.

The statue is kept in good repair. In December, 1934, the arm holding the torch began to weaken; three years later the entire figure was repaired and made safe. The spikes of the crown were placed in new iron frames and "a heating system was installed to keep her feet dry." Because of all this care, as Elsa Debra stated in an article, "Symbol of Freedom":

> Instead of deteriorating with age this 75-year-old [in 1961] Goddess, like the truths she represents, grows more beautiful with time. Wind, rain, and sun have oxidized the original shiny exterior with an attractive patina of light green.

Nearby Ellis Island was abandoned in 1954 as the immigration center. It had served, it is claimed, as the gateway to America for 16 million newcomers. In 1965 President Johnson proclaimed Ellis Island as part of the Statue of Liberty National Monument. An appropriation of $6 million was set aside by Congress to develop Ellis Island as a park and museum. A causeway for pedestrians will connect it with the New Jersey shore. A highway to Liberty Island is also a possibility.

VISITING THE STATUE

Visitors may enter the statue any day in the week, Sundays and holidays included, from 9 A.M. to 5 P.M.—until 6 P.M. when daylight saving time is in force.

The trip takes about eighteen minutes each way. The *Miss Liberty* ferry leaves Battery Park every hour, with half-hour trips in the summer. The dock is at the extreme tip of Manhattan's Battery Park.

The structure consists of three parts: the base, the pedestal, and the statue. The base—an eleven-pointed star—is entered by a tunnel leading to the lower elevator landing. (Or you can walk ten stories to the top of the pedestal.) For 10 cents you can ride in the elevator, which was installed in 1908, while a record gives a short historical outline. This ride takes you to the foot of the statue. (Although one can go down on this elevator, it is advisable to walk and see the interesting exhibits displayed at different levels.)

The remaining twelve stories must be climbed on winding stairs with steep steps. A heavy guard wire has encircled the stairs since 1947. People are admitted to all parts of the statue except the torch. It can hold twelve persons but has been closed to visitors since 1916.

The observation platform in the head is about 260 feet above sea level. Thirty people can stand on it at one time. Twenty-five small windows form the jewels of the crown. These afford a magnificent view of the harbor and city of New York, also of New Jersey. On a clear day you can see for 15 miles.

There have been some unusual occurrences at the statue. Once a man broke the lock that barred the way to the uplifted arm and draped a Hungarian flag round the torch. This was removed by the National Park Service. A circus acrobat asked for permission to balance himself on his index finger on the balcony. An inventor suggested that smoke should be simulated as coming from the torch; and a woman artist asked to paint pupils in Miss Liberty's sightless eyes.

There has been some criticism of the statue by Americans. One source states:

> The Statue inspired meager emotional response here until World War I, when doughboys from all over the country sailed past her, and the 77th Division, which fought in France as the Statue of Liberty Division, chose her as their insignia.

As many as 10,000 people have visited Miss Liberty in a single day. And each year thousands "lift their eyes to her, on luxury liners and from wartime transports, a catch in their throats, as they glide silently into the harbor of home."

> There, with her head above the haze, she welcomes them . . . as re-dedicated Americans, aware of their heritage and ready to put patriotism into action.

And as they come, the stately lady bids them welcome, her 42-foot arm upraised in greeting, her glowing lamp signifying a new vista and a hope, a dream rising real out of the troubled fog of the past.

THE STATUE OF LIBERTY STAMP

The Statue of Liberty was brought strongly to public attention all over the United States when in 1954 an 8-cent stamp in red, white, and blue was designed by the Post Office Department, with the statue on it.

At that time 8 cents was the standard price for sending a letter overseas. The stamp "was designed to carry a message of faith and hope throughout the world." Since it would have its greatest use on international mail, Postmaster General Summerfield declared that at least 200 million of this issue, each one of which he termed "a postal ambassador," would spread the message around the globe.

The new 8-cent stamp was well described in *The Los Angeles Times:*

> Majestically simple in design, the stamp is centered by the Statue of Liberty, printed in red. Around the head and upheld torch is a brilliant white halo, fading off into a rich blue background that frames the whole. The words, "In God We Trust," appear above the statue. At the top is "U.S. Postage 8¢" and across the bottom, in white-faced Gothic, is the spaced-out word: "LIBERTY."

When this stamp was issued, it received the greatest sendoff of any postal issue. President Eisenhower appeared on a television show, with Vice-President Nixon, the members of his Cabinet, and several representatives of the nation's largest religious groups.

The reason so much attention was paid to this particular 8-cent stamp was that it could claim several "firsts." It was the original one to incorporate a religious tone; it had the honor of being first to bear the national motto, "In God We Trust." The stamp was also our first issue to be printed in more than one color, and was first to be presented to the entire nation by a President.

In early 1968, when postage on first-class letters went to 6 cents, a new 6-cent stamped envelope went on sale. The stamp showed the head of the Statue of Liberty embossed in white against a green background.

The statue has not been depicted only on our stamps; it has been reproduced many times in different ways. For example, a well-known illustrator, Joseph Pennell, often used it in his lithographs and etchings. The Statue of Liberty was the central figure in his famous Liberty Loan poster in World War I days. During President Lyndon Johnson's administration a cartoon showed the Statue of Liberty carrying aloft a sign with the words "Great Society."

At times it has been used in a humorous way. For example, the noted short-story writer O. Henry once represented the statue as speaking these words:

I was made by a Dago and presented to the American people, on behalf of the French government, for the purpose of welcomin' Irish emigrants into the Dutch city of New York.

THE MUSEUM

Franklin Delano Roosevelt rightly pointed out to us that we are a nation of immigrants. All of us except the American Indians are immigrants or the descendants of immigrants. No longer do they come as they did in the nineteenth and early twentieth centuries, many traveling in ship steerage, the men in ill-fitting clothes, the women with shawls over their heads, accompanied by shy, wide-eyed children. Now most newcomers arrive by plane. And they do not come in such great numbers as before, for the government has placed restrictions on immigration, with priorities granted those with special skills.

During the 1840's there were several potato-crop failures in Ireland, where the potato was the chief food. This caused many Irishmen to leave their old homes to seek better lives in the new world. Long-continued famines in Canton province, China, between 1850 and 1881 brought at least 200,000 Chinese to our country. It happened luckily that such workers were badly needed after the discovery of gold in California, and also for the building of railroads.

From 1905 to 1907 there was much migration to the United States from southern Europe, with over 3 million arriving during this short period. In 1914, at the outbreak of World War I, 1.2 million persons came here from various parts of Europe.

Our government in 1921 decided to set quotas and limit entrance of those living outside the Western Hemisphere. No restrictions were put on our neighbors in the two Americas. This quota of course cut down greatly the numbers of those permitted to enter the United States and see looming up before them, and welcoming them, the Statue of Liberty. After World War II a number of Jewish refugees from the horrors of war in Europe were allowed to come in on special quota.

Since 1886 the statue has symbolized freedom to countless immigrants. In a brochure issued by the National Park Service are these impressive words:

One of the colossal sculptures in history, the Statue has greeted many millions of the oppressed and venturesome from other lands who crossed the ocean in search of greater freedom and opportunity. To the world the Statue has become a symbol of those ideals of liberty upon which our nation and its form of government were founded.

Today those immigrants and their descendants are sponsoring a museum built at the base of the statue. It will be a permanent record of those who looked for liberty when immigrating to America.

The American Museum of Immigration, now building at a cost of $2.5 million, is a nationwide project to tell the story of the many immigrants who have aided in developing our country. It will honor them and their accomplishments. It has taken years of work by patriotic organizations and scholars to plan the new institution, which will open officially in 1969.

The museum will have permanent exhibits showing the chief reasons for migration here, trace the course of this migration, and illustrate the achievements of the newcomers. The largest space will be given over to the period between 1815 and 1915, when about 35 million people reached the United States.

Many objects in the collections will serve for use in special shows, illustrating a particular day such as Pulaski Day or St. Patrick's Day. George J. Svejda, a historian, in a letter dated October 18, 1966, wrote of the purpose of the museum. He concluded with this paragraph:

> We do believe that the museum upon its completion will become a showcase for the United States, as it will reflect the growth, development and achievements of the people who over the years have come here in the pursuit of ideal and material betterment, and thus formed the "melting pot," or crucible from which our present nation has emerged.

Besides the displays on the general theme of immigration, there will be in the exhibit halls an auditorium for patriotic ceremonies, the showing of films, dance festivals, plays, and educational talks by museum staff members. There will be study rooms and a library.

Oscar Handlin, in an article in *This Week* in 1956 entitled "A Museum for Liberty," told of the plans for this new institution. He spoke of the fact that our immigrants and their descendants have left many marks on American culture; that their talents and works have improved the condition of all of us; that these people from foreign lands have made outstanding contributions in many phases of life.

Fortunately Americans are learning the importance of looking back to the sources of our culture. Therefore it is fitting that this museum be created to commemorate the contributions of immigrants to our national life. The exhibits will help us to understand better both our past and our present.

Some time ago the John Hancock Insurance Company issued a public message with a picture of the head of the goddess. The significance of the Statue of Liberty was set forth thus:

> Where can you find another country where Liberty stands bright and pleasant at the door, saying: "If you believe in me, come in and be one of us?"
>
> Long before the people of France gave us her image in metal, she was here in spirit, her light already in the door. She had come in storm-tossed vessels like the *Mayflower*, in sailing packets heavy with ice, in iron steamers caked with rust.
>
> Sometimes by first-class and sometimes by steerage, she came, sometimes in silks, sometimes in rags. But always she came in the hearts of the bold and hardy ones in every land, those who dared to choose freedom, those who could leave their settled ways and say: "Where she is, there is my home."

11

The Washington Monument

IN our national capital stands the noted monument to the "Father of His Country," the commander-in-chief of the victorious colonial forces during the American Revolution, and our first President.

This Washington memorial has been a constant inspiration to all the chief executives who have followed him. It can be seen from the White House, from almost every part of the city, and from the countryside for long distances outside the capital. "Looming majestically on the skyline," it rises above all other structures in the city.

It is truly fitting that the Washington Monument is located here. No better site could have been chosen, for George Washington was born, lived, and died in the state of Virginia—just across the Potomac River from the memorial. It is situated on land selected by George Washington for the national capital of the country he helped to create.

The gigantic obelisk stands on a grassy knoll on the two-mile-long mall, midway between the Capitol and the Lincoln Memorial. This "monarch of the Washington skyline" partly conceals the Lincoln monument and the long reflecting pool from the Capitol.

Washington Monument is in the center of "a grandly designed cross" whose arms extend across the Tidal Basin to the Jefferson Memorial, the White House, Lincoln Memorial, and the Capitol.

This 555-foot monument is a hollow shaft of white marble "severely unadorned." It has no decorations or embellishments, except for the entrance doorway on its east side and eight small windows, two on each of the four sides at the 500-foot level.

Upon reaching the capital, most tourists make a beeline for the Washington Monument, which seems to beckon people to visit it. For it is the most prominent feature of the landscape, and by law, it will always be the physical high point of the city.

> It is one of America's most popular year-round tourist attractions, year in, year out, but it is more than just another point on a sightseeing tour to those who visit it. It is hallowed ground. For it is a symbol of the fulfillment of the American dream of the first American President.

While most persons praise its graceful simplicity, some critics believe the obelisk suffers by comparison with the Lincoln and Jefferson memorials. However, many maintain that the slender shaft "is indeed a true reminder of George Washington's precise and lofty character."

One writer has said that although the memorial was planned many years ago, it is well fitted for the supersonic age. Pilots watch for it at all times when they are coming into the city, for

> Bathed in floodlight by night, and in sunlight by day, its shimmering, gleaming beauty signals to them that they are nearing the capital of freedom.

When a British ambassador, Sir Cecil Spring-Rice, saw the gigantic column for the first time, he termed it "George Washington's finger, pointing to the sky," and asserted:

> It is a fitting description of the tallest memorial in the world, as well as the perfect ideal of beauty in a monument—a combination of beauty and grace.

Someone has said that it punctuates the capital's skyline "like a giant exclamation point"; also that it is "eye-catching and absorbing from a dozen different viewing points."

When the monument was completed and dedicated, many tributes to it rang through the halls of Congress. But none was truer than these words spoken by an anonymous orator:

Taken by itself, the Washington Monument stands not only as one of the most stupendous works of man, but also as one of the most beautiful of all human creations. It is at once so great and so simple that it seems almost to be a work of nature. . . .

One hearer remarked that day, "George Washington would have liked that."

THE DESIRE FOR A MONUMENT

The history of the memorial really begins with the end of the Revolutionary War and even before all the British troops had left the country. Its legislative history is filled with "stumbling blocks and hesitations" that would have tried the patience of Washington himself.

In recognition of the general's popularity and because of the distinctive services he had rendered his country, the Continental Congress on August 7, 1783, passed a resolution that "an equestrian statue of General Washington be erected at the place where the residence of Congress shall be estabished."

The national hero was to be clad "in a Roman dress, holding a truncheon in one hand, and his head encircled by a laurel wreath." However, Washington himself objected to its erection because of the great expense and the shortage of funds in the new treasury. Therefore, at his request the matter was dropped.

However, when the noted French architect Pierre Charles L'Enfant in 1791 drew up the plans for the new federal capital, he designated a place where this proposed equestrian statue should stand. As matters turned out, the shaft dedicated to our first President is located close to L'Enfant's original spot.

The feeling back of the desire to honor Washington was appreciation for his superb leadership and his sacrificial services to the new nation. As one person foretold, the General was already destined to take his place among the immortals:

In July, 1775, when George Washington stood under an elm tree on Cambridge Common and took charge of the raw recruits of the newly formed Continental Army, his star was beginning to shine in the sky of the great. Known already as a hero of the French and

Indian War, the quarter of a century ahead was to aim him straight to the hall of fame.

In the American Revolution he had more than proved his right to greatness. When the thirteen struggling colonies dared to match arms with the richest and most powerful empire in the entire world, Washington headed the small disorganized Continental Army, which was bent on achieving independence from the mother country.

His resources were scanty and the forces untrained. But the general's driving, unceasing enthusiasm, along with his remarkable ability to use his resources to the utmost, won the admiration and support of both military and civic leaders. And during the first years of the difficult and uneven struggle Washington's men actually won some victories against their highly experienced opponents. Because of this the colonials gained aid from France. They made an alliance with the French and succeeded in gaining their independence.

> General Washington, by the close of the Revolution, was held in honor by all Americans. He was the symbol of the Revolution and its triumphant conclusion.

Then, as head of the convention of 1787, he presided over the assembly that drew up our federal constitution. And after his election as the first chief executive, George Washington continued to demonstrate that he "was a man among men."

The following are some of the many tributes paid to General George Washington by his contemporaries:

> In the summer of 1799 I again saw the Chief. He rode a purely white horse, 17 hands high; well proportioned, of high spirit; he almost seemed conscious that he bore on his back the Father of His Country. . . . I have seen some highly accomplished riders, but not one of them approached Washington; he was perfect in this respect.
> —Lafayette

> There is something charming to me in the conduct of Washington. A gentleman of one of the first fortunes upon the continent, leaving

his delicious retirement, his family and friends, and hazarding all in the cause of his country!

His views are noble and disinterested. He declared when he accepted the mighty trust that he would lay before us an exact account of his expenses, and would not accept a shilling for pay.

—John Adams

Once when Patrick Henry was asked who was the greatest man in Congress, he replied:

> If you speak of eloquence, Mr. Rutledge of South Carolina is by far the greatest orator, but if you speak of solid information and sound judgment, Colonel Washington is unquestionably the greatest man on the floor.

> His mind was great and powerful . . . his penetration, strong . . . no judgment was ever sounder . . . certainly no general ever planned his battles more judiciously. Perhaps the strongest feature of his character was prudence, never acting until every circumstance, every consideration was maturely weighed; refraining, if he saw a doubt; but, when once decided, going through with his purpose, whatever obstacles opposed.

> —Thomas Jefferson

> To the memory of the man, first in war, first in peace, and first in the hearts of his countrymen.

> —Colonel Henry Lee

Later on, Daniel Webster in a speech on June 17, 1843, at the completion of the Bunker Hill Monument summed the matter up in this way:

> America has furnished to the world the character of Washington. And if our American institution had done nothing else, that alone would have entitled them to the respect of mankind.

When Washington died, in 1799, the subject of erecting a memorial to him was brought up again, just eight days after his passing. John Marshall proposed that a marble monument be set up in his memory by the United States in the city of Washington. This mausoleum was to be of American marble and granite, in the form of a pyramid 100 feet square at the base and of proportionate height.

Marshall's resolution also included the idea that our first President's body be interred in this memorial.

(From time to time Congress tried to have the casket brought to Washington, but the family did not agree to this. Today the body of George Washington lies in a modest mausoleum at the foot of a hill below his home at Mount Vernon. A perpetual guard marches back and forth in front of the tomb, and an American flag waves at its iron gate.)

THE DESIGNS FOR THE MONUMENT

For more than three decades the matter of building a Washington memorial was debated, but action was delayed. Congress could not decide on any definite plan. One source says that it was not indifference that postponed the project, but indecision.

In 1832, when the Senate disagreed with plans submitted by the House of Representatives, Henry Clay made this fervent plea: "As a monument, rear it; spend on it what you will; make it as durable as the Pyramids, eternal as the mountains!"

Exasperated by the indecision and delays of Congress, a band of influential public-minded citizens joined in 1833 to organize the Washington National Monument Society. George Watterson, librarian of Congress, was prominent in the group which elected John Marshall as their first president. (After Marshall's death, in 1835, former President Madison succeeded in office for a short time. Madison himself died in 1836.)

The idea of the group was to promote on their own the building of the memorial to Washington, and thus to atone for the failure of Congress to do so. They planned a suitable and fitting monument that would cost at least $1 million. The group soon called for designs; in 1836 American artists were asked to participate.

Someone once said that the monument, like Topsy in *Uncle Tom's Cabin*, "just growed."

> As are many other parts of our national life, it is an amalgam of many thoughts, many hopes, many dreams.

The simple shaft that is the Washington Monument today is a contrast to the ornate designs offered in its "stump" days. It is evident that in other, more lurid forms, it would never have won the place it holds today in the minds and hearts of the American people.

Numerous individuals competed for the privilege of designing the Washington memorial. Plans by at least six highly competent persons came close to being accepted. But "compared with the completed monument, all these were grotesque."

Henry R. Searle, a well-known architect of Washington, submitted a design for "three terraces with battering walls," adorned with sculptured panels and surmounted by a pointed tower.

A Philadelphian, John Fraser, offered a campanile of seven stages, like the Italian belltower of the Middle Ages. The stages would be of similar heights, rising from a base of four miniature campaniles. Over the main entrance, and topped by a shield and an angel with a trumpet, was to be an equestrian statue of General Washington.

Another campanile design was made by the poet and sculptor William Wetmore, "with a bow to the Florentine masterpiece." He had planned a Renaissance framework for the statue of our first President; at the top would be a figure of Fate, with a wreath of laurel for the national hero below.

A Boston artist, M. P. Hapgood, presented a design featuring an English Gothic tower with a lantern at the summit. A statue of Washington would stand in a niche at the base, with an angel at the top of the shaft.

"The design to end all designs" was submitted by a California architect, representing the modern French style. It had many details and showed "affinity with some of the better Hindu pagodas." This plan called for a statue of George Washington, seated on a throne, "attended by ladies gracefully leaning on their elbows." It was lucky for following generations that such bizarre designs were not accepted.

Robert Mills's idea was to have at the base of an obelisk a circular colonnaded building, like a Greek temple, 250 feet in diameter and 100 feet high. There would be 30 columns, each 12 feet across and 45 feet in height. The architect wanted the structure to be an American pantheon, with a colossal figure of Washington; later, figures of other Presidents and national heroes could be added. Rising from the temple would be a 600-foot Egyptian column, decorated with gigantic stars. The shaft would be topped by a statue of Washington in a Roman chariot, driving four horses.

Although Mill's design was accepted by the society, construction on the monument was delayed; there were not enough funds to pay for the "frills" he designed for the base. In fact, the obelisk was the only element of his elaborate conception of the monument that actually survived. But strange to say, this outstanding architect estimated the complete cost of the structure at $1.26 million—a figure "amazingly close" to the final cost.

ROBERT MILLS, THE DESIGNER

Robert Mills, the first native-born professional architect in the United States, was "one of the chief exponents of the Greek revival."

Born in Charleston, South Carolina, on August 12, 1781, he was the son of William Mills, a Scotsman from Dundee who had married Anne Taylor, "a lady of ancient and honorable Carolina lineage." Early in life the red-haired boy decided to become a trained architect. This was unusual, for at that period there were few such professionals in this country.

The education for this work was a costly undertaking. In order to earn money for attendance at Charleston College, the youth obtained a part-time job in the office of James Hoban, designer of the capitol of South Carolina.

From him young Mills learned "the rudiments of construction, and draftsmanship and rendering." He graduated at the age of nineteen and soon designed a combined chapel and library for the University of South Carolina. When Hoban moved to Washington, D.C., Mills went with him. There the young architect worked with Hoban as a draftsman on details of the plans for both the White House and the Capitol.

Mill's willingness to work and his determination to get ahead in his chosen profession inspired confidence in others. He soon attracted the attention of Thomas Jefferson, who invited him to visit at Monticello in 1803. This was fortunate; there Mills had access to Jefferson's books on architecture, then the finest collection in the country. The young man made an extended stay at Monticello, with the rare chance of studying and working under Jefferson's excellent direction.

Because Robert Mills was eager to do worthwhile work in architecture, Jefferson advised him to study with Benjamin H. Latrobe, Hoban's successor as architect for the Capitol. From 1803 to 1808 he worked as clerk and draftsman with Latrobe. At twenty-six he supervised for his employer the construction of the Bank of Philadelphia; he was also chosen that year to design wings for historic Independence Hall—a great honor for a man of any age.

During his entire life Robert Mills, who was a very religious man, concerned himself with church architecture. He designed a number of churches and incorporated in them new ideas on acoustics and the use of fireproof materials. Among his important church buildings were the Octagon Unitarian Church in Philadelphia and St. John's Episcopal in Washington.

Mills was versatile, and because of his dependable personal habits and exceptional genius he received many important commissions, including that of building the new capitol in Harrisburg, Pennsylvania. In 1814 he designed a $160,000 Washington monument for the city of Baltimore. It was a striking circular shaft of Doric design which was acclaimed both here and abroad. This statue, which towered over Baltimore, is said to have spurred on the citizens of the national capital and of the nation to build such a memorial on the Potomac, to symbolize their respect and admiration for General Washington.

Robert Mills also constructed a bridge on the Potomac River in Washington and one over the Schuylkill River near Philadelphia. The latter had a span of 344 feet, 98 feet longer than any other bridge in the world at that time. In Richmond, Virginia, he planned the new courthouse and several outstanding residences, including one for Dr. John Brockenborough that later was used as the White House of the Confederacy.

The architect also showed much interest in his fellow men. He designed nine hospitals, one of them still in use—the State Hospital for the Insane at Columbia, South Carolina. It was decades ahead of its time in providing accommodations for the insane as sick persons, not criminals.

Mills also used his broad abilities in designing a transcontinental railroad, a system of hard-surfaced roads, a rotary steam engine, and a reaping machine. He was interested in geology, and especially in the study of earthquakes and how they could damage buildings.

In 1836 his friend President Andrew Jackson appointed him

federal architect. For fifteen years Mills worked continually with the purpose of making Washington one of the most beautiful cities in the world. He designed the old Patent Office and the Treasury Building. The latter was considered by competent critics as the best contemporary specimen of American architecture.

From 1830 until his death, in March, 1855, he lived in the national capital, "where his charm and genius as an architect made him a celebrity." His religious principles remained unchanged, and he regularly attended church with his good friend President Franklin Pierce. "The crowning success of his life was his victory in competition for the design of the Washington Monument."

ACTION AT LAST

In January, 1848, Congress authorized the Washington National Monument Society to go on with their project. The President of the United States and the board of managers of the society were to choose the site. They agreed upon a location on the Mall some distance directly west of the Capitol.

During the 1840 and 1850 censuses, United States marshals, who were in charge of our early census-takings, were authorized to collect money that would be used to pay for the Washington Monument. Contributors to this cause were given lithographs as mementos of their participation.

Although the society worked hard to collect funds, they made progress slowly. However, by 1847 they had obtained about $70,000 from private individuals; finally enough money had been received to justify starting the work.

Next came the important ceremony of the cornerstone-laying. This took place on July 4, 1848, with impressive Masonic rites. Grand Master French was in charge of the event; he used the same trowel that General Washington had employed when the cornerstone of the Capitol was laid in 1793.

It was reported that a crowd of between 15,000 and 20,000 "picked its way across swamps, canals, and creeks, toward the knoll," the site of the new monument.

Among the prominent persons there that day were President Polk, Dolly Madison, and Mrs. Alexander Hamilton. A live American eagle was perched on a decorated arch—the same eagle, so the story went, that had sat on the Arch of Welcome when the Marquis de Lafayette made a triumphal visit to the old town of Alexandria, just across the Potomac River.

At the ceremonies Mrs. Hamilton and Dolly Madison placed in the cornerstone the following items, typical of the period: By-Laws of the Powhatan Tribe, No. 1; *Memoirs of a Tour to Northern Mexico, 1846–7,* by R. B. Anderson; Maury's Wind and Current Charts of the North Atlantic; Constitution of the First Temperance Society in America; copies of the Cayuga, New York, *New Era* and the Vicksburg, Mississippi, *Weekly Whig.*

(There is an unsolved mystery in regard to the cornerstone of the monument; today no one knows its location.)

That evening there was a great showing of fireworks to end the festivities. The display was followed by a gala reception at the White House.

The work on the Washington Monument continued slowly for seven years. By 1854, $300,000 had been raised, and the shaft had been finished to about 150 feet. By this time it had become evident that the memorial would be more beautiful "in simple majesty" than it would be with columns and a temple around the base, as planned at first.

An old photograph shows the memorial under construction during the 1850's. It depicts the partially built shaft with many workmen busy around it cutting stones into proper sizes, while teams of oxen are pulling carts filled with great slabs of rock. Drivers are walking alongside as the materials are being conveyed to the base of the monument.

Then several things happened that stopped the work for more than twenty years—money troubles and the coming of the Civil War, when Americans were trying to decide whether to be one nation or two.

But the main obstacle was a political dissension, when the monument became involved in the notorious "Pope's Stone" affair. This event angered many Americans; contributions ceased; it was not until 1876 that the project was resumed by the government. Then at last it was completed—after its building had been "the plaything of an indifferent Congress, the despair of its patriotic sponsors, and the focal point of a religious battle."

Thus the Washington Monument stood unfinished for more than two decades, during which time the "stubby shaft" was an eyesore. When the Centennial Year was approaching, Congress seemed to wake up and redeem itself for its indecision and long neglect of the memorial.

The two houses united in passing resolutions to take over and complete construction; an appropriation of $200,000 was made; both measures were approved by President Ulysses S. Grant. On August 17, 1880, work was resumed under government engineers. It was found that the monument had settled somewhat out of plumb since it had been worked on before, so the "leaning-tower" effect had to be corrected.

In bringing about the completion of the Washington Monument, one man, George P. Marsh, later minister to Italy, should be given much credit. It was discovered that the foundation was not strong enough for the heavy weight of the proposed shaft; Mr. Marsh made a detailed study of this matter and of others. His excellent recommendations were followed.

Under the new sponsorship, construction proceeded continuously; by August 9, 1884, the walls had reached the 500-foot mark.

Then came the "crowning" event—putting the capstone in place. It weighed 3,000 pounds and was topped by a pyramid of pure aluminum weighing 100 pounds. It was the largest piece of this metal ever cast up to that time. On the faces of the point were inscribed the names of individuals connected with the building of the monument.

(The story is told that when the aluminum pyramidion was being exhibited in New York and Washington prior to its emplacement, several persons asked permission to step over it so they could later say they had "hopped" over the Washington Monument.)

The capstone was put in position, "to the enthusiastic applause of a joyous crowd," on December 6, 1884, marking the completion of the long-drawn-out project. The ceremony happened while "a howling gale" was "blowing fiercely around the memorial." Thus, after a total period of 36 years, 5 months, and 2 days, the Washington Monument was a reality. It was the tallest building in the world at that time. "The completion of the unadorned 555-foot shaft of the Washington Monument seemed to contemporaries to give the city its crowning touch."

At the dedication program, on February 21, 1885, Robert C.

Winthrop, who thirty-seven years before had given the address at the laying of the cornerstone, was once more the chief speaker. Three years later, on October 9, 1888, the memorial was opened to the general public. It has been welcoming millions of visitors ever since.

The memorial is in the shape of an Egyptian obelisk and follows the same proportion, though it is much larger than those columns were. The 555-foot height is ten times the width of its base. "According to Greek concepts of grace and strength combined, this is perfect proportion."

The sides gradually slant inward as they rise to the base of the pyramidion—55 feet high—which tops the monument. At this point, each side of the pillar is a few inches over 34 feet.

At the bottom of the obelisk the walls are 15 feet thick, at the top 18 inches. The memorial contains more than 90,000 tons of stone, but it has settled less than 2 inches. It was built to withstand Washington weather, and its sway in a 30-mile gale is very slight.

The obelisk is "dressed" with white Maryland marble in 2-foot courses. The first thirteen are from the same vein and were laid in 1854. When work was resumed in 1876, the marble came from another quarry and had a slightly different color; this is noticeable and is called "George's Ring." Visitors are warned not to believe the story that the stones of the lower part of the shaft were discolored when waters of the Potomac River reached that point.

Inside, the walls up to 150 feet are backed with bluestone; higher up, with New England granite and marble.

The cost of Washington Monument was $1.2 million. It is believed that a duplicate today would cost at least $5 million, or perhaps closer to $10 million, to buy the land and pay for the materials and labor. It is said that the land alone, because of the enormous growth of the city around it, is worth several million dollars.

THE MEMORIAL STONES

Anyone who is vigorous enough to skip the elevator and walk up or down the long stairway in the Washington Monument has a special privilege. For he can pause and examine the memorial stones—about 200 of them—that are set in the interior walls of the gigantic obelisk. These especially appeal to historically minded individuals.

These stones were presented by individuals, states, territories, state militias, churches, schools, various organizations and lodges, labor unions, and foreign nations. "The carvings on the stones run from that of a whale to the most exalted sentiments of patriotism," declared one writer. Most of the stones, properly inscribed, were inserted between 1848 and 1885. The last one placed in the shaft was that of Hawaii, in 1936.

> The hiker is rewarded by the unfolding panorama of memorial stones at each ten-foot interval, on the landings. He soon becomes aware that nearly every race, creed, and color of man has made its contribution to the construction of the monument, memorializing the man who was "first in war, first in peace, and first in the hearts of his countrymen."

When money gifts for the building were coming in slowly, the state of Alabama suggested that the different states each give a stone in place of money. This idea was eagerly accepted by the Washington National Monument Society, and it sent out immediately an urgent call for such gifts. The state of Maine has the honor of being the first one to respond to the call; its stone can be seen on the 30-foot landing.

On the same platform is one sent by Delaware; its inscription declares that this state, "first to adopt, will be the last to desert the Constitution." At the same height are memorials given by Arkansas, by the Franklin Fire Company of Washington, D.C., and by two individuals, Timothy O'Neale and George Watterson, first secretary of the Washington National Monument Society.

An interesting memento came from New Bedford, Massachusetts; it bears the carving of a whale, "symbolic of the economic founding of the city's life at that time—the great American whaling industry, which centered there."

Utah—then termed "Deseret"—has a stone. The one for Indiana proclaims that "she knows no North or South, nothing but the Union." North Carolina proudly boasts that Mecklenberg, within her borders, had adopted its own Declaration of Independence in

May, 1776, some time before the adoption by all the colonies on July 4, 1776.

One slab is inscribed with the name of an early locomotive made by a Philadelphia company. There are memorial stones also from the Revolutionary battlefields of Bunker Hill and Long Island, and from the field in Pennsylvania where George Washington as a young man won his spurs, and where the English officer General Braddock was defeated by the French and Indians.

The tribe of Cherokee Indians paid tribute to their Great White Father by giving a memorial stone. An unusual inscription appears on the gift of the Pennsylvania Sons of Temperance: "The Surest Safeguard of the Liberty of Our Country Is Total Abstinence from All That Intoxicates."

During the years the memorial was building, gifts of stones kept arriving from distant parts of the globe. Greece sent a fine marble block from the ruins of the world-famous Parthenon. It was marked: "From the Mother of Liberty." Others came from the remains of ancient Carthage, from the tomb of Napoleon on St. Helena, from the historic old library in Alexandria, and from Egypt, Wales, Brazil, Siam, Switzerland, and the Free City of Bremen.

A stone from Turkey was in a strange script and consisted of a poem dedicated to George Washington and composed by the Sultan's court poet. The Chinese rated our first chief executive as far above "a whole constellation of celestial patriots." Another stone from that same country was the gift of Americans living in Foo Chow Foo in 1857, the heyday of swift clipper ships and the China trade.

In 1853 Commodore Matthew C. Perry made his long-remembered expedition to Japan and opened up that isolated country to Western influence. That very year a memorial stone for the monument was sent, one of the first exports from the island empire to the United States.

Among the varied stories, none is more fantastic than the tale concerning one presented by the state of California. The contributions of all other sources to the society amounted to less than $1.2 million, yet when California decided to give a stone, it unintentionally made a gift which cost the state more than $2 million.

California entered the Union in 1850, just two years after the cornerstone of the monument was laid. Other states were sending contributions, so when the new legislature met and discussed its gift, that body decided to send a block of gold quartz. There were no funds in the young treasury. A "due note" for $975 was signed to pay for the stone and its shipment.

This note carried interest at 3 per cent monthly, a common rate in those days. At the next meeting of the legislature, members discovered they owed more than $1,000. At once they replaced the note by a small bond issue, with annual interest at 15 per cent.

For some strange reason that no one seems able to explain, the bonds were overlooked. By 1857 the amount exceeded $5,000. Still no payments were made, and the bonds were refinanced again and again.

In 1943 the California legislature discovered to its horror that the original debt of $975 at compound interest then amounted to the staggering sum of $2,277,550. Later that same year, Governor Earl Warren signed checks to pay off the stupendous debt of almost a century's standing.

If you walk up or down the monument, you can see that famous gold quartz block. Then you will realize that California did more than her rightful share and that the state really meant what is engraved on the stone: YOUNGEST SISTER OF THE UNION BRINGS HER GOLDEN TRIBUTE TO THE FIRST PRESIDENT.

THE POPE'S STONE

Few Americans who visit the slender shaft that rises above the city know about the "sordid intrigue," the decades of long effort, the typical American confusion, the long delay, the construction blunders, and the sacrifices represented by this memorial to George Washington.

Perhaps, too, not many have heard the story of the "Pope's Stone," which was the prime cause of discord and delay. It was a block sent by Pope Pius IX from the Temple of Concord in Rome, to be set into the wall of the monument. Its coming and intended incorporation in the memorial angered a political party calling itself the American, or Know Nothing, party. The members expressed their resentment and declared that they were strongly opposed to accepting the "papist gift."

This organization was a secret society which existed in the United States from about 1852 to 1860. It was antagonistic to immigration and the election or appointment of Roman Catholics and foreign-born persons to official positions. Its meetings were held in secret, and actions were not openly discussed.

When asked about their beliefs, members would answer, "I don't know." In 1854 they carried Massachusetts and received many votes in New York and Pennsylvania. They had a big following, too, in the South. The group finally split on the slavery question.

The party slogan was "Americans must rule America." Members were bitterly anti-Roman Catholic; they were opposed to the control of large eastern cities by immigrants of German or Irish extraction. They wanted immigrants to live in the United States for twenty-one years before attaining citizenship.

On the night of March 5, 1854, a number of masked men attacked the watchman at the Washington Monument and stole the "Pope's Stone." It is reported that this band of raiders either had been sent by the Know Nothing party or was made up of its members. The stone was never seen or heard of again. Some believe it was shattered by sledgehammers and the pieces dropped into the Potomac River, just a few hundred yards from the monument.

This act of vandalism enraged many people and discouraged the collection of contributions for the completion of the memorial. With the stoppage of gifts, the society appealed to Congress for help. That body agreed to pass an act, on Washington's birthday, 1855, to make an appropriation of $200,000 for the construction.

But on the night before—February 21—the Know Nothings broke into the office of the society and stole all the books and records. After putting out the elected officials and placing their own members in office, the Know Nothings announced they were in possession of the monument. They declared they would finish it as "an American institution, supported by all Americans." These actions so angered members of Congress that they refused to pass the promised appropriation.

So for a time there were two competing societies. But when the Know Nothing party began to disintegrate, they surrendered control of the true society's records, in October, 1858.

VISITING THE MONUMENT

By April, 1948, more than 22 million persons had visited the landmark. On May 9, 1953, there was a record attendance for one day of 13,127 visitors. This number included a youth safety group of 8,460 that was touring the city. That year had the highest attendance, up to that date—1,022,269 persons.

By 1958 more than 25 million sightseers had gone to the top, and by 1961 more than 35 million had made the ascent. Usually there are from 3,000 to 5,000 visitors each day.

The monument is open from 8 A.M. to 11 P.M. from March 20 to Labor Day, and from 9 A.M. to 6 P.M. the rest of the year. It is open every day of the year except Christmas Day.

There are two ways of getting to the top: by riding in the elevator and by walking up the iron stairway, which has 50 landings and 898 steps.

During 1953, 817,905 persons used the elevator, while 204,364 walked up the stairs. For several reasons numerous "stouthearted walkers" prefer the "shoe-leather express" to the elevator. The thrilling climb takes about half an hour. It is a recognized feat though not one advocated for those with weak hearts.

Up to 1958, over 5 million people had snubbed the elevator and trudged up the stairway. Also, believe it or not, at least two persons have gone down the steps on their hands.

The favorite way of seeing the memorial, with many persons, is to ride up, then walk down to inspect the tribute stones in the interior walls.

A custodian, Charles Herman, who had climbed the steps at least a thousand times, said that even though the elevator makes the trip in about a minute, the fact doesn't seem to impress the high-school seniors, many of whom prefer to run up the 898 steps.

I don't know why people insist on taking those steps anyway. Nearly all of the staircase visitors count the steps and hardly anybody ends up with the right number. . . . They complain that there's only 896. I tell them to go back and count them over again. And, by golly, some of them go back and do it.

The first elevator was a steam hoist which took twelve "precarious" moments to reach the top. One newspaperman wrote a booklet about his experience in ascending in those early days, calling it "The Ascent: Its Horrors and How Mundane Things Appear 550 Feet in the Air."

This steam elevator was used until 1900, when an electrical device was installed. Then, in 1926, the old one was replaced by a modern affair that took only seventy seconds to get to the summit.

On November 17, 1958, Washington Monument was closed while a newer elevator was being put in place. The memorial reopened on February 23, 1959, with a short program honoring Washington's birthday. Officials of the Interior Department made the first trip to the 500-foot platform in the new elevator. This has steel cab doors on two sides, allowing simultaneous loading and unloading at the ground floor and observation platform.

At first there was no cost for the ride; however, when Harold Ickes was Secretary of the Interior, he placed a charge of one dime on the trip. The story is told that Mr. Ickes himself flounced past the guards without paying when he and President Truman ascended to survey a site for a bridge over the Potomac.

While the elevator is making its up and down journeys, passengers hear a recording through an amplification system. This gives background facts and vital statistics and tells of the memorial stones and of the significance of the memorial. At the top the record describes the view.

Since April, 1943, the same voice has been heard, which one visitor claimed "had no peer the world around." Some time ago the superintendent of parks declared that this record was good for at least ten more years, during which period at least a million more persons would hear it.

The voice is that of Sherman Allen. He served as the head of special projects in the office of the army adjutant general and was concerned with such things as television shows, displays, conventions, and like events in which the government was interested.

After World War II Mr. Allen joined the foreign service. However, his recorded voice remained at the Washington Monument. Once Sherman Allen commented:

I never dreamed I would speak as the Washington elevator went up and down so many times in ten years, and who knows how many more? Thank Heaven, I had it recorded! I can't stand height—and that many trips up and down each day would drive a man daffy.

The recording was installed—so someone has said—to distract passengers' minds from "the eerie ascent into the upper atmosphere." Percy Porter, in charge of the elevator, once remarked:

> There are lots fewer cases of old ladies' fainting in the elevator now that they can listen to that nice announcer's voice. . . . However, no scheme that the monument has been able to devise has altered one of the ladies' worst habits.
>
> Every day some lady goes to the top, sticks her head out of the window, and says, "I can see the Lincoln Memorial all right. But where's the Washington Monument?"

Visitors have the chance of a lifetime to look out from the eight small windows, in all four directions. From here they get a splendid panoramic view.

At this lofty height spectators have a sight of the city and the surrounding countryside, the rivers, bays, islands, and bridges. The public buildings seem to be set in a great park; and the "L'Enfant plan of the city of Washington is as obvious as if on a drawing board."

> To the north across the Ellipse is the White House; across the Tidal Basin is the domed Jefferson Memorial; the Mall and Capitol can be seen to the east; to the west is the stately Lincoln Memorial; and across the Potomac, the hallowed slope of Arlington Cemetery and Robert E. Lee's home.

You see the Potomac slowly winding its way south toward Mount Vernon; and to the west, the hills of Virginia, through which George Washington passed so frequently on private and public errands.

Directly across the river is Alexandria, in which Washington, as a young officer, drilled the Virginia militia before and after Braddock's ill-fated expedition.

On the Washington side of the Potomac is quaint old Georgetown, where our first President was often the guest of friends; at its southern edge is the Chesapeake and Ohio Canal, which is a partial realization of a navigable waterway connecting the national capital and the West.

SOME STORIES ABOUT THE MONUMENT

In 1951, when Charles Herman was in charge of the monument, he was interviewed and told some tales about unusual things that had happened in the memorial. The writer Leslie Lieber described Mr. Herman as the "Grandpa of the Washington Monument," with "gray hair and rosy red nose"—a man whose glasses sometimes got blown off when a heavy gale whistled around the "marble beanstalk." According to Mr. Lieber, Charles Herman "carried everything inside his head worth knowing about the Washington Monument."

The custodian told of a mouse that for several years had lived in the pyramid on top of the shaft, on chewing-gum wrappers and "whatever spiritual vitamins it could get from gazing at the White House from the north windows." Mr. Herman also told a story about a cat that fell or jumped from the monument. However, it landed safely on four feet. After its death, this remarkable animal was stuffed and placed in the Smithsonian Institution. The custodian also made this remark to his interviewer: "A few years ago, some college professor stated that the Washington Monument had sunk 2 inches in the past fifty years. I don't know; I ain't felt nothing." One of Mr. Herman's assistants did some figuring and assured him that, at the present rate of settling, the top of the memorial wouldn't be underground until many centuries from now.

Although it is forbidden to throw anything out from the top, some people disobey the rule, thus endangering the lives of others waiting in line below. Objects that have been thrown include steel spikes, roller skates, whiskey bottles, and rifle shells. Of the last-mentioned Mr. Herman commented: "The kids seem to visit the F.B.I. building first. The F.B.I. gives them rifle shells as souvenirs. Maybe if the F.B.I. reads this in the paper, they won't give away rifle shells anymore."

In August, 1908, Preston Gilbert, a descendant of Patrick Henry, rolled thirteen baseballs out of a trough from the top. Down below, a baseball player, "Gabby" Street (then with the Washington Senators), was waiting. He was not able to retrieve any of the first twelve, but did manage to catch the thirteenth, winning a reward of $500. (Some years afterward, that ball was auctioned off at a War Bond rally for $40,000). On another occasion the pitcher Walter Johnson threw several softballs over the side of the monument to eager youngsters waiting on the grass below.

Sometimes the government uses the shaft as a test tube for mysterious experiments. For a while the Civil Aeronautics Administration officials kept cruising up and down in the elevator. All Charles Herman would say was, "They ain't testing elevators." Once some army officers threw a small weighted parachute from a window, and it landed in a tree on Connecticut Avenue.

Only one person—according to Custodian Herman—has ever spent a night in the Washington Monument. After attendants had closed the memorial and gone home, Mrs. S. E. Longwell, of Middlebury, Vermont, found to her horror that she was locked in with bats, howling winds, and "the flitting memories of a score of vanished administrations." But ever since that episode, one of the guards looks the place over carefully each evening, by walking down the 898 steps.

Although this mishap was not planned by Mrs. Longwell, many other individuals have tried to use the monument for publicity purposes. Officials flatly refused to let one couple be married in the memorial.

One day Mr. Herman was told a man wanted to see him at the entrance. There he found the noted magician Blackstone seated on a black-and-white pony. He said he wanted to go to the top of the monument and make the animal disappear. The custodian called the Interior Department, but the officials denied Blackstone's unique request. Then Charles Herman returned to tell the magician the decision, declaring, "Mr. Blackstone, I'm a better magician than you are. I'm going to make both you and the pony disappear. Now move on!"

However, the government at times has permitted certain experiments to be made at Washington Monument. In 1910, for example, Dr. Alfredo Warsaw, formerly a member of the National Opera Company, sang an aria from the top of the memorial. He was trying to find out if his voice could be heard on Constitution Avenue. There is no record of the results.

Some years ago authorities of the Interior Department allowed a musician in the National Symphony to try an experiment. He aimed his trumpet toward Constitution Avenue, where members of the orchestra and other persons were gathered. When he played a theme from Beethoven's Leonore Overture, No. 3, those below heard the notes distinctly, proving, as Leslie Lieber declared, that "the trumpet can make a helluva racket."

In concluding the interview, Charles Herman sadly reflected that our Presidents do not make the trip to the top; he stated that Harry Truman was the only Chief Executive to do so, adding,

> But there's one President who is with us all the time. They say he's out at Mount Vernon. I don't believe it. I feel in my bones that George Washington's spirit is in this stone, and this stone is as immortal as the nation he founded.

CARING FOR THE MONUMENT

The Washington Monument is under the jurisdiction of the National Park Service and is well taken care of. In 1934 some masonry was repaired, and the entire surface of the great shaft was cleaned and thoroughly scrubbed for the first time. Scaffolding was built completely around the structure. It extended up to the apex for this gigantic "housecleaning." Steel brushes, sand, and water were the chief agents used for the job, which took five months. It is said that the cost of building and dismantling the scaffold and the washing was about $100,000. In 1964 the monument had another outside scrubbing, the first in thirty years.

There is a semiannual interior cleaning, to get rid of the dust and dirt that 2 million visitors yearly leave behind them. Then employees wash the elevator shaft and roof. In addition, they spend much time trying to get rid of the crayon, pencil, and lipstick remembrances that many tourists enjoy leaving behind them. These men also repaint the benches and the room on the ground floor where patrons sit and wait for the elevator.

In 1954 Custodian Herman, in speaking of the fact that so many young people walk up instead of using the elevator, stated that he inspected the inside walls twice a week. And he always found mementos left by them, such as "John loves Mary," with a heart and arrow. "I don't mind the pencil so much," he said. "The lipstick is the worst to get off."

THE CHERRY BLOSSOMS

When the famous Japanese cherry trees are in bloom in Washington, they symbolize the beginning of spring, and they are a big drawing card to the vicinity of the monument.

> April brings a million tourists to Washington every year, drawn by the cherry blossoms. . . . The trees bordering the Tidal Basin flourish, making the city's finest spectacle. Drifts of these snowy white flowers pile up in delicate blizzards, as their petals fall to the ground.

This mass planting in West Potomac Park makes for a most striking display. However, East Potomac Park, on a peninsula that runs 2 miles downstream into the Potomac River, southeast of the Tidal Basin, is a strong rival.

In this park, one of Washington's most attractive, the cherry trees are an important part of the landscape. Here are found several varieties of cherry, including the Kwanzan; it is one of the most popular types and produces "heavy clusters of deep-pink double blossoms, and is among the latest of the Japanese cherry tree varieties to bloom." Its deep-pink color adds a lovely effect to the massed plantings in East Potomac Park.

Soon after William Howard Taft was inaugurated as President, on March 4, 1909, Mrs. Taft became interested in the idea of planting Japanese cherry trees in Potomac Park. It happened that a noted Japanese chemist, Dr. Jokichi Takamine, the discoverer of adrenalin, was in Washington and heard of the First Lady's interest in planting such trees. He was instrumental in having the city of Tokyo, through its mayor, Yuhio Ozaki, present a gift of cherry trees to Washington as a gesture of friendship. The generous gift—3,000 trees of 12 varieties—was shipped from Yokohama on the SS *Awa Maru* on February 14, 1912.

When they reached Seattle they were put in insulated freight cars; after the long journey across the continent, they arrived in the national capital on March 25, 1912.

Two days later a small group of people attended a simple ceremony on the northern bank of the Tidal Basin, about 125 feet south of Independence Avenue.

Mrs. Taft planted the first tree. Viscountess Chinda, wife of the Japanese ambassador, planted a second one. At the conclusion of the ceremony the First Lady gave a bouquet of American-beauty roses to Viscountess Chinda. At the bases of the two trees they planted are bronze-inscribed markers honoring the work of these two ladies.

At once workmen continued to plant the Yoshino type trees around the Tidal Basin; then the rest of this variety and eleven other kinds were set out in East Potomac Park.

About 650 trees are maintained around the Tidal Basin, 90 per cent being Yoshino and 10 per cent Akebono. The former, a favorite cherry tree in Japan, was developed about 1870. It has a great profusion of single white blooms. The latter was developed by a nursery in the United States in 1920. It has deep-pink buds which open as "delicate pale-pink, single flowers." The two varieties are in bloom at the same time and provide an attractive color contrast.

In 1927 schoolchildren commemorated the original planting of the gift of the Japanese cherry trees. A three-day celebration of the 1912 event occurred in 1934; this was sponsored by the commissioners of the District of Columbia. By the next year various civic groups had joined to cooperate in carrying out the Cherry Blossom Festival.

This delightful affair was interrupted by the two world wars, but it has grown in scope and popularity. In 1940 a pageant was added to the program. Eight years later Cherry Blossom princesses were selected from each state and territory. Then, from this group a queen of the festival was chosen, by using a wheel of fortune.

There are several outstanding attractions in this fete, which is officially opened by lighting a 300-year-old Japanese lantern presented to Washington in 1954 as a token of friendship.

On Pearl Harbor Sunday, December 7, 1941, "Some misguided persons" chopped down several of these beautiful Japanese gifts. But fortunately the rest of the trees bloomed during the war years and continued to add their beauty to Washington after peace came.

With the close of hostilities some citizens of Tokyo offered to send over a thousand new seedlings. However, as Japan had been so badly bombed, many cherry trees had been destroyed; also the plantings had deteriorated because of lack of proper care. Therefore, the Japanese could not supply the cuttings, and in 1952 they requested some from us in order to restore their trees. The National Park Service gladly sent over the needed cuttings. These were from the very trees that had been shipped to us forty years before by the Japanese of Tokyo.

History repeated itself fifty-three years after the beginning of this distinctive project, when on April 6, 1965, there was a second token planting. This occurred near the spot where Mrs. Taft and Viscountess Chinda had planted the first two trees.

On this occasion Mrs. Lyndon B. Johnson, who has taken so much interest in beautifying our country, received a similar gift of 3,000 to 4,000 Japanese cherry trees from the government of Japan, "in a renewed symbol of national friendship."

According to the Japanese ambassador, Ryuji Takeuchi, the number was left open and would depend on need. These were to be placed around the grounds of the Washington Monument.

At a rainy ceremony, Mrs. Johnson and Mrs. Takeuchi each planted a blossoming cherry tree, using the official gold-plated ceremonial spade. This rite opened the 1965 Cherry Blossom Festival. There was a crowd of several hundred present; it included the fifty-three pretty festival princesses, who sat under umbrellas to hear the forty-minute ceremony of speeches and band music.

The time of blooming varies from year to year and can be predicted only about ten days ahead. Since 1924 the Yoshino and Akebono trees have blossomed as early as March 20 and as late as April 17 with the average tree of this variety in full bloom on April 5. The Kwanzan has varied from April 14 to May 1, with the average date April 22.

Cherry blossoms are short-lived; their petals begin to fall at the end of a week. But during what the early-American poet Philip Freneau in his poem *The Wild Honeysuckle* called "the frail duration of a flower," thousands throng to the Potomac parks to see the lovely, fragile beauty of these Japanese cherry blossoms and to recall their symbolic meaning—promoting ties of friendship between two widely separated lands.

INDEPENDENCE DAY AT THE MONUMENT

Following the Cherry Blossom Festival, the next important observance near the Washington Monument is the celebration of Independence Day, long associated with the memorial. As early as 1850, two years after the laying of the cornerstone, patriotic ceremonies were conducted at the foot of the uncompleted structure.

In 1913 a gala party was held on the large circular greensward between the Washington Monument and the White House. Large crowds gathered for a late-afternoon "song fest." Everyone was happy when Uncle Sam appeared; bugles rang out; and lovely young girls, dressed in red, white, and blue costumes, carrying bouquets, heralded the coming of Miss Columbia.

With each year the Fourth of July celebrations have become of more importance. In 1926 great throngs assembled to note the one hundred and fiftieth anniversary of our independence from England.

There was an especially important, and somewhat different, observance at the towering shaft in July, 1948—a momentous birthday celebration. The ceremonies commemorated the one hundredth anniversary of the cornerstone-laying. Thousands attended. There was a reenactment of the original event, and the same trowel was used. As customary, long speeches were given by prominent orators, and a fine display of fireworks concluded the event.

The annual Independence Day celebration continues, with patriotic programs and fireworks. The monument grounds are also the scene of varied events, including political rallies, Veterans' or Boy Scout encampments, and ceremonies honoring national heroes. Often members of senior high-school classes arrive from far and near to visit the shrine. Near it, outdoor dance festivals and dramatic presentations are given during the spring and summer months, such as the annual Shakespeare Festival, staged in the nearby Sylvan Theater in July and August.

IN THE NEWS

In February, 1965, the Washington Monument got on the front pages of our newspapers, when in New York City four persons were arrested: three American men and a Canadian woman. They were charged with planning to blow up the Washington Monument, the Liberty Bell, and the Statue of Liberty. But their plans failed, due to the fine work of the New York police, the F.B.I., and the Royal Canadian Police.

The major credit for foiling the plot was given to a rookie New York patrolman, who had cleverly infiltrated the group. Police declared that the Canadian drove a car from Canada with thirty sticks of dynamite, which were found in the possession of the group.

The woman pleaded guilty to smuggling in the dynamite and testified for the government. The three men were convicted in Federal Court in New York City of bringing in the dynamite and planning to damage government property.

OTHER WASHINGTON MEMORIALS

Many Americans are not aware of the fact that there are two other memorials to George Washington in our national capital. One of them stood for many years in Statuary Hall, in the Capitol. It was executed in marble in the 1830's by a well-known sculptor, Horatio Greenough, who worked on it for eight years. It depicts George Washington clad in a Roman toga. This piece of sculpture was severely criticized by some persons. When the Capitol architect declared it was too heavy for the floor, it was placed in the plaza in front of the Capitol. Then, in 1908, the figure was taken to the basement of the Smithsonian Institution.

The other statue of the "Father of His Country" stands in Washington Circle. Designed by Clark Mills, it shows the general in the uniform of the commander-in-chief of the Continental Army. This work cost $50,000 and was unveiled by President Abraham Lincoln on February 22, 1860.

THE SYMBOL

Like other national memorials and shrines, the Washington Monument has become an important symbol to Americans. Someone once said that the monuments citizens raise in their national capitals reveal their beliefs and show past trends in their histories. Thus the outside world can see what a nation holds in honor, also what it considers art.

The unnamed writer of the book *Washington, City and Capital* (Federal Writers' Project, 1937) made this comment:

> To Americans the monument is the material symbol of Washington, the city, and Washington, the man. As a landmark, visible for miles by day and by night, when it is illuminated by floodlights, it is a fitting introduction to the capital of the nation. As a monument, its simplicity and austerity of line make it an appropriate memorial to our first President.

Here are statements by various other persons about the monument as a national symbol:

> The pure line of Washington Monument, piercing the sky, is shown everywhere, and is often taken as the emblem of the capital. When it was built, it was the tallest structure on earth. It remains the tallest in stone, surpassed of course by high climbing steel and concrete.

> The Washington Monument symbolizes to the world our fast faith in the principles of its founders, and represents the admiration of all Americans for those qualities of devotion to ideals that set George Washington apart as a great leader.

> A striking illustration of the fact that one man can be an object of admiration to all lovers of liberty, wherever they live. It is both a national and an international expression of respect for Washington and the nation he helped to weld.

Appropriately enough, the monument is surrounded by fifty American flags, representing each state. These have been there permanently since Washington's birthday, 1959. Before, they had been flown only on July 4 and February 22. Because of popular demand the National Park Service decided to fly them permanently, stating that, "since the Washington Monument is a Federal memorial of national significance, the flying of the National Colors is symbolic of our nation united under one Flag."

12

The Lincoln Memorial

ONE of the highlights of a stay in Washington, D.C., is a visit to the Lincoln Memorial. This stately templelike edifice crowns a high terrace and is reached by an impressive flight of steps.

Classic in design, the building has been termed the "American Parthenon"; it is said to be to the United States what the temple to Athena, located on the Acropolis in Athens, was to the ancient Greeks. Although its design received some criticism at first, it has now been accepted as an excellent expression of American ideals.

It is not only a thing of beauty by daylight; but: "The magnificent memorial at Washington, erected to the Great Emancipator, makes a striking blaze of light against the murky sky at night."

Another especially charming view of this monument can be obtained in the spring from across the Tidal Basin when the flowering cherry trees are seen in the foreground.

The following is a comment made about the memorial:

> Perhaps no other building in Washington has been more duly admired than the Lincoln Memorial.
>
> The Lincoln Memorial with its unrivalled setting at the end of the Mall—a great temple with Greek Doric columns executed in white marble—is perhaps the most impressive and stately memorial in Washington.

In a booklet published by the U.S. Interior Department, concerning the history of this monument, the unnamed writer has well summed up the significance of this building:

Had Lincoln been an ordinary President—even an ordinary hero—an ordinary monument would have sufficed, and no doubt would have been quickly built. More than half a century elapsed, however, before an appropriate memorial to the man arose in the nation's capital.

It seemed as if time stood aside until coming generations could fashion the perfect tribute to their benefactor. The Memorial is neither temple, palace, nor tomb, but partakes something of all. It seems to gather within its marble walls the spirit of the man's character, his belief, that all people should be free, free to think, and express themselves, and free to apply their natural talents and ambitions in lawful enterprise.

PLANNING THE MEMORIAL

As early as two years after Abraham Lincoln's assassination there was some talk about erecting a monument to honor his memory. The first organized effort came when Congress passed an act incorporating the Lincoln Memorial Association.

The group at once appealed to the general public for subscriptions to enable them to build a memorial. However, there was no practical response. Also because of some "political embroilment," the plan for the monument had to be shelved.

On January 20, 1909, Senator Charles Dick introduced a resolution in the Senate to make the one hundredth anniversary of Lincoln's birth a legal holiday. He also recommended the construction of a suitable monument to the martyred President.

Two more years passed; then, in 1911, on February 19, Congress approved the legislation necessary to bring about the construction and dedication of the Lincoln Memorial in 1922. By this act, the Lincoln Memorial Commission was created "to secure plans and designs for a monument to the memory of Abraham Lincoln." Chief Justice William Howard Taft served as head of this commission all during its existence.

The body held its first business meeting on March 4, 1911. At its tenth gathering, February 3, 1912, the commission made the vital decision to locate the Lincoln Memorial in Potomac Park, which comprises all the lands south of Constitution Avenue and west of the Washington Monument. The site was recommended by the Committee on Fine Arts.

The group selected this site—in an area of 394 acres redeemed from Potomac swamp—even though there was strong opposition. Many citizens considered the location as "remote and inaccessible."

However, some farsighted persons recognized the possibilities in its development. In 1901 the McMillan Park Commission had begun the work of reclaiming and filling in the swamp, thus allowing for an extension of the Mall, which would make available a site for the Lincoln Memorial.

Today the Potomac Park region is one of the city's largest and most popular parks. The recreation spot has many features that interest travelers.

After choosing the site, the commission selected a New York architect, Henry Bacon, to prepare the design for the memorial. Congress on June 29, 1913, approved his plan and made a contract with him for his full professional services "in connection with the designing and construction of the Lincoln Memorial."

Bacon believed the location of the memorial was the best possible one, and after its completion, he was completely convinced. He declared that the memorial was thus free from the near approach of vehicles. "Reverence and honor should suffer no distraction through lack of silence, or repose in the presence of a structure reared to noble aims and great deeds."

It is said that the chief congressional proponent of erection of this monument was Senator Shelby M. Cullom of Illinois (1829–1914), who served on the planning commission.

On February 12, 1914, workmen broke ground for the monument. The cornerstone was laid a year later, on the one hundred and sixth anniversary of Abraham Lincoln's birth.

At the informal ceremony forty different items, including a Bible, were placed in the stone. An American flag was draped over it. The ceremony was completed when officials placed mortar beneath the cornerstone.

As the building progressed, the commission selected Daniel Chester French, a well-known American sculptor, to create the Lincoln statue, and Jules Guerin to design and execute murals for the end walls and to ornament the bronze ceiling beams.

The Lincoln Memorial was completed at a total cost of $2,940,-000; it was dedicated in 1922.

THE SETTING

The original plans for the setting of the Lincoln Memorial called for a cruciform body of water near it. This was changed, and a shallow rectangular basin was designed, extending along the Mall axis to the memorial. This pool forms "a shimmering vista of water about 2,000 feet long."

> The tall shaft of the Washington Monument, a half mile to the east, as well as the white marble colonnade of the Lincoln Memorial, is mirrored in the surface of the long reflecting pool which lies between them.

The pool, it is said, was suggested by the beauty and dignity of the canals and waterways at the Palace at Versailles, near Paris, and also by the long reflecting basins at the Taj Mahal in India.

In the summertime, the pool is the scene of model-yacht races and fly-casting contests, while in the winter ice skaters move swiftly over its long course.

> The Reflecting Pool gains dignity and distinction from the broad, grassy terraces and walks around it. English elms, planted in memory of the soldier dead, border the Pool. Elsewhere upon the grounds are dwarf box and English and Japanese yews.

Just in front of the memorial is the Rainbow Fountain, whose waters are turned on twice weekly. This forms a striking spectacle when colored lights illuminate it. The surroundings of the memorial are beautifully landscaped, and visitors find there "the solemn dignity and nobility that enshrine the meaning of Lincoln in the hearts of his people."

ARCHITECTURE

The superstructure of the Lincoln Memorial is about 80 feet high, 188 feet long and 188 feet wide. It rests on a base of three large marble platforms, their outer edges forming steps.

The landscaped approach ascends from a terrace, confined by a 14-foot-high granite wall. The flight of steps to the terrace is 130 feet wide. At either side is a large tripod, nine feet high. These were carved from single blocks of pink Tennessee marble by the Piccirilli brothers of New York. The entrance is a wide doorway facing the Washington Monument and the Reflecting Pool.

The building has a large hall surrounded by 36 Doric columns. "Within the broad framework of classical design, the structure has a motif that symbolizes the Union of the States." The columns, more than 40 feet high, surround the walls and represent the 36 states in our country at the time of Abraham Lincoln's death in 1865.

Above the colonnade is a running border of forty-eight festoons; each is inscribed with the name of a state and the date of its admission. These states made up the United States when the Lincoln Memorial was dedicated. The garlands are supported by the wings of elaborately carved eagles, "the end of each garland being affixed to the wall with a ribbon having flowing ends, at the top of which are two palm leaves." Ernest C. Bairstow of Washington carved the frieze and the decorations on the attic wall.

THE INTERIOR

The interior of the hall, of Indiana limestone, is divided into three sections by 8 Ionic columns. The main chamber is 60 feet wide and 70 feet long. The central part is open in front and contains the gigantic statue of Lincoln.

The 60-foot ceiling includes bronze girders, which are decorated with oak and laurel leaves. Between the girders are panels of Alabama marble. These were saturated with paraffin to make them translucent. The floor of the main chamber and the wall base are of pink Tennessee marble.

In the two side sections—smaller halls each 63 by 38 feet—opening to the right and left, are tablets inscribed with two of Lincoln's most notable speeches. The decorations of the Gettysburg and Second Inaugural speeches were done under the direction of Daniel Chester French by Evelyn Beatrice Longman, his assistant.

Above the inscriptions are two murals by Jules Guerin, each 60 feet long and 12 feet high. The canvas for each mural weighed about 600 pounds, and the painter needed 150 pounds of paint for each picture.

The murals are unusual and reveal in allegorical fashion principles of thought and conduct characteristic of Lincoln, such as justice, law, freedom, liberty, fraternity, unity, and charity.

One painting, *Emancipation,* above the Gettysburg Address, shows an Angel of Truth freeing a slave, while *Union,* executed above the Second Inaugural, symbolizes the union of the North and South.

> The daylight reaching the inner hall through the eastern opening is supplemented and softened by the quiet glow diffused through the marble ceiling.

According to one expert, the Lincoln Memorial contains structural features not usually found in modern buildings. For instance, the columns are not really in vertical position; they are inclined slightly inward, with the four corner columns having the most incline. The outer facade, above the columns, and the wall are inclined inward somewhat. Such a structural characteristic "eliminates the optical illusion of a building bulging at the top."

Someone has said that although the memorial has features based on Greek-temple architecture, it departs in some respects from traditional conception. The entrance is unique, being at one side; the high base adds much to the impressiveness of the edifice; and the wide steps increase this effect. This critic asserts that the exterior is superior to the interior, "with its somewhat dubious skylight arrangement."

> Undoubtedly, the monument was conceived far more in the spirit of an abstract affirmation of national idealism than as a personal interpretation of the Great Emancipator.

Clearly, the building is a symbol—not perhaps so much of Lincoln as of our noblest aspirations. With this end in view, Henry Bacon doubtless turned for inspiration to the Greek Doric-temple form as the highest expression of pure classicism. Roman pomp was laid aside in favor of the more chaste and abstract beauty of Greek architecture.

THE LINCOLN STATUE AND ITS CREATOR

Daniel Chester French, a friend of Henry Bacon, the architect, was chosen after much deliberation to create the colossal statue of Lincoln. The wisdom of this choice was proved by the magnificent portrayal of our Civil War President which this artist produced. Bacon once said of the work:

> The outstanding feature of the memorial is the statue of Lincoln. . . . It is placed in the central hall of the memorial, where by virtue of its imposing position, in the place of honor, it predominates. The gentleness, power, and determination of the man has been wonderfully expressed by the sculptor, not only in the face, but also in the hands which grip the arms of the massive seat.

Daniel Chester French was an outstanding American sculptor who also created numerous other pieces of lasting fame. His works are distinguished for their "plastic beauty and grace." Mr. French was preeminent in the field of monuments and memorials. Some critics assert that his work "is more profoundly American than that of any of his contemporaries."

Born on April 20, 1850, at Exeter, New Hampshire, Daniel Chester French died at Stockbridge, Massachusetts, on October 7, 1931. He came from a long line of distinguished ancestors. His family was connected with those of John Greenleaf Whittier and Daniel Webster. His father, Judge Henry F. French, was Assistant Secretary of the U.S. Treasury under three presidential administrations.

The French home in Exeter is said to have had a charming environment, so the boy grew up in happy surroundings. However, sadness entered the home, because Mrs. French died when Daniel was only six years old. He had two sisters and a brother who later became director of the Chicago Art Museum.

When Daniel was ten the family moved to Cambridge, Massachusetts, where the judge remarried. The children all became very fond of their stepmother.

The boy attended public schools in Cambridge and later the Massachusetts Institute of Technology for a year. The judge did not try to force Daniel into choosing a profession. He let him decide for himself what his life work would be.

The story goes that young French really stumbled into his talent and life-long career by a fortunate incident. One day the mood took him to carve a turnip into "a grotesque image of a frog dressed in clothes." The boy took it into the house and showed it to his family. The wise stepmother recognized his talent and exclaimed, "Daniel there is your life work!" Both parents encouraged him to get the necessary training for this profession.

The French and Alcott families were neighbors and good friends. Mary Alcott, an artist and sister of Louisa May, the noted writer, helped Daniel by lending him her modeling tools. The evening he first got them from her all members of the French family sat around a big table and tried their hands at this new craft.

At first the boy modeled birds and animals, but he turned from this to portraiture and made several busts of neighbors. Mary Alcott gave him constructive criticism of his pieces of sculpture.

There was no art school in Boston, but Daniel did study anatomy there for a time. Then he had the opportunity of working for a month in Brooklyn at the school of John Quincy Adams Ward, "the Dean of American sculpture."

In 1875, just before the centennial of the Battle of Concord, the people of Concord wanted to erect an appropriate memorial at the spot where the raw colonists had met the trained British redcoats in 1775. The council asked for plans.

Young French modestly presented his design. It was accepted, and the sculptor received his first commission when he was only twenty-three years old. He asked only $400 to cover his expenses; later the town paid him $1,000.

On July 4, 1875, the *Minute Man* was unveiled and dedicated. It depicts a young farmer standing by a plow with one hand on it while the other grasps a musket. His head is alert, as if he were awaiting a summons, and his body is held ready for an advance.

> The little town of Concord might well reckon itself fortunate. It had furnished the men for the battle, the poet for the celebration, and the sculptor . . . all without going beyond its borders.

The first stanza of Emerson's *Concord Hymn* is inscribed on the base of the statue. Copies of the figure are now seen in several New

England towns, and during World War II the *Minute Man* was depicted on defense bonds, stamps, and posters.

Soon after this, French spent a year abroad studying with Thomas Bell, one of the best American sculptors of the period. This was practically all the formal training that French was to receive; he learned his art mostly by himself. When he came home, he brought with him his *Sleeping Endymion,* done in the classic Greek style.

Between French's first triumph in 1875 and his Lincoln statue in 1922, "there issued from his studio a constant stream of sculpture." In 1884 he created the seated figure of John Harvard, at Cambridge, Massachusetts, praised for its "fine dignity and simplicity." Now the artist was becoming well known and was kept busy doing huge figures for the custom houses at Philadelphia, Boston, and St. Louis. At the latter building he created an enormous statue of War and Peace.

In 1886 French went to Paris and studied there for a time. In 1893 he modeled the gigantic figure of Republic, a stately goddess that stood in the Court of Honor at the Columbian Exposition in Chicago. In the same year he created *Death Staying the Hand of the Sculptor* at Forest Hills Cemetery in Boston. Many consider it his masterpiece; it is a memorial relief for the tomb of the Boston sculptor Martin Milmore (1844–1883).

French was a hard worker and a prolific one. His many works include varying subjects, such as the Palmer Memorial, Wellesley; Gallaudet and his deaf-mute pupil; Flanders Field, Boston; General Lewis Cass; Admiral Farragut; the Marshall Field Memorial, Chicago; and the Dupont Fountain, Washington, D.C.

When he was commissioned to do an equestrian statue of George Washington, to be set up in Paris, the sculptor did the figure of the general, but he had the assistance of Edward C. Potter in creating the horse.

French made three pairs of bronze doors for the Boston Public Library, 1902; groups of the four continents for the New York Custom House, 1907; the "standing" Lincoln, for the city of Lincoln, Nebraska, 1912; the statue of Emerson for the Concord Public Library, 1914; the Alma Mater, at Columbia University, 1915; and the First Division Memorial, Washington, 1924.

The monuments characteristic of Daniel Chester French are said to be idealized personifications, broadly handled, the sentimental element being stronger in them than in the works of Augustus Saint-Gaudens, who influenced the sculptor in several ways.

Frequently honored by awards and degrees, French was important in setting the standards of official monumental sculpture for several decades.

J. Walker McSpadden called French:

> . . . A sculptor who has probably contributed more than any other one man to the public memorials, historic and personal, of his country; whose output has been uniformly high in quality; and whose fertility of invention and grace of flowing line have invested each and every subject with potent charm. . . .

French's work coincided with the rise of American art. In his younger days, American artists had looked to European and classic models. Now America had developed its own native art, which the sculptor believed was as good as that of any other country at the time, and asserted:

> It is my proudest boast that I have had a part in this movement—that I and a group of men I knew have worked in this formative period. With the group of men now working, the future of American art, and particularly sculpture, is assured.

The majestic marble statue of Lincoln completely dominates the interior of the memorial. It is enshrined in a dignified setting and shows Lincoln as the wartime President, in an attitude of contemplation. The realistic figure is seated in a flag-draped chair, facing outward.

The work is made from crystalline Georgia marble, constructed of blocks so perfectly interlocked that the statue seems like one huge monolith. It rests on an oblong pedestal of Tennessee marble, about 10 feet high, 18 feet wide, and 19 feet deep at the base. This in turn is placed on a platform of Tennessee marble.

At first the statue was to have been 10 feet in height. However, when experiments were made with the sculptor's original model, it was decided that if a figure of that size were used, it would be "dwarfed and out of scale" in the large hall where it was to be placed. Therefore the commission made a change in their contract with the artist, doubling the size of the Lincoln figure, making it 20 feet tall. The scale is such that if Lincoln were standing, he would be 28 feet high. The extreme width of the statue, including the drapery over the chair, is the same as its height.

Above the figure of the Civil War President are these words:

IN THIS TEMPLE
AS IN THE HEARTS OF THE PEOPLE
FOR WHOM HE SAVED THE UNION
THE MEMORY OF ABRAHAM LINCOLN IS ENSHRINED FOREVER

For the statue, twenty-eight blocks of white Georgia marble were quarried and each portion had to be perfect. The pieces were of different sizes and weights. To aid in the work of carving the sections, French called to his assistance a remarkable group of six brothers of an Italian family in New York. They were the sons of Giuseppe Piccirilli, who was an artist of great ability in the line of marblecutting. His sons were not only skilled in doing individual work but also expert in carrying out designs of other sculptors.

The artist prepared a small working model, about 3 feet in height (later he executed the head, full size). Then for four years, assisted personally by French, the Piccirilli brothers carved and assembled the sections of the figure in their New York studio.

THE DEDICATION

Finally, seven years after the laying of the cornerstone, the Lincoln Memorial was completed. Dedication ceremonies were conducted on the afternoon of Memorial Day, 1922. Some 3,500 engraved invitations had been sent out to President Harding, high civilian and military government officials, officers of the various patriotic societies, and distinguished citizens.

An honored guest was the venerable Robert T. Lincoln, oldest son of the martyred President. He had served as Secretary of War in the cabinets of Presidents Garfield and Arthur and as minister to Great Britain under President Benjamin Harrison. When Robert Lincoln arrived that day at the memorial and took his seat, he was given a tremendous ovation.

The day was bright and sunny, but not too hot. The grounds around the memorial were thronged with people, a crowd estimated at about 50,000. Amplifiers aided in hearing the program, which was broadcast to all parts of the nation.

Chief Justice Taft had been the chairman of the Lincoln Memorial Commission since its inception. He was in charge of the program.

In the prayer of dedication Bishop Samuel W. Fallows included these words:

> We thank Thee that the wrath of war has been settled, that brother no longer strives against brother, and that the whole people have come to realize the excelling greatness of Abraham Lincoln, that we once again have one country, one flag, and one destiny. . . .

Dr. Robert R. Moton, president of Tuskegee Institute, gave an excellent address, in which he touched on racial relations. (Although spoken forty-five years ago, his words are applicable today.) In part, Dr. Moton said:

> The claim of greatness for Abraham Lincoln lies in this, that amid doubt and distrust, against the counsel of chosen advisers, in the hour of the nation's peril, he put his trust in God and spoke the word that gave freedom to a race and vindicated the honor of a nation conceived in liberty and dedicated to the proposition that all men are created equal.
>
> Lincoln has not died in vain. Slowly through the years that noble spirit has been permeating every section of our land and country. Sixty years ago he stood in lonely grandeur above a torn and bleeding nation, a towering figure of patient righteousness.
>
> Today his spirit animates the breasts of millions of his countrymen, who unite with us to pay tribute to his lofty character and his immortal deed. . . .
>
> I somehow believe that all of us, black and white, both North and South, are going to strive on to finish the work which he so nobly began, to make America an example for the world of equal opportunity for all who strive and are willing to serve under the flag that makes men free. . . .

Edwin Markham read one of his greatest poems, *Lincoln, the Man of the People*. He dedicated the work to the Lincoln Memorial, "this far-shining monument of remembrance erected in immortal marble to our deathless martyr, the consecrated statesman, the ideal American, the ever-beloved friend of humanity."

Following the singing of *The Battle Hymn of the Republic* Chief Justice Taft made the speech of presentation of the Lincoln Memorial to President Harding. In his address, the Chief Justice told how the idea of the monument had been conceived and carried out, and he described the structure as

> a shrine at which all can worship, an altar upon which the supreme sacrifice was made for liberty; a sacred religious refuge in which those who love country and love God can find inspiration and repose. . . .

VISITORS' REACTIONS TO THE LINCOLN MEMORIAL

The memorial is under the care of the National Park Service. It is open to the public daily from 8 A.M. until midnight and is closed only once a year, on Christmas Day. Annually about 2.5 million persons visit it.

It is interesting to note their varied reactions. One source has stated: "Many come, but few linger at a shrine that for all its beauty is remote, aloof, and unreal."

In the magazine *This Week* in 1958, Ralph Newman in an article, "Lincoln Was One of Us," has given vivid descriptions of the kinds of spectators who stand before the seated figure: "Chatting and laughing, they come by ones and twos and busloads to the imposing marble memorial to Lincoln. They leave, most of them, solemn and subdued."

There is always an especially large number of visitors each year on Abraham Lincoln's birthday—February 12—when the annual ceremony of laying wreaths at his statue occurs. But every day in the year hundreds of ordinary citizens, from far and near, arrive to pay their respects to the best-loved of American Presidents.

One visitor from the West Coast said that although he had been there many times before, he always left with "a feeling of peace and confidence." This man especially enjoyed coming at night, when the soft lighting made Lincoln seem very close to him.

Some tourists take time to stand at the south wall and read through the Gettysburg Address, ending with those inspiring words that still ring down through the ages—words that have a vital message for all Americans today:

> . . . It is for us the living rather to be dedicated here to the unfinished work which they who fought here have thus far so nobly advanced. It is rather for us to be here dedicated to the great task remaining before us; that from these honored dead we take increased devotion to that cause for which they gave the last full measure of devotion—that we here highly resolve that these dead shall not have died in vain—that this nation under God shall have a new birth of freedom, and that government of the people, by the people, for the people, shall not perish from the earth.

Other visitors may pause at the north wall, where inscribed in stone is another incomparable Lincoln speech, his Second Inaugural Address, delivered in March, 1865. In this, Lincoln touched on the events of the past four Civil War years and noted the fact that both sides had prayed that God would aid them. He asserted:

> It may seem strange that any men should dare to ask a just God's assistance in wringing their bread from the sweat of other men's faces, but let us judge not that we be not judged. . . .

The President prayed that "the mighty scourge of this war may speedily pass away" and declared his belief that "the judgments of the Lord are true and righteous altogether." He ended with words that continue to thrill all who read them. He stated his attitude toward both North and South and revealed his plans and determination to conclude the unhappy struggle and to bring the two sections of our nation together again. This Second Inaugural reveals Lincoln's great spirit and shows what might have happened much sooner if he had lived "to bind up the nation's wounds":

> With malice toward none, with charity for all, with firmness in the right as God gives us to see the right, let us strive on to finish the work we are in, to bind up the nation's wounds, to care for him who shall have borne the battle, and for his widow and his orphan—to do all which may achieve and cherish a just and lasting peace among ourselves and with all nations.

The well-known author Catherine Marshall told of a childhood incident in an article, "What I Learned About Lincoln," which appeared in the *Christian Herald* for February, 1959. When she was eight years old she stood with her parents before the statue in the memorial and listened intently as her father read the inscription. Then she startled her parents by saying, "I think I'll climb up and sit on his lap."

At that, her mother grasped her hand tightly, so she was not able to carry out her wish. However, Mrs. Marshall felt that even if the guard had objected, Abraham Lincoln and Daniel Chester French would have approved. The President had always attracted small girls because of his kindly manner toward them. And in this work of sculpture, its creator "had captured in marble, compassion and tenderness, fatherliness and humor, strength and humanity."

THE SOUTHERNERS JOIN IN

The Los Angeles Times for February 13, 1954, had this headline, "The Southerners Join Lincoln Observance, Sons of the Confederacy Break Tradition at Capital Rites."

Johnny Reb broke with nearly a century of tradition today and honored the Civil War President, Abraham Lincoln, on the 145th anniversary of his birth.

President Eisenhower took part in this annual wreath-laying ceremony, which is sponsored by the Military Order of the Loyal Legion. His wreath of red, white, and blue carnations was the largest floral offering; but the 1,000 or more persons who had braved the windy, subfreezing weather to see the yearly rite appeared to be more interested in a magnolia wreath with two small Confederate flags attached to it.

This wreath was brought by Colonel John Virden, whose grandfather had served in the Second Arkansas Cavalry with the Confederate Army. The officer was representing the Sons of the Confederacy; they had resolved, for the first time, to accept the offer made them by the Sons of Union Veterans to participate in the wreath-laying ceremony. The colonel said: "We decided ninety years was long enough to hold a grudge; Lincoln belonged to all the people. He was a good deal more than just an Illinois Republican."

Colonel Virden, a native of Seminole, Oklahoma, was then helping publish the *Air Force Daily*. During World War II he had been General Eisenhower's press officer.

When the President's car rolled up to the Lincoln Memorial that February day, the colonel greeted the chief executive warmly, and both saluted. Then President Eisenhower walked up the long flight of steps, accompanied by military aides. Before the giant statue of Abraham Lincoln, he paused, removed his hat, and laid his wreath beside the one of southern magnolias. For a moment he stood silent with uncovered head. Then he turned and walked briskly down the steps.

That year's ceremony had a unique feature in that it was directed by General Ulysses Grant III, grandson of the eighteenth President. General Grant told reporters that he was very pleased that the Confederate group had taken part in the ceremony. "It's time," he commented, "old wounds were healed."

A 1963 MEETING AT THE MEMORIAL

An entirely different kind of meeting occurred near the Memorial in August, 1963.

In June, a short time before, President John F. Kennedy had recommended to Congress a Civil Rights Bill. He asserted:

> This nation, for all its hopes and all its boasts, will not be fully free, until all its citizens are free. . . .
>
> The heart of the question is whether we are going to treat our fellow Americans as we want to be treated. If an American, because his skin is black . . . cannot enjoy the fullest free life, which all of us want, then who among us would be content to have the color of his skin changed, and stand in his place?

Hoping to help speed the Civil Rights Bill through Congress, 200,000 persons from many states took part in a march on Washington. Most of them were Negroes, but about 20,000 were white men and women who joined in the march because they believed the cause of the Negroes was a just one.

On the morning of August 28 the great throng gathered in the Mall. As they waited for the formal program to begin, they picnicked on the grass and sang. Often the words of their favorite freedom song were heard:

> We shall overcome,
> Black and white together,
> We shall overcome someday.

Early in the afternoon the immense gathering made its way to the Lincoln Memorial, where the solemn statue of the Civil War President looked down on the assembly.

Among the speakers was Dr. Martin Luther King, Jr., who spoke of his hope that in the future his children would not be judged by the color of their skin. He said: "I have a dream that one day this nation will rise up and live out the true meaning of its creed—we hold these truths to be self-evident that all men are created equal."

Dr. King believed the new Civil Rights Bill would help in the realization of his dream for his people. However, the courageous and far-seeing young President was killed before Congress passed this important measure. But under his successor, Lyndon B. Johnson, the bill became law in 1964.

PRESIDENT JOHNSON AT THE MEMORIAL

At Christmas the same year there was another notable gathering at the Lincoln Memorial attended by the chief executive. More than 15,000 people waited in freezing temperatures to see a new and unique ceremony.

This rite was under the direction of the Interreligious Committee on Race Relations. The group was headed by three religious leaders of different faiths: a Negro Baptist, the president of a Jewish community, and a Roman Catholic priest. They lighted a candle at John F. Kennedy's grave and carried it across the Potomac River to the Lincoln Memorial.

When the candle was given to the President, he cupped it in his hands, then an aide took it. At once thousands of other candles began to dot the twilight with their glow, in front of the huge memorial.

President Johnson made a brief speech which one reporter said "rang with phrases sounded at Gettysburg one hundred years and a month ago."

> We have been bent in sorrow, but not in purpose. We buried Abraham Lincoln and John Kennedy, but we did not bury their dreams or their visions.
>
> Thirty days and a few hours ago, John F. Kennedy, thirty-fifth President of the United States, died a martyr's death. The world will not forget what he did here. He will live on in our hearts, which will be his shrine.

President Johnson also asserted that Kennedy, like Lincoln, had "malice toward none," and he would be remembered for his "fight for a better life for our people."

> Let this be for all people in need of the light of an era of new hope. May God bless this land and all who live in it.
>
> Let us determine that John Kennedy did not live or die in vain, that this nation, under God, shall have a new birth of freedom, and that we shall achieve in our time the ancient vision of peace on earth, goodwill to men.

TRIBUTES TO LINCOLN

Ever since Lincoln's death, in 1865, untold volumes, poems, and articles have been written about him, and each year such material increases.

One poet, Edmund Vance Cook (1865–1932), in writing of Lincoln's birth, told of the bad luck that had come by the birth of a son to Tom and Nance Lincoln: "Poor youngster, born without a chance!"

> A bronzed, lank man; his suit of ancient black,
> A famous high top hat and plain worn shawl.
> —Vachel Lindsay

> Lincoln . . . six feet one, in his stocking feet,
> The lank man, knotty and tough as a hickory rail. . . .
> —Stephen Vincent Bénet

> Giant, he walked among his people then,
> Homely of features, beautiful of soul. . . .
>
> —Elaine V. Emans

> Here was a man to hold against the world,
> A man to match the mountains and the sea.
>
> —Edwin Markham

Walt Whitman, who idolized Abraham Lincoln, wrote his famous poem *O Captain! My Captain!* to his memory. In it he stated that

> The ship has weathered every rack, the prize we sought is won . . .

But on

> . . . the deck, my Captain lies, fallen cold and dead.

In his quatrain *In a Back Alley*, Carl Sandburg writes that newsboys were pitching pennies with a dead man's face on them:

> Remembrance for a great man is this . . .
> Dear lover of boys, what do you ask for now?

What was it that made this plain man of the people what he was, the human being who was so worthy of the mighty memorial that has been raised in his honor? Through the many decades which have passed, men have tried to discover and express the qualities that made him great. Here are some samplings of the varied estimates that have been made of his life and works:

> Abraham Lincoln . . . who was at home and welcome with the humblest, and with a spirit and a practical vein in the times of terror, that commanded the admiration of the wisest. His heart was as great as the world, but there was no room in it to hold the memory of a wrong.
>
> —Ralph Waldo Emerson

> He leaves for America's history and biography, so far, not only its most dramatic reminiscence—he leaves, in my opinion, the greatest, best, most characteristic, artistic, moral personality.
>
> —Walt Whitman

The best loved face in the world, also the best known face, is that of Abraham Lincoln.

Sometimes you look at it and wonder why. It has no form or comeliness nor beauty in it that we should desire him. . . . It calls to mind the fact that one's beauty is not in the features nor form, but in the soul. . . . America is truly fortunate in having a figure like Abraham Lincoln, standing out like a peak in history, and moulding the characters of the coming generation.

—Dr. Frank Crane

In 1959, at the one hundred and fiftieth anniversary of Lincoln's birth, Carl Sandburg, "the white-maned poet with a cowlick over his left eye," appeared before a joint session of Congress. He was introduced as "the man who probably knows more about Abraham Lincoln than anyone else in the world."

Then for eighteen minutes the 81-year-old poet "brought members of Congress to the verge of tears," as he spoke of the incomparable Lincoln. Sandburg painted a full picture of the Civil War President:

The man of compassion, who, controlled by events, became a dictator to save the Union, the man, who tried, unsuccessfully, to persuade the North to compensate the South for the loss of its Negro slaves, and who, failing, freed them by fiat and thereby confiscated nearly four million dollars' worth of property. But Lincoln's policies were aimed at saving the Union. . . .

The most enduring memorial to Lincoln is in the hearts of lovers of liberty. . . . It is these who understand that wherever there is freedom, there have been those who have fought and sacrificed for it. . . .

Not often in the story of mankind does a man arrive on earth who is as hard as a rock and as soft as drifting fog, who holds in his heart and mind the paradox of the terrible storm and peace unspeakable and perfect.

In the Los Angeles *Examiner* for February 15, 1959, Harry Golden wrote an article, "Lincoln Was Great and He Was Human"; here are some excerpts from this writing:

I do think we sometimes disguise Lincoln's greatness by trying to pretend that he was some sort of a romantic hillbilly. The reason for this is that Lincoln has not yet become remote history.

And because he is not yet remote history, it amazes us that this country could have produced a Lincoln. . . . More than an American embodiment, Lincoln was a supremely moral man. . . . He was not simply a rawboned son of the Illinois frontier. . . . He was a superior man.

"Stevenson Pays Tribute to Republican Lincoln" is the title of an article in the Los Angeles *Examiner* for February 2, 1959. Adlai Stevenson declared that since his death Abraham Lincoln has become a symbol not only to Americans but also to men everywhere.

But the universality of his appeal is more than that, and is found in the character of the man himself. Other statesmen have become remote in greatness—Lincoln never did. He has lived on for the people as a man. . . .

Lincoln believed firmly in social evolution, a kind of inevitability for human improvement, and saw the democratic form of government as the most promising environment for that evolution. . . .

How did Lincoln arrive at this deep faith in mankind? Because he was one of them. He knew nothing of privilege; born in poverty, schooling himself, working incredibly hard for every personal advancement, he knew the people, good and bad, ridiculous and sublime—and he believed there was more good than bad in most of them. . . .

And so, while statesmen come and statesmen go, Lincoln in his person and in his life work remains the greatest democrat of us all, and a continuing inspiration to all mankind.

13

The Jefferson Memorial

======

If you are fortunate enough to be in Washington, D.C., in the spring when the world-famous Japanese flowering cherry trees are in bloom, you will get a charming picture of the handsome memorial to our outstanding third President, Thomas Jefferson.

It is at this time that the monument receives the most notice from the public. For the white and pink blossoms make an incomparable setting for the stately building. (These trees were a gift from Japan, as related in the Washington Monument chapter.)

On the south bank of the Tidal Basin, with the flowering trees in the foreground, the Jefferson Memorial with its great columns and rounded dome rises in impressive fashion. This distinctive national monument is under the supervision of the Capital National Park System, United States Department of the Interior, and is open to the public from 8 A.M. to 12 P.M.

When the time came to erect a memorial to Thomas Jefferson, those to Washington and Lincoln had already been completed. The fact of Jefferson's great importance as one of the foremost men in our national history required that an impressive monument be erected in his honor. The average citizen believes that these three men "have contributed the most to our independence, to the preservation of the Union, and to its concepts of liberty and democracy."

The Jefferson Memorial, its curved outline contrasting with the rectangular mass of the Lincoln Memorial and the sheerness of the Washington Monument, gives Jefferson a noble memorial, worthily

236

placed in conformity with his importance and with the plan of the city of Washington.

—Stanley W. McClure

THE BUILDING OF THE MEMORIAL

Provision to erect this monument to Jefferson was made by an act of Congress approved on June 26, 1934. At once a commission of twelve members, including three appointed by the President, three by the President of the Senate, and three by the House of Representatives, was set up. Their duties were to plan the edifice, by securing a suitable design, then to supervise the erection of the monument.

The president of the Thomas Jefferson Memorial Foundation was Stuart G. Gibboney of New York City. The commission held its first meeting on April 22, 1935. When Mr. Gibboney died, in 1944, Senator Elbert D. Thomas of Utah was elected chairman of the commission.

Several sites were suggested, and on February 18, 1937, the group selected the final location. The erection of the monument at this spot necessitated the removal of some cherry trees, and there was considerable public criticism about this. However, the opposition subsided when it was learned that only 171 of the 2,700 cherry trees in Potomac Park had to be cut down.

At this same 1937 meeting the commission designated the National Park Service as the agency to construct the memorial and accepted the design by John Russell Pope, called the "Circular Plan."

This noted architect was born in New York, on April 24, 1874. He attended the College of the City of New York and in 1894 graduated from the School of Mines at Columbia University. Afterward Mr. Pope studied in Rome and Paris and then practiced architecture in New York City. He designed several important structures in various cities, including the Terminal Station in Richmond, Virginia; the Lincoln Memorial in Hodgenville, Kentucky; the Roosevelt memorials in New York and Washington; and the National Gallery of Art, in Washington.

The Thomas Jefferson Memorial was designed by Pope in the classic Greco-Roman style so much admired by our third President.

(When Mr. Pope died, in August, 1937, the surviving members of his firm, Daniel P. Higgins and Otto R. Eggers, were appointed to serve as the architects.)

These men showed their respect for President Jefferson's wishes by erecting a monument to his memory that was in keeping with his individual liking. They were strongly influenced by his own tastes, as expressed in his writings, also in the buildings which he designed. Jefferson was a great admirer of the Pantheon in Rome and of the work of Andrea Palladio, a sixteenth-century Italian architect. In planning the capitol at Richmond, the rotunda at the University of Virginia in Charlotteville, and Monticello, his own distinctive residence nearby, he showed his fondness for circular features and the classic approach which he is said to have introduced into the New World.

On December 15, 1938, there were groundbreaking ceremonies for the Thomas Jefferson Memorial, attended by hundreds of spectators, in which President Franklin D. Roosevelt took part. The same gilded spade was used on this occasion as had been utilized for the groundbreakings for the Tomb of the Unknown Soldier and the Lincoln Memorial. The President handed the spade to Stuart G. Gibboney, who turned over the first spadeful of earth.

Then, on November 15, 1939, the laying of the cornerstone occurred under ideal weather conditions. About twenty-five hundred persons saw President Roosevelt lay the cornerstone; members of the Thomas Jefferson Memorial Commission were present, as were several Cabinet members and other high government officials. President Roosevelt made a short address on the life and works of Thomas Jefferson and commented on the memorial to be erected in his honor. The ceremonies were broadcast all over the United States.

Following is a list of the articles which were placed in the cornerstone: a copy of the Declaration of Independence; a copy of the U.S. Constitution; *The Life and Morals of Jesus of Nazareth*, by Thomas Jefferson; *The Writings of Thomas Jefferson*, by Paul Leicester Ford (10 volumes); a copy of the annual report of the Thomas Jefferson Memorial Commission for 1939; and one copy each of the Washington *Post*, *Evening Star*, *Times-Herald*, and *Daily News*.

About four years later, on April 13, 1943, the two hundredth anniversery of Jefferson's birth, the strikingly handsome Jefferson Memorial was dedicated. It is a splendid circular building enclosed by a colonnade and surmounted by a great dome in classic style, similar to the work of Palladio. The cost was $3 million.

The walls and dome are of white Danby Imperial Vermont marble and reach about 96 feet above the level of the walk, which encircles the structure inside the colonnade. The building is 152 feet in diameter.

Leading from the edge of the Tidal Basin to the building are three wide flights of steps on which at intervals are level platforms. The entrance steps are flanked by beautifully planted terraces. Twelve massive columns support the portico, with eight of them extending across the front.

The visitor enters the Jefferson Memorial on the north side. As one walks up the steps, he can see in the pediment above the entrance a large sculptured group created by Adolph A. Weiman.

Weiman was born at Karlsruhe, Germany, on December 11, 1870, and came to the United States as a child. He studied art in New York under the famous Augustus Saint-Gaudens and became a member of the National Academy. Like those of John Russell Pope, the works of Weiman may be seen in various places. Besides pieces of sculpture, he created the victory button in 1919 and designs for a new dime and a half-dollar.

Weiman's pediment depicts the committee of five men who had been selected by the Continental Congress to draft the Declaration of Independence. They are shown at the end of their labors; Thomas Jefferson is reading the completed draft to his associates. The members, from left to right, are Benjamin Franklin, John Adams, Jefferson, Roger Sherman, and Robert Livingston.

As you enter the memorial, you are in a central room 86½ feet in diameter. In its center stands the heroic bronze figure of Jefferson, by Rudulph Evans, which completely dominates the room. You can look up at the high-domed ceiling of Indiana limestone, which reaches 67 feet above the head of the gigantic statue. The floor is of pink Tennessee marble.

Evans was born in Washington, D.C., on February 1, 1878. His art education was obtained in Washington, at the Corcoran Art School, and also in New York and Paris. He was given a bronze medal at the Paris Salon in 1914, and the French Cross of the Legion of Honor in

1934. Among his many fine works are busts of such noted persons as Longfellow, Robert E. Lee, and John D. Rockefeller. His model for the Jefferson figure was chosen in competition in 1941.

The 19-foot statue shows Thomas Jefferson standing—in marked contrast to the "seated" Lincoln in *his* memorial. The figure is mounted on a pedestal of black Minnesota granite that reaches 6 feet above the floor. The dates of Jefferson's birth and death—1743 and 1826—are inscribed in bronze at the front of the pedestal. A temporary figure in plaster was set up here in 1942, and then in April, 1947, the final huge bronze figure was put in position.

Some of the most important words ever written by Thomas Jefferson appear in the circular frieze around the memorial room:

I HAVE SWORN UPON THE ALTAR OF GOD ETERNAL HOSTILITY AGAINST EVERY FORM OF TYRANNY OVER THE MIND OF MAN.

At a meeting on October 19, 1939, the commission chose these words—suggested by Dr. Fiske Kimball—to be used in the frieze. This sentence appears in a letter which Thomas Jefferson had written to his good friend Benjamin Rush on September 22, 1800, from Monticello, at the time Jefferson was in his campaign for the Presidency. In these words he was complaining about the attacks that had been made upon him in the state of Connecticut and in other places in regard to his religious beliefs. The quotation was well chosen, for it expresses his strong opposition not only to religious tyranny but also to all forms of tyranny.

Opening from the circular interior are four colonnaded doorways, each having two large columns. Thus visitors can look at the towering statue of Jefferson from several different angles and see it in varying lights and shades.

On the interior walls, of white Georgia marble, are four large oblong panels surmounted by festoons. The panels, carved in bronze, are inscribed with selections from Jefferson's writings that affirm his fundamental beliefs and philosophy.

You can read on the southwest wall passages from the Declaration of Independence. These well-known phrases are most appropriate here, in the first space; for it was Jefferson's earnest wish that he be remembered, first of all, as the author of the most celebrated American document: the Declaration of Independence.

> WE HOLD THESE TRUTHS TO BE SELF-
> EVIDENT: THAT ALL MEN ARE CREATED
> EQUAL, THAT THEY ARE ENDOWED BY THEIR
> CREATOR WITH CERTAIN UNALIENABLE
> RIGHTS. THAT AMONG THESE ARE LIFE, LIBERTY
> AND THE PURSUIT OF HAPPINESS. THAT
> TO SECURE THESE RIGHTS GOVERNMENTS
> ARE INSTITUTED AMONG MEN. WE . . .
> SOLEMNLY PUBLISH AND DECLARE THAT
> THESE UNITED COLONIES ARE AND OF RIGHT
> OUGHT TO BE FREE AND INDEPENDENT
> STATES . . . AND ASK FOR THE SUPPORT OF THIS
> DECLARATION, WITH A FIRM RELIANCE
> ON THE PROTECTION OF DIVINE
> PROVIDENCE. WE MUTUALLY PLEDGE
> OUR LIVES, OUR FORTUNES AND OUR
> SACRED HONOUR.

The second panel carries excerpts from Thomas Jefferson's Statute of Religious Freedom, which he promulgated in the Virginia legislature. It embodies his firm doctrine of the freedom of the mind.

> ALMIGHTY GOD HATH CREATED THE
> MIND FREE. ALL ATTEMPTS TO INFLUENCE
> IT BY TEMPORAL PUNISHMENTS OR
> BURTHENS . . . ARE A DEPARTURE FROM
> THE PLAN OF THE HOLY AUTHOR OF
> OUR RELIGION. . . . NO MAN SHALL BE
> COMPELLED TO FREQUENT OR SUPPORT
> ANY RELIGIOUS WORSHIP OR MINISTRY
> OR SHALL OTHERWISE SUFFER ON
> ACCOUNT OF HIS RELIGIOUS OPINIONS
> OR BELIEF. BUT ALL MEN SHALL BE
> FREE TO PROFESS AND BY ARGUMENT
> TO MAINTAIN, THEIR OPINIONS IN
> MATTERS OF RELIGION. I KNOW

BUT ONE CODE OF MORALITY FOR
MEN WHETHER ACTING SINGLY OR
COLLECTIVELY.

In the northeast quadrant, the third panel is devoted to Jefferson's strong belief in the freedom of the individual and to the great need for educating the mass of the population.

Thomas Jefferson was one of the first Americans to argue forcefully that slavery is inconsistent in a democratic state. Although his efforts to abolish slavery were not successful, he was among the first to oppose it. Hal Boyle says: "although he inherited 30 slaves at age 14, he detested slavery, signed a federal act outlawing the slave trade and freed his own slaves at his death."

Jefferson also believed that founding the University of Virginia was one of his greatest achievements. During his entire career, he continued to stress the fact that general education of the people "is necessary to efficient self-government."

Here is the third panel inscription:

GOD WHO GAVE US LIFE GAVE US
LIBERTY. CAN THE LIBERTIES OF A
NATION BE SECURE WHEN WE HAVE
REMOVED A CONVICTION THAT THESE
LIBERTIES ARE THE GIFT OF GOD?
INDEED I TREMBLE FOR MY COUNTRY
WHEN I REFLECT THAT GOD IS JUST,
THAT HIS JUSTICE CANNOT SLEEP FOR-
EVER. COMMERCE BETWEEN MASTER
AND SLAVE IS DESPOTISM. NOTHING
IS MORE CERTAINLY WRITTEN IN THE
BOOK OF FATE THAN THAT THESE
PEOPLE ARE TO BE FREE. ESTABLISH
THE LAW FOR EDUCATING THE COMMON
PEOPLE. THIS IS THE BUSINESS
OF THE STATE TO EFFECT AND ON
A GENERAL PLAN.

Jefferson's words on the fourth panel show his unusual vision in matters of government. In a letter to a friend, he wrote that "the laws and institutions must go hand in hand, with the progress of the human mind." So, from the words here we learn that Jefferson's far-seeing mind realized that changes in laws and institutions would be necessary in a democracy, as circumstances changed.

> I AM NOT AN ADVOCATE FOR FREQUENT
> CHANGES IN LAW AND CONSTITUTIONS.
> BUT LAWS AND INSTITUTIONS MUST GO
> HAND IN HAND WITH THE PROGRESS
> OF THE HUMAN MIND. AS THAT BECOMES
> MORE DEVELOPED, MORE ENLIGHTENED,
> AS NEW DISCOVERIES ARE MADE, NEW
> TRUTHS DISCOVERED AND MANNERS AND
> OPINIONS CHANGE, WITH THE CHANGE
> OF CIRCUMSTANCES, INSTITUTIONS
> MUST ADVANCE ALSO TO KEEP PACE
> WITH THE TIMES. WE MIGHT AS WELL
> REQUIRE A MAN TO WEAR STILL THE
> COAT WHICH FITTED HIM WHEN A BOY
> AS CIVILIZED SOCIETY TO REMAIN
> EVER UNDER THE REGIMEN OF THEIR
> BARBAROUS ANCESTORS.

Outside, on the portico and along the colonnade, you may study interesting architectural details. It is worthwhile, too, to see the way the terrain has been landscaped, its simplicity in harmony with the character of Jefferson. This work was supervised by "the dean of American landscape architects," Frederick Law Olmstead of Brookline, Massachusetts.

Plants from Jefferson's native Virginia and from lands where he served abroad have been used here. Flanking the portico are English and Irish yews, while at both sides of the steps are seen American holly trees and pines. In addition, firethorn, winter jasmine, and flowering dogwood add to the beauty of the landscape—as well as the cherry trees.

As at the Washington and Lincoln memorials, observances occur regularly at the Jefferson Memorial. One of the most important and well attended is the yearly celebration of Jefferson's birthday, on

April 13; this is a colorful affair that started in 1942, sponsored by the District of Columbia Society Sons of the American Revolution and the National Park Service. Also, each Wednesday during June, July, and August, at 8:30 P.M., the Torchlight Tattoo, a military pageant, is held.

Jefferson, the "Sage of Monticello," was also dubbed the "Inventor President." Among his most important traits were his unusual versatility and the remarkable practical application of his vast knowledge to many fields of endeavor. He was especially outstanding in architecture. One contemporary said of him:

> He may have been our most remarkable American, a gentleman who could calculate an eclipse, survey an estate, tie an artery, plan an edifice, try a cause, break a horse, dance a minuet, and play a violin.

In 1769, at the age of twenty-six, Thomas Jefferson was a member of the House of Burgesses, where he employed his brains in building up the then rather slipshod laws and government of his native Virginia.

When the American colonists began to rebel against their unjust treatment by the mother country, young Jefferson "plunged into the dawning struggle for American liberty." Soon Great Britain declared him an outlaw.

For the tall, red-haired Virginian, the greatest day of his entire life was July 4, 1776, when the Declaration of Independence was accepted and approved by the Continental Congress.

In the eighty-three years of his productive life, Jefferson founded the University of Virginia, was governor of Virginia, our first Secretary of State, minister to France, Vice-President under John Adams, and third President, serving two terms. As President he founded West Point, halted the slave trade, engineered the purchase of the Louisiana Territory, originated the decimal system of our money—in short, he was "master of all he undertook."

He was a prolific writer and turned out millions of words before the era of typewriters. Jefferson collected 10,000 books; these became the nucleus of the Congressional Library. Although Thomas Jefferson died a poor man, he enriched our country and the world beyond all calculation.

He was never afraid to express himself or to state his firm convictions on many different and highly controversial subjects. His great belief in several kinds of freedom expressed itself in these words already quoted: "I have sworn upon the altar of God eternal hostility against every form of tyranny over the mind of man."

This may be called "the creed of his political and social philosophy." His stern opposition to tyranny in all of its forms was voiced repeatedly. In the Declaration of Independence it appears in the famous phrase ". . . that all men are created equal, that they are endowed by their Creator with certain unalienable rights . . ." It is also seen in his Virginia Statute of Religious Freedom as ". . . well aware that Almighty God hath created the mind free . . ."

Thomas Jefferson believed in a simple, democratic form of government, freedom of the press, and education of the masses, asserting:

> If the children are untaught, their ignorance and vices will, in future life, cost us much dearer in their consequences than it would have done in their correction by a good education.

He also waged continual war on bigotry and declared:

> Bigotry is a disease of ignorance, of morbid minds; education and free discussion are antidotes of both.

Jefferson worked earnestly all his life for religious freedom.

> I have considered religion as a matter between every man and his Maker, in which no other, and far less the public, has a right to intermeddle.

He advised everyone to:

> Adore God; reverence and cherish your parents; love your neighbor as yourself; and your country more than life. Be just; be true; murmur not at the ways of Providence—and the life into which you will have entered will be one of eternal and ineffable bliss.

President Jefferson hated war and said of it:

> The evils of war are great in their endurance, and have a long reckoning for ages to come. . . . I have seen enough of one war never to wish to see another.

As an early and vigorous champion for the natural and civic rights of each individual, Thomas Jefferson fought for principles which still today are the chief doctrines of Americanism. His policies were of their own day; and he himself said, "The earth belongs always to the living generation." But in its emphasis on "the centrality of human rights" and the supreme importance of freedom, his philosophy is universal. "He remains the best American exemplar of hostility to every form of tyranny."

TRIBUTES TO THOMAS JEFFERSON

For sixty years of public service, which he endured against his wishes, he fought for human freedom on every front.

—Hal Boyle

He was a tall man, not especially prepossessing in appearance, and rather indifferent as to externalities of dress as he grew older, but amiable and gracious in all his personal relations. In his time he was the most conspicuous American patron of learning, science, and the useful arts—making distinctive contributions of his own in natural history and architecture.

—The *Encyclopedia Americana*

Stanley W. McClure, in a brochure on the Jefferson Memorial, has given this evaluation of Thomas Jefferson:

In person Jefferson was 6 feet, 2 inches tall, with a bony but strong frame, angular features, ruddy complexion, sandy or reddish hair, and light hazel eyes. In dress and bearing he was so far removed from the formal that he was almost slovenly. His manners were remarkably winning, and his disposition was very kindly not only to his family and friends, but to his slaves as well.

While not precisely learned, he probably had the most receptive mind of his generation; and it is by no means certain that, although he was on the whole a far from strong executive, he was not the most influential statesman of his day. In religion, it is probable that he was not far from what was then known as a freethinker. As an idealist, he did not underestimate the sublimity of Christ's character, but he had no belief in the orthodox theological ideas as to redemption.

His views on slavery were far beyond those of his time, but all of his efforts to effect a reform in Virginia were unavailing. The influence that he has had through the Democratic party has been but the most open expression of the deep influence he has had in the democratizing of all American ideas. The unfailing trust which the people of his day put in him was due largely to the deep and steady confidence he had in them.

The late John F. Kennedy was a great admirer of Thomas Jefferson and often referred to him in his speeches and writings. Fred Blumenthal told this story in one of his articles:

Perhaps the most fitting latter-day tribute to his greatness was that of President Kennedy at a White House dinner honoring all living Nobel Prize winners in the Western Hemisphere.

"I think," Mr. Kennedy said to the brilliant assemblage, "that this is the most extraordinary collection of talent, of human knowledge, that has ever gathered together at the White House—with the possible exception of when Thomas Jefferson dined alone."

Thomas Jefferson wrote these unpretentious words for his epitaph, not even mentioning the fact that he had twice been elected to the presidency of the United States.

HERE WAS BURIED
THOMAS JEFFERSON
AUTHOR OF THE DECLARATION OF
AMERICAN INDEPENDENCE,
OF THE STATUTE OF VIRGINIA FOR
RELIGIOUS FREEDOM, AND FATHER OF
THE UNIVERSITY OF VIRGINIA

14

The Tomb of the
Unknown Soldier

═══════

On a high slope in Arlington National Cemetery stands the Tomb of the Unknown Soldier with its unforgettable inscription:

HERE RESTS IN
HONORED GLORY
AN AMERICAN
SOLDIER
KNOWN BUT TO GOD

This snow-white block, one of our most distinctive and cherished national symbols, is set on a broad terrace of marble. It overlooks the city of Washington, with its three impressive memorials to Washington, Lincoln, and Jefferson.

After World War I the body of the first Unknown Soldier was interred here in 1921; in 1958 two unidentified men of World War II and the Korean conflict were placed beside the first.

Arlington National Cemetery, established on June 15, 1864, contains several hundred acres; it is the largest of ninety-seven such burial grounds belonging to our country. Administered by the Department of the Army, it is visited by more than two million people each year.

This land has an interesting history. Originally, Governor

Berkeley of Virginia deeded 6,000 acres (of which the cemetery is a part) to a sea captain who had brought a load of colonists to the colony of Virginia. It is reported that this skipper soon traded the vast holding for six hogsheads of tobacco.

The property changed hands several times. George Washington bought it, and during the summers of the 1790's lived on it while overseeing the building of the new "Federal City." (The land was part of the District of Columbia from 1791 to 1847, when Congress returned Arlington County to Virginia.)

It became the property of George Washington Custis, a grandson of Martha Washington and adopted son of the general. The new owner began to build a colonial house with tall pillars—a typical southern mansion—and named it Arlington. His daughter, Mary Ann Randolph Custis, was married in 1831 in one of the parlors to a young army officer, Robert E. Lee. Afterward she inherited the property, and the Lee family lived here until the coming of the Civil War.

One day Robert E. Lee was called into Washington and offered the command of the Union forces. Although he disapproved of slavery and had freed his own slaves, he felt he could not fight against his relatives and friends.

It was in one of the rooms of Arlington that the general made his decision, and on April 20, 1861, he wrote his resignation from the Union army. Then he rode away to Richmond to offer his sword and services to the Confederacy. He never saw his beloved Arlington again. Soon Mrs. Lee and her children followed him to Richmond.

At once the Union forces occupied Arlington as their military headquarters. Great trees were cut down and grounds cleared for building Fort Whipple, now Fort Myer. Here General George B. McClellan drilled his troops.

In Richmond Mrs. Lee received news that taxes of $12 were due on Arlington. She sent the money by a messenger, but it was refused. He was told that the money must be paid in person by the owner of the property. Of course Mrs. Lee could not fulfill this condition; therefore, Arlington was put up for sale at auction for delinquent taxes. United States commissioners bought it in 1864. The house served as a hospital for a time. Union officers sent away for safekeeping some of the valuable Custis-Lee family heirlooms.

Quartermaster General Meigs suggested to President Lincoln that the estate be dedicated as a National Cemetery. His idea was approved by Congress, and 2,111 bodies from the North were interred in a single grave.

When the Civil War was over and General Lee and his wife were gone, the eldest Lee son sued the United States government for the return of his land and home. The case went on for years; finally it reached the Supreme Court, where the Lee family received justice. In 1883 the owner could have ordered that all graves be removed; instead, he relinquished claims to the property of Arlington for the sum of $150,000.

Originally, on the slopes below the Arlington mansion, Union officers had been buried, while their men were interred across the lower meadows. In 1910 a large number of Confederate soldiers was brought from scattered points and laid to rest here, in the nation's "Field of the Dead."

Arlington house was restored to its old gracious beauty in 1925, and various mementos of the family, along with reproductions of the original furniture, were placed in it.

In 1955, by an act of Congress, the house was officially designated as the Custis-Lee Mansion. Today it is administered by the National Park Service and can be visited daily (except on Christmas Day) October through March, from 9:30 A.M. to 4:30 P.M.; and April through September, from 9:30 A.M. to 6 P.M.

In Arlington National Cemetery a total of 136,567 interments had been made as of March 31, 1966, including 4,724 unknown dead. Many graves have small simple markers; however, there are several large memorial buildings, such as the Temple of Fame. There is a monument to the Canadian soldiers who served with Americans in World War I.

The Maine Memorial (with the mast from the warship which was blown up in Havana Bay on February 15, 1898) is in memory of the 167 men who lost their lives at that time. The Daughters of the Confederacy raised a monument to their dead; there is another to the memory of fallen Union heroes of the Civil War; there is also a Spanish-American War memorial—a granite pillar surmounted by a great American eagle. The Coast Guard, too, has a fitting monument in Arlington.

In this impressive burial place, generals and admirals rest beside seamen and privates. Two Presidents—William Howard Taft and John Fitzgerald Kennedy—are here, as are many other notable civilians, including William Jennings Bryan, John Foster Dulles, Justice Oliver Wendell Holmes, Pierre L'Enfant, Robert Todd Lincoln, Kenneth Roberts, George Westinghouse, the Polish pianist and patriot Ignace Paderewski, and James Forrestal.

Among the army and navy officers are H. H. Arnold, Richard E. Byrd, Claire L. Chennault, William F. Halsey, William D. Leahy, George C. Marshall, John J. Pershing, Walter Reed, Phil Sheridan, and Jonathan Wainwright.

"A dazzling white amphitheater" of Vermont marble was built at Arlington by the Grand Army of the Republic in memory of the men killed in battle. It is an open-air theater, with marble benches that seat about 4,000 persons.

Many impressive services are held here, including the Easter Sunrise Service; programs are always presented on Memorial Day and Veterans Day, formerly Armistice Day. Countless wreaths are placed here by individuals and organizations, also by visiting American and foreign notables.

After World War I each of the Allied countries had countless unidentified dead. The governments of Great Britain, France, Belgium, Italy, and the United States decided it would be most fitting and proper to honor the memory of these men who had made the supreme sacrifice.

Great Britain buried her Unknown Soldier with her kings and great men in Westminster Abbey. France buried hers beneath the Arch of Triumph in the center of Paris, where a flame burns eternally. Belgium placed her dead hero at the base of the Colonnade of the Congress in Brussels. Italy's Unknown Soldier lies in front of the outstanding monument to Victor Emmanuel in Rome.

When the United States decided to honor its Unknown Soldier, the selection was made in Europe on October 23, 1921. The American army of occupation had been in Germany for about two years.

One day, to his great surprise, Sergeant Edward F. Younger was told by his commanding officer to report to Koblenz, where he would meet five other soldiers from occupied territory. The six then went by train to Châlons-sur-Marne to be assigned as pall-bearers to the Unknown Soldier of World War I. None of these men had the slightest idea of the important job one of them would be called upon to perform.

After reporting, all were interviewed by General Henry Huddle-ston Rogers. Then he announced his decision that Sergeant Younger was to make the vital selection of the Unknown Soldier. The six men, officers, a bugler, color bearers, and a company of French soldiers walked quietly and solemnly to the City Hall in Châlons-sur-Marne.

In it a chapel had been improvised, and four coffins containing bodies on whom no personal identification had been found were placed there. The remains had been brought from American ceme-teries in different parts of France. At once the officer placed a bunch of white roses in Edward Younger's hands. His orders were to proceed alone, make his selection, and place the flowers in the chosen casket.

Sergeant Younger told later of the experience. As he walked in and saw four coffins in the dim light, at first he couldn't move. But when he heard the strains of a familiar hymn, Edward Younger instinctively bowed his head in prayer.

He began his march around the biers, asking himself, "Is this the one?" When he had circled the caskets three times and had begun the march for the fourth round, he felt he had found the right one—the second casket. Younger's hand trembled as he laid the roses on this coffin. Then he stepped back and saluted the newly selected Unknown Soldier. By this simple act, an unknown man became the symbol of all our war dead.

After he had made the choice, Edward Younger started toward the door and heard the band playing "The Dead March" from *Saul*. The young soldier said he felt a strange exhilaration as he saluted his officer and told him he had carried out his order.

The body of the Unknown Soldier was first taken to Paris, then to Le Havre, and placed aboard the *Olympia*, which had been Admiral Dewey's flagship at the Battle of Manila Bay. As the *Olympia* with its unusual cargo passed through the harbor, it was saluted by the French fleet.

The casket was received in Washington with much acclaim. It lay in state for two days in the Rotunda of the Capitol, while thousands of visitors passed by in silent homage.

At 8:30 A.M. on Armistice Day, November 11, 1921, gun salvos sounded from Fort Myer and continued every sixty seconds during the five ceremonial hours.

There was a long procession to Arlington National Cemetery. Then the Unknown Soldier was entombed amid a program of hymns, prayers, and speeches in the presence of civilian and military dignitaries, including former Presidents William H. Taft and Woodrow Wilson and General John J. Pershing, commander of the American expeditionary forces in Europe during World War I. President Harding made the main speech, in which he asserted: "There must be, there shall be, the commanding voice of a conscious civilization against armed warfare."

The Unknown Soldier was placed in a temporary tomb at the east front of the Arlington Memorial Amphitheater. (The completed tomb was dedicated in 1932.) The casket rests forever on soil brought from American battlefields in France.

Wreaths were reverently laid at the base of the tomb. Then the slow bugle notes of taps were heard. When three final salvos of minute guns sounded, the great throng dispersed, after having witnessed an important event in our national history.

Sergeant Younger was invited to take part in the Memorial Day program at Arlington National Cemetery in 1930. He died in 1942 and was buried with honors not far from the Tomb of the Unknown Soldier. Many visitors to the cemetery place flowers on his grave.

After World War II and the Korean War, Congress decided that two more Unknown Soldiers should be honored at Arlington, one from each of the conflicts—and that they should be placed beside the first. One would be chosen in Europe and the other in Hawaii.

At Epinal, France, in May, 1958, a gray mist hung over the cemetery where 5,000 Americans had been buried. Thirteen coffins had been brought from all the American cemeteries in France. These symbolized the nation's war dead of World War II, including 7,500 unidentified bodies and another 75,000 listed as missing in action.

General Edward O'Neill, of St. Albans, Vermont, was to select one of the thirteen, all of whom had died as Unknowns. The graying, fifty-six-year-old veteran of three World War II assault landings at first stared straight ahead at the monument in the cemetery. Someone had said of this burial ground, "This is their memorial—the whole earth is their sepulcher."

After pausing for a full minute, the general walked forward and placed a red-and-white wreath on the fifth coffin from the left. Three military chaplains, a Jew, a Roman Catholic, and a Protestant, prayed for God's grace on the anonymous hero. A priest from Upper Darby, Pennsylvania, said:

> He is symbolic and will remain symbolic of the fact that, in spite of lofty words, the real foundation of our liberty is solidified by the warm blood of all who died for the ideas of our great nation. In honoring one, even though he must remain forever nameless, we are honoring all.

The Jewish chaplain, Lieutenant Colonel Edward Ellenbogen, of Omaha, Nebraska, prayed: "Father of all, continually bless and cherish our fallen comrades."

After the ceremonies, the chosen casket was taken to an airfield near Nancy and later flown to Naples. There it was put aboard the U.S. destroyer *Blandy* for the voyage to a rendezvous off Norfolk, Virginia, with the vessel carrying two other Unknowns.

Also in May, 1958, in the National Memorial Cemetery of the Pacific, at Punchbowl, near Honolulu, an American sergeant, Ned Lyle, selected a casket from those of four unidentified soldiers of the Korean War and placed on it the traditional lei.

A second Unknown was chosen at Hickham Air Force Base, not far from Honolulu. Colonel Glenn T. Eagleston (who had downed twenty-three enemy planes) made the selection from six flag-draped coffins, by laying a Hawaiian garland of white carnations on one of them.

The two chosen thus in Hawaii would be transferred to the cruiser *Canberra* for the final selection. One of the World War II heroes would be interred at Arlington National Cemetery, the other buried at sea with full military honors.

On the *Canberra* the caskets were guarded by two "ramrod straight marines." Late in May the final choice was made on the ship. Before the solemn ceremonies, Rear Admiral Lewis S. Parks looked down on the biers and made this statement:

> Two of them gave their lives in battle during the Second World War. The third gave his life in battle preserving the independence of the Republic of Korea, and even more important, defending against further Communist aggression in the Free World.
>
> These men did not fail when the chips were down, and we must not fail them in the days and years ahead when Communist forces will press ever harder to drive the Free World into slavery. America must remain alert, strong and dedicated to the task of preserving the kind of world that these three knew and loved so well; they gave that which was dearest to them, their lives, so that all of us could continue to enjoy the fruits of victory.

On the *Canberra* waiting to make the choice was William R. Charette, of Ludington, Michigan, a navy hospitalman, first class, who had won the coveted Congressional Medal of Honor. He was to select one of two caskets, one on his right, the other on his left. It is said that he seemed "visibly moved" by the great task assigned him. He stopped, dramatically, then made a brisk half-face to the right coffin and placed the red-and-white wreath on it. Later he said:

> I didn't make up my mind until I picked up the wreath and stood there at the foot of the coffins for a while. I prayed that I'd do the right thing, an informal sort of prayer, I guess you'd call it.

After the selection the *Canberra* with the casket of the "Unchosen" sailed farther out to sea, about 33 miles off the Virginia coast, where the water was 15 fathoms deep. Six men carried the flag-covered pallet to the slanted platform on the afterdeck of the vessel. Chaplains of four faiths, all dressed in their vestments, said prayers for this Unknown.

> The bearers tilted the platform. Out from under the covering slid the shrouded body, weighted to carry it down. A little cloud of foam drifted back from the stern of the *Canberra*, to mark the spot, briefly on the quiet sea.

The two chosen Unknowns were placed on the *Blandy*, "a grim, gray warship"; and on its deck, under the care of an honor guard, they rested throughout the night. The vessel was accompanied up the Potomac River by the Coast Guard ship *Ingham* and docked at Pier 1 of the Naval Gun Factory.

Next morning, at 8:30, the band played *Nearer, My God, to Thee* in muted tones. At 9:03 A.M. the official welcome began, with "four ruffles and flourishes" and a hymn by the Navy Band. From the dock came six military pallbearers, preceded by chaplains; they marched up the gangplank of the *Blandy*, on which flags hung at half-mast. To a ruffle of drums, the men picked up the caskets and carried them ashore, through a military corridor made up of various officials, headed by Secretary of Defense Neil McElroy.

As the motorcade started for the Capitol, the gun factory gave a twenty-one-gun salute. A composite guard of honor of men from the Army, Navy, and Air Force escorted the black hearses as the cortege moved slowly to the Capitol.

When the procession reached it, ceremonies were repeated at the plaza. To the accompaniment of hymns, the bodies were taken up the long steps, in full military fashion. The Korean Unknown was first, followed by the European, each preceded by two clergymen. A silent crowd watched the passage up the steps. As soon as the second coffin was within the doors, the flag on the Capitol was lowered to half-mast.

The two caskets were placed on catafalques in the center of the Rotunda, just under the vast dome. Side by side they lay in state. The chaplains took their positions at the foot of the identical bronze caskets, while the honor guards stood at the heads.

In a semicircle in the Rotunda stood Vice-President Nixon, Speaker of the House Rayburn, senators, representatives, diplomats, and other dignitaries. The Vice-President, the House Speaker, and Dr. Don Guillermo D. Sevilla-Sacase, of Nicaragua, each placed at the caskets identical 4-foot wreaths of white carnations in behalf of the two houses of Congress and of the foreign emissaries.

Others in the audience included Gold Star Mothers whose sons had not been identified. Perhaps each was wishing that one was her son.

For two days people filed past the honored biers at the rate of 1,200 per hour to pay silent homage to these heroes. Every half-hour a new wreath was laid, and each hour, both day and night, the guard was changed. On Memorial Day, 1958,

. . . down sunlit steps and to the cadence of muffled drums, bearers carry them to Arlington National Cemetery for enshrinement—symbols of a nation's homage to all who gave their lives.

The caskets were placed on horse-drawn caissons for the trip to Arlington. The air force flew some of its newest jets over the procession as it crossed Memorial Bridge on its way from the Capitol. Following the caissons were units of all the armed forces together with civilian and military officials and foreign diplomats. This time the coffin of the soldier of World War II was ahead of the Korean.

It was estimated that about 115,000 persons lined the route to the cemetery, while thousands crowded into the marble amphitheater where services were conducted by President Eisenhower and Vice-President Nixon.

Seated before the dais were 216 men who had won the Congressional Medal. Also present that day were generals and other officials, Supreme Court justices, members of the diplomatic corps, Gold Star Mothers, and thousands of other Americans.

President Eisenhower laid a red-and-white wreath of carnations at the base of the tomb. As he placed Congressional Medals of Honor on the flag-draped coffins, he said simply:

> On behalf of a grateful people, I now present Medals of Honor to these two Unknowns, who gave their lives for the United States of America.

Protestant, Roman Catholic, and Jewish chaplains said prayers for the men who represented 293,000 unidentified Americans killed in action in World War II, and 33,000 who lost their lives in Korea.

Rather than construct a second monument and disturb the simplicity of the distinctive war memorial, the newly honored men were buried in the same vault.

In the gloaming the two Unknowns were interred. The superintendent of Arlington National Cemetery released chains holding the caskets, and in the dying light the bronze coffins sank slowly from sight. The uniformed pallbearers stood at hand salute, while civilians placed their hands over their hearts. Thus with pomp and ceremony the honored soldiers were laid to rest, overlooking the capital of the land for which they had given their lives.

Now two more Americans had come home; and the Tomb of the Unknown Soldier had become the Tomb of the Unknowns.

The Honor Guard for the tomb made up of "the proudest soldiers in the army," consists of sixteen enlisted men, carefully selected from Company A, Third Infantry, and known as the "Old Guard." They are stationed at Fort Myer, Virginia.

Those who maintain this classic vigil are among our finest fighting men. All of them volunteer for this special service, and the selected ones are chosen from hundreds of applicants for their splendid bearing, proficiency, smart appearance, and military records.

Each must have a high intelligence score; weigh between 145 and 200 pounds; be between 5 feet, 11 inches, and 6 feet, 2 inches, in height; and have commensurate weight and build, fine physical appearance, and no defects.

They go through a rigid course of training. When a volunteer has acquired the routine on the parade ground, he walks each evening for two weeks beside the sentry, when the gates are closed to visitors.

At the conclusion of his term of duty, which may be from six to eleven months, he receives a certificate of achievement, in recognition of outstanding performance of duty while a member of the guard.

Visitors to Arlington National Cemetery thrill to watch the guard as he walks the path, regardless of the weather, turns, clicks his heels, and paces along the rubber mat on the paved surface. His precision is outstanding; he walks before the tomb at 128 steps a minute. The sentry never speaks except to rebuke a disrespectful visitor.

> Entrusted to these men for whom every day is Memorial Day, America's Unknown Soldier "rests in honored glory."

EVENTS AT THE TOMB

During recent years several outstanding events have occurred here. On Memorial Day in 1960 a special ceremony honored the memory of Lieutenant General Claire L. Chennault, who had died three years before. He had achieved fame in World War II as the leader of the Flying Tigers and the Fourteenth Air Force in China.

Also on this date there was a notable wreath-laying rite at the grave of General John A. Logan, commander of the Grand Army of the Republic, who in 1868 had issued an order designating May 30 ". . . for the purpose of strewing with flowers, or otherwise decorating the graves of comrades who died in defense of their country, during the late rebellion."

On Veterans Day in 1960 an unusual gift was presented to Arlington National Cemetery. A torch that had been lighted in Belgium was flown to Washington and presented by an officer of the Belgian Air Force. It was at the eleventh hour of the eleventh month—forty-two years after World War I had ended.

This Belgian torch that flamed at the Tomb of the Unknown Soldier was accepted and cited as "the symbol for the timeless effort for peace." Then the former commandant of the United States Marine Corps, General Lemuel C. Shepherd, led the assembly in paying "symbolic tribute in this bivouac of the dead to the immortal members of the veterans of all wars."

The general declared that there was no end in sight in the conflict between the communists and the Free World and warned that the United States and its allies "will continue to be constantly assaulted on our ideological, political, and economical fronts."

On November 11, 1961, several months after he had been inaugurated, President John F. Kennedy stood bareheaded in bright, clear 50-degree weather before the Tomb of the Unknown Soldier and pledged "that the United States would fight if necessary, to maintain the frontiers of freedom."

He also used that emotional occasion to pray that "there will be no veterans of any further war—not because all shall have perished, but because all have learned to live together in peace."

The young chief executive was born in 1917, the year we entered World War I. Then, forty-three years to the day after its ending, John Fitzgerald Kennedy stood in Arlington National Cemetery and said:

> In a world tormented by tension and the possibilities of conflict, we meet in quiet commemoration of a historic day of peace.

In an age that threatens the survival of freedom, we join together to honor those who made our freedom possible.

The President also declared that it was tragic that the hopes surrounding the end of World War I had not been fulfilled, but he believed that November 11, 1918, signified the beginning of man's great effort in recent times to solve the problems of war by international cooperation.

There is no way to maintain the frontiers of freedom without cost and commitment and risk.

The only way to avoid war is to be willing to face it—and to mean it.

Let no nation confuse our dislike of war. . . . We can convince friend and foe alike we are in earnest in the defense of freedom. . . .

And I can assure the world we are.

President Kennedy urged that no one feel that such a ceremony as that day's was in vain. He begged them not to forget that November 11, 1918, was a beginning as well as an end and that "World War I produced the first great effort to solve the world's problems, short of war." (He was, of course, referring to the League of Nations, which continued its efforts for peace until World War II broke out.)

In the fateful year of 1963, on Veterans Day the dynamic young chief executive, flanked by his military aides and Marine General David M. Shoup, appeared promptly at the tomb, before a crowd of more than 5,000.

A twenty-one-gun salute was fired in the background, after which Platoon Sergeant Allen Eldridge of Fort Lauderdale, Florida, assisted the President in laying a wreath of red and white carnations. Then the President, with his aides, Defense Secretary Robert F. McNamara, Army Secretary Cyrus Vance, and others stood at attention during the sounding of taps.

Newspapers featured shots of the scene and one of young John Kennedy, who seemed enthralled by his surroundings as he walked past a row of wind-whipped flags when leaving Arlington National Cemetery, after seeing his father place a wreath at the Tomb of the Unknown Soldier.

President Kennedy did not speak on this Veterans Day, but listened to General Shoup, who asserted: "It is what Americans stand for and what Americans are willing to fight for that has made America great."

Then, just a year later, on November 11, 1964, at Arlington, America again honored the 31 million military veterans living and dead who have waged its wars and protected its peace. Veterans' Administrator John P. Gleason placed a wreath in solemn ceremonies. At 11 A.M. the traditional moment of silence was observed. Mr. Gleason recalled the fact that just a year before, in the nation's most hallowed cemetery, at the Veterans Day exercises, John F. Kennedy had placed a wreath at the tomb, little knowing that he himself in exactly two weeks would, like them, rest forever here.

The Unknown Soldiers and John F. Kennedy together gave all that men can give so that you and I and our children would inherit a free land.

VISITORS TO THE TOMB

Millions of visitors from the United States and abroad have come to this distinctive tomb—a huge block of marble mined in Colorado and carved in Vermont, with its eternal flame burning. On one Veterans Day alone 146 wreaths were placed here.

Foreign notables who visit Washington rarely fail to make a journey here to pay homage. For instance, in the fall of 1952, on a rainy day, King Paul and Queen Frederika of Greece visited the tomb.

In January, 1953, a tall, dignified man placed a wreath of white carnations at the base. He was Admiral J. C. Qvistgaard, chief of defense for Denmark. He had just witnessed the burial in Arlington of his own son, killed in action with the United States First Marine Division in Korea. The wreath also saluted all the boy's comrades who had died for freedom.

Also in January, 1953, the president of Turkey, Celal Bayar, was so impressed by the ceremony at the tomb that he asked for instructions so he could repeat it at the tomb of Kemal Ataturk, Turkey's great national hero.

West Germany's Chancellor Adenauer, in April, 1953, after placing his tribute, stood deeply affected before onlooking Americans. And on September 9, 1953, his Imperial Highness Crown Prince Akihito of Japan placed a wreath as representative of his country. He stood silent as the band played national anthems.

Another impressive wreath-laying rite occurred in April, 1953. A group of officers from Allied nations had been attending conferences at nearby Fort Belvoir and asked permission to pay their respects before returning to their countries: Great Britain, France, Canada, Belgium, Greece, Turkey, The Netherlands, Korea, Iran, Norway, Nationalist China, Portugal, and Thailand.

In *Together*, May, 1962, in the article "Through a Child's Eyes," Charles R. Goff told of taking his three daughters to visit the tomb. The eldest climbed the wide stone steps and came back to him with a troubled look.

"This," she said, "isn't the grave of the Unknown Soldier." When her father tried to assure her it was, she insisted it didn't say that; for the inscription says he is "known but to God."

No one knows the names of these three heroes or their race, religion, branch of the service, or rank. "Their anonymity is perfect." Since identification was impossible, the three have become symbols.

And this splendid, solemn resting place reminds the millions who stand reverently before it of the young lives that were sacrificed to keep America safe and free. Visitors watch the sentry, who, never looking to right or left, passes back and forth before this cherished national shrine.

Now they sleep at the Tomb of the Unknown Soldier. Each Memorial Day, along with all they represent, they will receive the wreaths, prayers, the eternal honor of the nation for which they gave their lives.

Bibliography

BOOKS

ABBOTT, SAMUEL. *Dramatic Story of Old Glory.* New York: Boni Liveright, 1919.

BARTLETT, JOHN. *Familiar Quotations.* Boston: Little, Brown and Company, 1955.

———. *The Shorter Bartlett's Familiar Quotations.* New York: Pocket Books, Inc., 1937.

BENET, WILLIAM ROSE. *The Poetry of Freedom.* New York: Random House, 1945.

CAVANAH, FRANCES. *Our Country's Freedom.* Chicago: Rand McNally & Company, 1966.

COLMAN, EDNA. *Seventy Years of White House Gossip.* New York: Doubleday Page and Company, 1925.

DESMOND, ALICE C. *Your Flag and Mine.* New York: The Macmillan Company, 1960.

GIBBONS, CROMWELL. *Republic U.S.A.* New Haven, Conn.: Country Press, 1960.

GOLENPAUL, DAN, AND ASSOCIATES. *Information Please Almanac Atlas, and Year Book.* New York: McGraw-Hill, Book Company, 1961.

HALE, E. E. *The Man Without a Country.* New York: Franklin Watts, Inc., 1960.

HARBOURT, JOHN. *Our Flag.* New York: Lothrop, Lee & Shepard Company, 1940.

HARTMAN, GERTRUDE. *The Making of a Democracy.* New York: The John Day Company, 1926.

HEAL, EDITH. *The First Book of America.* New York: Franklin Watts, Inc., 1952.

HOOVER, IRWIN H. *Forty-two Years in the White House.* New York: Houghton Mifflin Company, 1934.

KRYTHE, MAYMIE R. *All About American Holidays.* New York : Harper & Row, 1962.

LEWIS, ETHEL. *The White House.* New York: Dodd, Mead & Company, 1937.

LONG, E. JOHN. *The Real Book About Our National Capital.* Garden City, N.Y.: Garden City Company, 1959.

LONG, LUMAN H., ed. *World Almanac.* New York: New York World Telegram and New York Sun, 1966.

MALONE, DUMAS, ed. *Dictionary of American Biography.* New York: Charles Scribner's Sons, 1934.

McSPADDEN, J. WALKER. *Famous Sculptors of America.* New York: Dodd, Mead & Company, 1924.

NESBITT, HENRIETTA. *White House Diary.* Garden City, N.Y.: Doubleday and Company, 1948.

PARTON, MARY FIELD. *Your Washington.* New York: Longmans Green and Company, 1938.

QUAIFE, MILO M., et al. *The History of the United States Flag.* New York: Harper & Row, 1961.

ROSEWATER, VICTOR. *The Liberty Bell.* New York: D. Appleton and Company, 1926.

SMITH, IRENE. *Washington, D.C.* Chicago: Rand McNally & Company, 1964.

SMITH, MARIE, and LOUISE DURBIN. *White House Brides.* Acropolis Books, 1966.

STAFFORD, MARIE PEARY. *Discoverer of the North Pole.* New York: William Morrow & Company, 1959.

STEWART, CHARLES. *The Stars and Stripes from Washington to Wilson.* Washington, D.C.: Navy Publishing Company, 1914.

TAPPEN, EVA. *The Little Book of the Flag.* Boston: Houghton Mifflin Company, 1937.

TERRELL, JOHN UPTON. *The Key to Washington.* Philadelphia: J. B. Lippincott Company, 1962.

THOMAS, LESLIE. *Long May It Wave.* New York: William Morrow & Company, 1914.

TRUMAN, MARGARET. *Souvenir.* New York: McGraw-Hill Book Company, 1956.

WRIGHT, RICHARDSON. *Forgotten Ladies.* Philadelphia: J. B. Lippincott Company, 1928.

————. *Washington City and Capital.* Washington: Federal Writers' Project, 1937.

MAGAZINE AND NEWSPAPER ARTICLES

ANDERSON, JACK. "America's First Ladies," *Parade*, November 21, 1965.

——. "Our Capitol Gets a New Fix," *Parade*, July 7, 1959.

BENGSTON, BENNIE. "The Statue of Liberty," *Classmate*, November 7, 1948.

BLUMENTHAL, FRED. "A Most Remarkable American," *Parade*, June 28, 1964.

——. "The White House Is Their Beat," *Parade*, June 6, 1961.

BOYLE, HAL. "Jefferson's Great Career Ended on July 4th," *Long Beach Press-Telegram*, July 4, 1963.

BREED, OLIVE. "First Ladies," *Southland Magazine*, March 6, 1966.

BUTTERFIELD, ROGER. "The Liberty Bell," *Collier's Magazine*, July 5, 1951.

CASEY, JEWEL. "First First Ladies," *Classmate*, February 15, 1948.

——. "Washington National Monument Today," *Classmate*, February 22, 1948.

CHILTON, CARL. "The Three Unknown Soldiers," *Classmate*, August 2, 1959.

COLE, MARTHA. "Fame's Eternal Bivouac Will Wear Flags Today," *Los Angeles Times*, May 30, 1965.

COLLINS, L. A., SR. "Religion in Schools, Part of Education," *Long Beach Press-Telegram*, July 17, 1966.

CONSIDINE, BOB. "Unknown Hero Chosen for Arlington," *Long Beach Press-Telegram*, May 27, 1958.

CORKERY, LOIS. "Fads That the White House Started," *Southland Magazine*, April 23, 1961.

CORNELL, DOUGLAS B. "Memorial to Lincoln, Peaceful, Powerful," *Long Beach Press-Telegram*, 1958.

CORNELL, GEORGE W. "Hostess to the Mostess—Liberty's Lamp Aflame for 70 Years," *Long Beach Press-Telegram*, October 28, 1956.

COOPER, JOEL A. "The Meaning of Patriotism," *Together*, July, 1966.

COWAN, RUTH B. "It's Moving Day—President Dodges," *Long Beach Press-Telegram*, March 1, 1952.

CURTIS, OLGA. "The Eagle Comes Home to Roost," *Parade*.

DAVIS, MARY. "The Lady on the Lantern," *Classmate*, April 18, 1948.

DE BRA, ELSA. "Symbol of Freedom," *Southland Magazine*, October 22, 1961.

DUCHE, THE REV. J. "First Prayer in Congress," *Thatcher's Military Journal*, December, 1777.

EMERSON, GLORIA. "The Statue of Liberty," *Life,* 1957.

FARRAR, LARSTEN D. "Exclamation Point of Freedom," *Western Family,* July, 1948.

FAY, ELTON C. "Unknown Warriors Laid to Rest," *Long Beach Press-Telegram,* May 31, 1958.

———. "Warships Near Rendezvous for U. S. Transfer," *Long Beach Press-Telegram,* May 16, 1958.

FERM, BETTY. "The Frenchman and the Liberty Bell, a Living Memorial to Freedom," *Twelve/Fifteen,* July 3, 1966.

GILBERT, NELSON B. "128 Steps a Minute," *Classmate,* November 17, 1957.

GOLDEN, HARRY. "Lincoln Was Great and He Was Human," *Los Angeles Examiner,* February 15, 1959.

GORDON, ARTHUR. "The Sound of Freedom," *Woman's Day,* July, 1964.

HALL, WARREN. "Uncle Sam," *This Week,* July 2, 1961.

HANDLIN, OSCAR. "A Museum for Liberty," *This Week,* January 29, 1956.

HARTMAN, ROBERT T. "Who Is Uncle Sam?" *Los Angeles Times,* March 26, 1952.

HOOVER, J. EDGAR. "America Needs Full Time Patriots," *This Week,* July 1, 1956.

HOYTEN, FRANK. "Special First Ladies," *Southland Magazine,* February 14, 1965.

HYMAN, WARREN. "Proudly We Hail, Allegiance Pledged to Liberty," *Leisure World News,* Laguna Hills, California, July 7, 1966.

HYMOFF, EDWARD. "Lest We Forget," *Blue Book,* 1958.

JORDON, WILFRED. "True Story of Our Liberty Bell," *Ladies' Home Journal,* July, 1910.

KELLY, V. W. "Visit at White House," *Long Beach Press-Telegram,* January 16, 1964.

KILGORE, MARGARET. "White House, Not much Fun—Ex-inmates Agree," *Long Beach Press-Telegram,* March 3, 1964.

LYNOTT, JOAN. "Improved Monument Will Open Today," *Los Angeles Times,* January 12, 1959.

LEWINE, FRANCES. "J.F.K. Lauds White House Work," *Long Beach Press-Telegram,* February 15, 1962.

LIEBER, LESLIE. "Ghosts in the White House," *This Week.*

———. "Washington Never Slept Here," *This Week,* February 18, 1951.

MACK, KENT E. "Robert Mills, Architect," *Classmate,* October 28, 1951.

MARTIN, PETE. "The Shrine They Almost Auctioned Off," *Saturday Evening Post,* September 4, 1948.

MATTHEWS, DORIS. "They Rang the Bell," *Classmate,* July 1, 1965.

MARSHALL, CATHERINE. "What I Learned About Lincoln," *Christian Herald*, February, 1959.

McDERMOTT, WILLIAM F. "In Honored Glory," *Coronet*, November, 1949.

———. "Known But To God," *Together*, May, 1962.

McMURTRY, DR. GERALD. "Lincoln Lore," June, 1963, and June, 1967.

MYERS, DEBS. "The New White House," *Holiday*, November, 1952.

NICHOLS, HAROLD M. "Voice Has Told Story to 8,066,000 People," *Long Beach Press-Telegram*, 1953.

OPSAHL, JOSEPHINE. "The Bells of Our Land," *California Highway Patrolman*, June, 1967.

PADDLEFORD, CLEMENTINE. "Dinner Fit for a King," *This Week*, October 12, 1958.

PEACOCK, MARJORIE, "Greatest Seal of All," *Southland Magazine*, July 24, 1960.

PEALE, NORMAN VINCENT. "The Pursuit of Happiness," *Long Beach Press-Telegram*, July 7, 1967.

PEATTIE, DONALD CULROSS. "Arlington, Where Sleep the Brave," *Reader's Digest*, August, 1952.

PEET, SAUL. "Pilgrims Awed by Bell," *Los Angeles Times*, July 1, 1951.

POLLOCK, JACK HARRISON. "It's Fun to Grow up in the White House," *This Week*, June 25, 1961.

RADEN, CAMILLE M. "A Wife Becomes First Lady," *Southland Magazine*, May 20, 1965.

REMINGTON, FRANK L. "Tribute in Stone," *Southland Magazine*, February 19, 1961.

ROSENTHAL, JOE. "The Picture That Thrilled the Nation," *Reader's Digest*, February, 1955.

SADLER, CHRISTINE. "McCall's Gallery of Children in the White House," *McCall's Magazine*, May, 1962.

SCHULTZ, ESTHER. "Miss Freedom Comes to Washington," *Coronet*, July, 1952.

SERLING, ROBERT J. "Kennedy Child's Kitten Follows Long Pet Line," *Los Angeles Times*, February 5, 1961.

SHELTON, ELIZABETH. "Lynda Bird Says Vows in White House Rites," *Los Angeles Times*, December 10, 1967.

SMITH, MARIE, and LOUISE DURBIN. "Monroe Wedding Story," *Los Angeles Times*, July 17, 1966.

STEVENSON, ADLAI. "Stevenson Pays Tribute to Republicans' Lincoln," *Los Angeles Examiner*, February 12, 1954.

STEWART, M. "Old Liberty Bell Will Ring Again," *New York Times Magazine*, December 27, 1925.

STRATTON, REP. S. S. "Should We Leave The Capitol Alone?" *Parade*, September 25, 1966.

SUGRUE, FRANCIS. "It's an Image—an Image of Us," *New York Herald Tribune*, September 29, 1961.

TERRY, MARY COLLIER. "Hats off to the Bell."

————. "Miss Liberty at the Golden Door," *Classmate*, May 18, 1952.

————. "Your House in Washington," *Classmate*, January 18, 1953.

ULLMAN, WILLIAM. "Christmas in the White House," *National Motorist*, November–December, 1947.

UNGER, HENRY F. "Monumental Birthday," *Highway Traveler*, February, 1948.

WASHINGTON, GEORGE. "Prayer After His Inauguration," April 30, 1789.

WIGGINS, PATRICIA. "U.S. Seal Placed in New Home," *Long Beach Press-Telegram*, January 8, 1956.

WILLIAMS, ALBERTA. "Lady of Liberty," *Coronet*, August, 1955.

WOOD, MADELYN. "Our Bird of Freedom," *Coronet*, July, 1954.

WRIGHT, MAJOR GEN. E. K. "The Tomb We Honor," *Parade*, May 30, 1954.

ENCYCLOPEDIAS

Collier's Encyclopedia. New York, Toronto: Crowell, Collier and Macmillan, Inc., 1967.

Compton's Pictured Encyclopedia. Chicago: F. E. Compton Company, 1960.

Encyclopædia Brittanica. Chicago, London: Wm. Benton, Publisher, 1967.

Encyclopedia Americana. New York: Americana Corporation, 1967.

Grolier Universal Encyclopedia. New York: Grolier, Inc., 1965.

World Book Encyclopedia. Chicago: Field Enterprises, Inc., 1955.

BOOKLETS, BROCHURES, LETTERS

CONKLIN, EDWARD. "The Lincoln Memorial in Washington," U.S. Office of Public Buildings and Parks of the National Capital, 1927.

McCLURE, STANLEY. "The Thomas Jefferson Memorial," United States Department of the Interior, National Park Service, National Capital Region, 1955.

SVEJDA, G. J. Personal letter, Historian of U.S. Department of the Interior, National Park Service, 1967.

WINSHIP, STEPHEN. "At the Bend of the River" (composed for Concord, New Hampshire, centennial)

———. "Birth of Liberty," Forest Lawn Memorial Park, Hollywood Hills, California, 1967.

———. *Capitol Dome Newsletter*, U.S. Capitol Historical Society, Washington, D.C.

———. "The Capitol, Symbol of Freedom," U.S. Government Printing Office, Washington, D.C.

———. "The Cherry Blossoms," U.S. Department of the Interior, National Park Service.

———. "Code of Conduct of the U.S. Fighting Man," Armed Forces Information and Education, Department of Defense, Washington, December 23, 1964.

———. "The Flag of the United States," John Hancock Mutual Life Insurance Company, 1960.

———. "Great Seal of the United States," Department of State, Washington, 1947, 1965.

——— "Independence National Park," Government Printing Office, Washington, 1963.

———. "Independence Hall," Walter Knott, Buena Park, Calif., 1966.

———. "Independence National Park," U.S. Department of the Interior, Washington, 1965.

———. "L. B. J., Family Start Yule Fetes Early," Long Beach, California, *Press-Telegram*, December 16, 1965.

———. "Lincoln Memorial," U.S. Department of the Interior, National Park Service, Washington, 1966.

———. "National Capital Parks," U.S. Department of the Interior, National Park Service, 1965.

———. "Our Flag," Historical Document #473, 89th Congress.

———. "Program—221st Anniversary of Birth of Thomas Jefferson," U.S. Department of the Interior, National Park Service, 1964.

———. "Program—'Torchlight Tattoo,'" Old Guard and U.S. Band, July 27, 1966.

———. "Statue of Liberty," U.S. Department of the Interior, National Park Service, Washington, 1964.

———. "Thomas Jefferson Memorial," U.S. Department of the Interior, National Park Service, Washington, 1953.

———. "We, the People," U.S. Capitol Historical Society, 1963.

———. "The White House," U.S. Department of the Interior, National Park Service, Washington, 1964.

———. "Within Sacred Grounds," Forest Lawn Memorial Park, and Mosaic, Hollywood Hills, Calif., 1967.

Index

DATE DUE

JAN 25			
APR 24			
MAY 28 85			
MAR 16 85			
MAR 28 85			
APR 18 85			
NOV 19			
NOV 16			
FEB 5			
FEB 1			
APR 28			
NOV 29			
NOV 15			
NOV 22			
30 505 JOSTEN'S